Soldiers and Citizens

Palgrave Studies in Oral History

Series Editors: Linda Shopes and Bruce M. Stave

Soldiers and Citizens

An Oral History of Operation Iraqi Freedom from the Battlefield to the Pentagon

Carl Mirra

SOLDIERS AND CITIZENS
Copyright © Carl Mirra, 2008.

First published in 2008 by
PALGRAVE MACMILLAN®
in the United States—a division of St. Martin's Press LLC,
175 Fifth Avenue, New York, NY 10010.

Where this book is distributed in the UK, Europe and the rest of the world,
this is by Palgrave Macmillan, a division of Macmillan Publishers Limited,
registered in England, company number 785998, of Houndmills,
Basingstoke, Hampshire RG21 6XS.

Palgrave Macmillan is the global academic imprint of the above companies
and has companies and representatives throughout the world.

Palgrave® and Macmillan® are registered trademarks in the United States,
the United Kingdom, Europe and other countries.

Cover image: U.S. Army Spc. Justin Towe scans his area while on a mission
with Iraqi army soldiers from 1st Battalion, 2nd Brigade, 4th Iraqi Army
Division in Al Muradia village, Iraq, March, 13, 2007. U.S. Air Force
photo by Master Sgt. Andy Dunaway. Reproduced under a Creative
Commons 2.0 license.

ISBN-13: 978-0-230-60155-0 (hardcover)
ISBN-10: 0-230-60155-3 (hardcover)
ISBN-13: 978-0-230-60164-2 (paperback)
ISBN-10: 0-230-60164-2 (paperback)

Library of Congress Cataloging-in-Publication Data

Mirra, Carl.
    Soldiers and Citizens : an oral history of Operation Iraqi Freedom
from the battlefield to the Pentagon / Carl Mirra.
        p. cm.—(Palgrave studies in oral history)
    Includes bibliographical references and index.
    ISBN 0-230-60155-3
        1. Iraq War, 2003—Personal narratives, American. I. Title.

DS79.76.M5565 2008
956.7044'3—dc22   2008019398

A catalogue record of the book is available from the British Library.

Design by Newgen Imaging Systems (P) Ltd., Chennai, India.

First edition: December 2008

10 9 8 7 6 5 4 3 2 1

Printed in the United States of America.

To
The Iraqi People,
soldiers and veterans of Operation Iraqi Freedom
and their families

Contents

Series Editors' Foreword

The 9/11 terrorist attack on the World Trade Center, the Pentagon, and the crash of United Flight 93 in a Pennsylvania field set off a series of responses felt around the globe. Not the least of which was America's invasion of Iraq and the toppling of its long-time leader, Saddam Hussein. Originally supported by a large segment of the U.S. population and premised on Iraq's possession of weapons of mass destruction, in the eyes of many Operation Iraqi Freedom (OIF) eventually transformed into a controversial and unpopular American imperial adventure. Carl Mirra's *Soldiers and Citizens* provides a gripping oral history of all parties to this event. His interviews include dissident veterans, pro-victory soldiers, affected families, and policy-makers. In so doing, he achieves his goal of developing a dialogue among all points of view.

This is not an easy task for the oral historian, who has a definite perspective about the subject under scrutiny. Yet a good interviewer ordinarily will permit the interviewee to tell his or her story without trying to bias the result. Here, the author has subordinated his point of view in the service of scholarship and employed oral history to achieve a dialogue across differences. In the words of scholar Andrew J. Bacevich, whose interview appears in chapter five, "I don't care if you tell me you are on the Left or the Right, what I care about is what you have to say. I am eager to hear all points of view." This is a good strategy for the oral historian, who has a responsibility to the reader to provide a reasoned narrative. Although this study began as a project of Historians against the War, it transcends any one perspective. Nevertheless, the oral histories collected herein should greatly contribute to historians and the public's assessment of OIF and the Bush administration's approach to foreign policy.

This volume, then, adds another important subject to the Palgrave Macmillan *Studies in Oral History* series, which already has discussed significant topics such as the Chinese Cultural Revolution, Japanese internment, Argentina's "disappeared," and the struggle for civil rights in the United States. With more volumes to come, the series strives to bring the best in oral history to a wide readership. In so doing, we hope to give life to history in the words of those ordinary and extraordinary people who live it and make it.

BRUCE M. STAVE
University of Connecticut

LINDA SHOPES
Carlisle, PA

Foreword by Christian Appy

Five years and counting, the Iraq War has already become the second-longest major U.S. military engagement since Independence. Only the Vietnam War still trumps it in sheer, will-it-ever-end persistence, and in both cases U.S. intervention continued years beyond the point when a majority of Americans concluded that their government had taken them into a war they should never have fought. In terms of the human cost, you would have to be what C. Wright Mills called a "crackpot realist" to find solace in the fact that the current death toll of about 4,000 Americans and nearly a million Iraqis is still below the nearly 60,000 Americans and 3 million Vietnamese killed in "America's longest war." As for the dollar cost—the bottom line supposedly honored by all realists (crackpot or not)—the current war has raced past its Asian predecessor, well beyond a trillion and climbing.

What a lot of history we have endured since 9/11. We need to remind ourselves how little of it our children can be expected to know or recall. Most high school students today have, at best, only the dimmest memory of those prewar months in 2002 when the Bush administration, with unbridled and unequivocal certitude, declared that Saddam Hussein possessed a huge stockpile of weapons of mass destruction posing a dire and imminent threat to us all. Barely aware of the original rationale for the war, students are even less likely to realize that it was based on "intelligence" that was long-outdated, badly distorted, or patently false. Nor can we assume they realize that not a single weapon of mass destruction has been found in Iraq; that the fundamental pretext of the war proved baseless.

As new justifications for the war poured from the White House to replace those found unconvincing, perhaps even many adults soon forgot the boldness with which the war was initially promoted— how essential it was to our security and how we could pull it off in a "cakewalk" for a mere $60 billion. Vice President Cheney assured us that our troops would be greeted as liberators. Secretary of Defense Rumsfeld scoffed at those who said we needed more troops to occupy Iraq. Less than six weeks into the war, President Bush, like a *Top Gun* stuntman, donned a flight suit and copiloted a naval jet onto the deck of an aircraft carrier—the *USS Abraham Lincoln*—strategically parked thirty miles off the California coast to accommodate the commander in chief's theatrical entrance. He issued a triumphal speech in front of a giant sign reading, "Mission Accomplished."

So many thousands have died in the years since Bush's premature victory party it seems as if it belongs to another era altogether. And the administration's apparent indifference to massive antiwar dissent makes it hard to remember how powerful the objections were even before the war began with "Shock and Awe" on March 19, 2003—how millions of people came together in small town squares and major cities throughout this country and the world to demonstrate, a massive and unprecedented effort to stop a war before it could start.

My point is that even vital recent history can be quickly forgotten, supplanted by the pressing events and diversions of the present, or, more alarmingly, transformed into mythic tales that may depend on gross omissions and outright fabrications but allow nations to preserve flattering views of their past, or at least easy and satisfying explanations for everything that went wrong. A full and candid reckoning with history may be particularly difficult in a culture like ours with such a strong tradition of looking ahead to a "new deal," a "new frontier," a "new world order," as if the past has no bearing on the present. It's enough to lead Gore Vidal to refer to us as the United States of Amnesia.

And so historians should feel a special obligation to remind us of important realities that may once have seemed obvious. Historical work thrives, of course, on new evidence and new interpretations, but it is also depends on the daily practice of remembering and recovering, the struggle to get things right. As Gloria Emerson put it in her brilliant, now largely forgotten, classic about the Vietnam War, *Winners and Losers*, "it is important to remember, to spell the names correctly, to know the provinces, before we are persuaded that none of it happened, that none of us were in such places."

Oral history has an important place in this memory work. As Carl Mirra makes clear in this compelling and important book, oral histories, like all sources, should not be taken on faith but weighed alongside other accounts and evidence. Our memories are not merely partial and flawed, but selective, all-too-human in the way they support our prejudices and predilections. Yet they can also be great reservoirs of unknown, unacknowledged, and disparaged historical knowledge and experience. When carefully probed and scrutinized, memory can take us to unfamiliar places that challenge every convenient or self-serving claim about the past. War, perhaps more than any other human activity, is promoted and sustained in the language of abstraction—sacrifice, freedom, duty, civilization. As Hemingway once noted, those words sound obscene alongside the concrete realities of war, especially the bodies of the dead. The accounts in this book are not like accounts we typically hear from government officials and the major media. Individual testimonies like these can help us connect the detailed, lived experience of war to the larger claims about the war we all, as citizens, must hazard.

Mirra is an unapologetic critic of this war. His political views were largely shaped by his decision to leave the Marine Corps as a conscientious objector during the Persian Gulf War. And yet he has a genuine curiosity about points of view on all sides of the Iraq War debate and he includes the testimonies of veterans and policymakers who support the war alongside those of its critics. And even the critics come from a variety of political perspectives—Left, liberal, libertarian, and even conservative. Indeed, one of the more remarkable aspects of the Iraq War has been the degree to which it has inspired opposition from a fascinating mix of people who might disagree on many other issues, but are united in viewing this war as an illegitimate and dangerous abuse of American power.

A final thought: The voices in these pages, however different, share an engagement with the most serious events of our time. However difficult and depressing the subject can be, it is always inspiring to be in the presence of people struggling to offer witness from their own experience and to make meaning of it in relation to a larger history. It doesn't seem too much to say that democracy depends, in some measure, on such crucial acts of citizenship and the work of historians like Carl Mirra to elicit and enrich them.

Acknowledgments

The idea for this book grew out of a conversation with Staughton Lynd. He insisted that historians should document the testimony of Iraq War veterans and argued that the Vietnam War was brought to an end by veterans who had turned against war. Recording the memories of Operation Iraqi Freedom veterans, his comments implied, might potentially alter the country's frame of reference on the war. The lifelong radical observed that any such effort should reach out to veterans whether their experience with the war was positive, negative or somewhere in between.

Together we launched an Oral History Working Group for the Historians against the War. Christian Appy, Monica and Kevin Benderman, Rosemary Feurer, Enrique Ochoa, Staughton, and I participated in the working group that was heartily supported by the historians. I compiled a pamphlet, which Jim O'Brien formatted and printed, entitled *Join Us? Testimonies of Iraq War Veterans and Their Families* in July 2006. It was the seed for this book.

The pamphlet was unapologetically antiwar and presented the voices of oppositional veterans exclusively. Marc Becker of Truman State University suggested that I interview veterans who supported the war, not necessarily in an attempt to achieve balance but to broaden the conversation. Since that time, what we call the "Left" has won the debate over the war. The administration's handling of the conflict has led a significant majority of the American populace to disapprove of the invasion.

Broadening the conversation seems worthwhile at this historical juncture. The voices of veterans of all political persuasions, who sacrificed the most among Americans, remain largely omitted from the public conversation on the war.

It occurred to me that I had little understanding of those veterans who supported the war. It also occurred to me that those who supported the war likely had an equally limited understanding of veterans (and citizens) who opposed it. Therefore, this book seeks to present both sides so that we gain a better grasp of one another, not simply for the sake of understanding, but to alter the for/against framework that limits our creativity and options for solving the dilemmas surrounding the war.

I hope that my presentation of the material is fair to all sides and illustrates each person's commitment and sacrifice in a respectful manner. Interviewing combat veterans has had a profound impact on me. People shared visceral and often tearful stories, which have forever altered my views of warfare. At one point, I told the series editor, Linda Shopes, that I could not complete the project. I did not know how to reconcile the conflicting accounts and opinions with my own views on the war. She gently allowed me to think out loud and work through this impasse, and I owe her a special debt of gratitude. Chris Chappell at Palgrave Macmillan was equally patient, and I was fortunate to have him as my editor. His skillful editorial remarks improved the manuscript.

Throughout this project, I have attempted to moderate my political views so as to better understand the "other" side. There was a time when I impulsively derided soldiers as brainwashed mercenaries. In talking with soldiers who support the war, I encountered complex human beings, driven by a diverse set of motivations. Readers who back the war are invited to see the same complexity in the antiwar voices contained in the following pages. Just as I wrestled to break through to understand the other side, I encourage the reader to do the same as they work through the pages of this book.

What struck me was that few of those soldiers who supported the war expressed anger toward soldiers who turned to the antiwar movement. Conversely, most of the antiwar soldiers held little animosity toward their pro-war counterparts. This is not to say that all soldiers feel the same about their opponents. Rather than portraying certain veterans as good, and others as bad, both the pro and antiwar soldiers are "good" veterans who have sacrificed a great deal. It is my hope that the sample of veterans in this book provides a worthwhile model for public dialogue.

Several people helped by reading drafts or by providing contacts with potential interviewees. Marv Gettleman read my original proposal to Palgrave Macmillan, and registered a sharp yet helpful critique. I should thank Randy Rydell, a senior political affairs officer in the Office of the UN Undersecretary General for Disarmament Affairs, who made it possible for me to get in touch with Dr. Hans Blix. Karl Grossman introduced me to Rydell, once again opening a door for me. Kelly Dougherty of Iraq Veterans against the War put me in touch with Camilo Mejía. Captain James McCormick and army historian Richard Killbane also assisted me in locating veterans to interview. I consider myself fortunate that Christian Appy read the complete manuscript and contributed a foreword. His supporting remarks at a panel (and after) where I presented some of the research on this book were most encouraging.

I especially wish to thank the interviewees in this book. They all graciously took time from their busy schedules to answer an array of questions. Listening to their stories has indeed been a transformative experience. Quite simply, I say to them all—thank you.

Introduction

This book preserves the raw and vivid memories of combat veterans and their families as well as those of public officials. The stories span from the battlefield to the offices of Washington to capture the broadest spectrum of voices, all of which depict the reality of the Iraq War. They uncover the emotional toll of war on its participants. What goes through a soldier's mind when he or she witnesses (or participates) in killing? How does a volunteer soldier evolve into an antiwar activist? How does it feel to lose a son or daughter in war? By examining the unfettered and often riveting words of soldiers and other individuals who were touched by the war, including some who came to reject what they saw, readers will better understand the true nature of war.

In March 2003, the United States invaded Iraq on the premise that Saddam Hussein's regime possessed weapons of mass destruction. In fall 2004, the United States' own "Iraq Survey Group" confirmed what many skeptics had maintained: that Iraq did not produce these banned weapons after 1991, and destroyed ones that remained after the First Gulf War. The Bush administration's inability to locate these weapons has incited a passionate debate over the legality and necessity of the war. High-ranking officials such as General Anthony Zinni, former head of the U.S. Central Command, have entered this debate. He sharply criticized the Bush administration's Iraq war plan. "I saw at a minimum true dereliction, negligence and irresponsibility; at worst lying, incompetence, and corruption" the general wrote. However, "don't blame the troops," cautioned Zinni.[1] Too often debates regarding the invasion have obscured the essence of combat and how it impacts the soldiers and their families.

The central argument of this book is that a sane civic dialogue is needed, one that can confront the errors of the Bush administration, while at the same time respecting the commitment of veterans and their families as we attempt to grasp the war's reality and move beyond sensationalized media images. The book uses oral history to transcribe interviewees' testimony into narrative form, with questions removed. Each chapter is organized around a common theme that unites the narrators in the section. The testimony of each narrator includes a head note that explains the person's service record and/or background.

Although the narrative foregrounds the oppositional voices, the reader can relate them to the contrasting accounts contained within the text. These separate and distinct perspectives give context and depth to the opposing voices, and allow readers to decide how they should reframe our understanding of the war. Whatever the reader decides, s/he will better understand the reality of war.

I claim that the testimony of soldiers is as valid as the memories and reflections of Pentagon planners and public intellectuals. It might be well to recall the words of Thich Nhat Hanh, the neutralist Vietnamese Buddhist Monk, who lived thorough the horrors of the Vietnam War. In his work with veterans, Nhat Hanh concluded that veterans "have experience that makes them the light of the tip of the candle, illuminating the roots of war and the way to peace."[2] Indeed, their experience with war can offer insights that might otherwise go unnoticed. That the book highlights veterans' voices does not mean it wishes to romanticize them. International relations scholar Andrew Bacevich warns that, "to assuage uneasy consciences, the many who do not serve proclaim their high regard for the few who do." Placing service members at the "top of the nation's moral hierarchy" is potentially dangerous, according to Bacevich.[3] Such a process promotes militarism, which is historically linked to authoritarian politics. Yet, veterans offer a unique and important perspective on the war based on their first-hand experience. Should this experience lead them to conclude that the mission is unattainable; the war will reach its conclusion. Paying attention to the soldier's perspective on the war does not require sanctification of the warrior.

This volume seeks to demonstrate that ordinary folks can participate in the wider process of historical interpretation and generalization.[4] This method follows oral historian Michael Frisch's concept of "shared authority." I understand that "the challenge of sharing authority is hardly unidirectional, as if authority were some dammed up reserve 'we' release so that it can flow down to 'them.'"[5] Each of the narrators brings expertise about their own experiences to the dialogue. Through shared authority, interviewees construct their own interpretative narrative. Interviewees have read and edited the transcribed interviews, which contributes to this sharing of authority.

I reach for a sense that these narratives hold the potential to reframe traditional narratives of war and patriotism, "creating opportunities for a more engaged public culture."[6] Experts with advanced degrees are not the only sources for historical interpretation. Iraq War veterans are capable of evaluating the causes and outcome of the conflict as a result of their individual experiences with war and their passionate investigations to make sense out of that experience. As historian Staughton Lynd has argued, oral historians should turn to interviewees not only for stories "but also for interpretation."[7] Indeed, we should not leave the evaluation of this war to the pundits; they should "share authority" with veterans over the meaning of the Iraq invasion.

This book attempts to contribute to a public conversation on the war, one that opens the reader to experiences and perspectives that usually remain undocumented. The history of modern warfare is all too often written from the perspective of generals, policy officials, presidents, and politicians. This book places the testimony of soldiers and family members side by side with policy makers and scholars. While my own antiwar prejudices have undoubtedly shaped the selection and presentation of interviews, the value of this book is in the testimony itself. I carefully attempted to preserve the authenticity of these voices by way of sharing authority with each narrator.

To avoid misunderstanding, I am not suggesting that the oral history narratives presented here are absolutely authoritative. I researched each interviewee's background as much as possible before interviewing them. All interviews started with an inquiry into the person's life history and personal background as much as they would permit. I have attempted to confirm the accuracy of each narrator's account, yet it is not feasible to track down every detail. In some cases, I could substantiate a narrator's testimony through public reports and military records. If someone shared something that seemed unlikely, I either found independent verification or omitted it.

The narrator's account of events is indeed not always accurate and oral history is not always perfect regarding the facts. I was fortunate to interview Hans Blix, and he cautioned me "to be careful" concerning the use of oral history. He cited a text on the United Nations that he believed relied on various statements that were not always fully reliable.[8] A Pentagon planner who declined my interview request acknowledged that he respected my attempt to interview a variety of subjects, but suggested that oral history often allows people "to retroactively reinvent" themselves.

Alessandro Portelli's extensive study on form and meaning in oral history reminds us that narrator's memories may manipulate facts and reorder chronological details. This modification is not caused by "faulty recollections," but is "generated by memory and imagination to make sense of crucial events and of history in general." Factual errors often reveal the narrator's interests, desires and aspirations. We gain a deeper meaning of any particular event, Portelli maintains, if we understand these mistakes as an attempt by interviewees to make sense out of the event in question. They serve as a window into the narrator's emotional world and state of mind. Most interviewees wish to "confer coherence to their stories" by following a consistent "mode of selection." For example, for soldiers who experienced the trauma of the battlefield, their narrative might be a response to the feeling of powerlessness and defeat, an emotion that many seek to avoid. It could be that the pro-war soldier adheres to a nationalist mode that preserves his or her identity and self-worth. The same might be said for antiwar soldiers (and families) who adopt a critical stance. An "upward, vertical shift" into the politics of the antiwar movement moves the narrator away from the trauma of the battlefield and shields one from powerlessness. Portelli maintains that this "discrepancy between fact and memory" enhances oral history insofar as it points to the deeper meaning behind individual and collective memory, a meaning that would be lost if we recorded only the facts. Though oral sources are "not always fully reliable," Portelli writes, "rather than being a weakness, this is however, their strength: errors, inventions, and myths lead us through and beyond facts to their meanings."[9] Sometimes the narrators may rearrange events, but this "skewed" memory may indeed offer a more poignant insight on the meaning of war and how we wish to remember it. The value of oral history does not reside in facts alone.

It might be well to note that even the most well-intentioned historian or scholar who relies on archival research is equally capable of distortions and omissions. Despite the risks, oral history remains an invaluable tool. In the following pages, we can read accounts of people who participated in the same events and immediately compare and contrast their experiences. Readers, of course, should consult outside sources to verify those items that interest them. Moreover, every narrator does not distort the record. Many soldiers whom I interviewed cited references; one even referred me to the U.S. Army historian for clarification. As with all historical accounts, we must approach the material with a critical eye, but avoid a wholesale debunking of oral history testimony.

Of special importance is the means by which the interviewee's answers are constructed and presented. The author of this volume is no empty vassal and brings his own biases to the public conversation. I am, as noted, "antiwar" and have spent a considerable amount of time studying and critiquing U.S. foreign policy. Part of my antiwar activity includes my resistance to the first U.S./Iraq War as a member of the U.S. Marine Corps.[10] Historical interpretation is always affected by the historian's prejudices. Nevertheless, the narrators in this volume are not proffered as data sources to confirm my interpretation of the war, but as individuals who are trying to make sense out of their experience.

While my sympathies reside with those soldiers who decided to speak out against the war, it does not mean that this book is somehow rendered incapable of presenting a range of opinions. The cynical reader might be tempted to dismiss the book as favoring antiwar sentiment. If the book does indeed lean toward an antiwar stance, it would be consistent with world opinion.[11] But we should recall one major aim of this book is to open dialogue, and there is a range of views here for readers to weigh and debate.

Dialogue presupposes understanding. Our rigid camps of Left/Right, pro-war/antiwar, and us/them inhibit dialogue and understanding. Scholars across disciplines have weighed in on the war, with new experts appearing daily. There is no urgency for another book dismantling the administration's handling of the war. We need to move from debate to dialogue, which paves the way for constructive solutions. Debates over the war, particularly in America's sound-bite television culture of screaming talk show hosts, are all too often what conflict worker Johan Galtung has called "continuation of war by verbal means."[12]

I observed in the acknowledgments that those who support the war (including its planners) and those who oppose it have little understanding of one another. This rift became painfully clear to me when I contacted an Iraq War veteran who backed the mission. At first, he was open to sharing his story. Then researched my background and discovered an antiwar activist, who he believed could not possibly function as an "objective" historian. He had little interest in talking to a peacenik. I explained that my goal was to understand, not to judge. This was not easy for me, I pleaded, but I nonetheless felt that we needed to start somewhere to move beyond solidified factions. Remarkably, he immediately embraced my gesture toward dialogue and we completed a rewarding interview.

"Dialogue is with persons, not with categories," Galtung reminds us. "We dehumanize the personal Thou by seeing that individual as representative of a category, of an It."[13] Although the chapter titles of this book admittedly slide toward categories of for/against, I implore the reader to read the testimony of each individual therein as a "Thou" not an "It." Wrestling with the individual voices can transform our grasp of the categories pro-war or antiwar. In doing so, we acquire a fresh perspective on those with whom we disagree, one that allows for understanding the person first, and the category second, which again, is the prerequisite for dialogue and creative solutions.

Christian Appy's oral history of the Vietnam War, *Patriots: The Vietnam War Remembered from All Sides*, provides a remarkable example of what I am reaching for in this book. Appy recorded the testimony of Anne Morrison Welsh, the widow of Norman Morrison, a Quaker who burned himself to death outside the Pentagon in November 1965, selecting the method of protest employed by Vietnamese Buddhist Monks. Anne Morrison Welsh reports that she was moved by former Defense Secretary Robert McNamara's 1995 book, *In Retrospect*. This chief war planner made headlines for admitting that the war was wrong. He also acknowledged that Morrison's act was a "tragedy" for both his family and the nation as it was an "outcry against the killing." "I reacted to the horror of his action," McNamara wrote, "by bottling up my emotions and avoided talking about them with anyone." Anne Morrison Welsh wrote McNamara to say that she too suppressed her emotions. The Pentagon planner telephoned Morrison Welsh shortly thereafter. As a result of their dialogue, she "felt this little bit of kinship with him...as a human being. It was almost as if we hadn't been on opposite sides of the chasm that had split our country apart."[14] Something similar, albeit in less personal and profound way, happened to me as I interviewed soldiers and others across the political spectrum. If Morrison, the wife of a Quaker who set himself on fire to protest the war could feel a kinship with a war planner, then Americans today can experience a kinship with their counterparts in the antiwar or pro-war camps. I am not asking the antiwar movement to enter into a "coalition with the Marines,"[15] or that "pro-victory" veterans enlist in the ranks of the socialist party. No one needs to compromise their political convictions in order to listen to the other side.

This book does not pretend to be a full account of Operation Iraqi Freedom or soldier attitudes. It provides an overview of the lives, experiences and aspirations of soldiers and family members and select policy makers. The voices of Iraqis, the people most devastated and traumatized by the war, are limited in this text.[16] With attention to Albert Camus' warning that we should avoid an "algebra of blood," Samir Adil reminds us in the following pages that, "Mothers in Iraq suffer the same as Cindy Sheehan and all the mothers in the United States." The reason for the small number of Iraqis here is largely due to the book's focus on an internal dialogue within the United States over its role and mission in the Middle East. Yet, readers outside the states will gain an acquaintance with battlefield experiences, the personal impact of the war, and the policy debates.

There is the danger that some in the antiwar movement will reduce my approach here to willy-nilly, milquetoast liberalism. The war's supporters meanwhile might see the book as the ruminations of another radical peace activist. To both groups I say—give dialogue a chance.

ONE

Iraq and the United States: A Brief Sketch

Iraq is located in the Middle East and shares its Eastern border with Iran. Kuwait sits at Iraq's southern border, while Saudi Arabia is located immediately to the west of Iraq. As can be imagined, Iraq has a dry, desert climate. However, in the north it is mountainous and experiences cold winters. A sergeant whom I interviewed encountered a hailstorm while in the north: "Hail came down all over the place. I mean ice covered sand in Iraq!" The country is roughly 4,300,000 square kilometers, slightly larger than the U.S. state of California. It is estimated that some 26 million people lived in Iraq in 2007 with concentrated populations in the capital city of Baghdad. Most Iraqis are Muslim; however there is significant tension between Shiite and Sunni Muslims as well as the ethnic Kurds who reside in the north.

These disparate groups were brought together as modern-day Iraq by European powers following World War I. Most Western accounts of the war focus on the European theater, but tumultuous events were unfolding in the Middle East during this time. The Ottoman Empire, which existed from roughly 1300 to 1923 AD, controlled a vast portion of the Middle East, including the region that is present-day Iraq. The empire was comprised of various ethnic groups, including Arabs, Assyrians, Armenians, Kurds, and Turks. The Turks were the largest ethnic group and the empire was ruled by the Sultan of Turkey at the outbreak of World War I. After the war, the empire was dissolved and modern-day Turkey was established in 1923.

The Ottoman Turks declared war on Britain and France in 1915. The British in turn encouraged Arab revolts throughout the Middle East, pledging independence to the nationalist insurgents at the conclusion of the war. The reasons for the revolts are complicated and beyond the scope of this brief introductory overview, but the British encountered eager nationalists in the region. Fabled stories of British officer T.E. Lawrence, dubbed "Lawrence of Arabia," traveling across the Middle East fomenting Arab revolt are well known. While the British (and French) were promising independence to the Arab insurgents, behind the scenes the European powers began devising plans to control the Middle East. The Sykes-Picot Agreement in 1916 divided the region into spheres of influence, with the British claiming control over Iraq and Palestine and the French laying claim to Syria and Lebanon.[1] This decades-old double-dealing lingers in the present-day memory of many Middle Easterners. Osama bin Laden's frenzied tirades play on this memory as he has compared George W. Bush and British prime minister Tony Blair's invasion of Iraq to the Sykes and Picot Agreement.[2]

Another significant pact occurred in Italy at the San Remo Conference of 1920. The European powers placed much of the Middle East under imperial mandate following the partition lines noted above. Insurrections abounded in the region and the European rulers harshly counterattacked the aspiring nationalist movements. In the hope of stabilizing the newly formed Iraq Kingdom, the British installed King Faisal in 1921. Faisal died in 1933, the year after Iraq gained its independence from Britain and joined the League of Nations. Before his death Faisal signed a treaty that permitted the British to station troops in Iraq. It was indeed a limited and constrained independence as many Iraqis resented the British military presence. Throughout this period, oil was discovered in the Middle East and the British-run Anglo-Persian Oil Company gained concessions in Iraq and elsewhere, as did some U.S. companies. Petroleum was one significant reason why the English and other European powers wished to exert control over the Middle East. To this day, Iraq's major natural resources and exports are petroleum and natural gas.

"Indirect" British rule over Iraq continued until 1958. In July that year Brigadier Abdul Karim Qasim overthrew King Faisal II, the last remnant of informal British rule. Qasim developed a republican constitution. He was also instrumental in establishing the Organization of the Petroleum Exporting Companies (OPEC) in 1960, which threatened to reduce Western influence over the flow of oil in the Middle East.[3] In 1963, a Baath Party military attaché ousted Qasim. Some researchers believe that the U.S. Central Intelligence Agency (CIA) aided the Baath Party to remove Qasim, owing to his "non-aligned" stance in the cold war and nationalist impulses concerning natural resources. Qasim was "seen as a grave threat in 1963," wrote Roger Morris who was on the senior staff of the National Security Council during the Johnson and Nixon administrations. "Washington's role in the coup went unreported at the time and has been little noted since. America's anti-[Qasim] intrigue has been widely substantiated, however, in disclosures by the Senate Committee on Intelligence," claimed Morris.[4]

Scholar Hanna Batatu discovered that the Yugoslav embassy in Iraq reported that the Iraqi Baathists had secret connections with the United States. Furthermore, King Hussein of Jordan, an ally of the United States, said that he "know[s] for a certainty" that American intelligence assisted the coup.[5] The importance of this alleged involvement resides in the fact that the Baath Party is the political group that Saddam Hussein belonged to and would later rule. We should not exaggerate the significance of the U.S. meddling in this affair; we should not ignore it either.

Factions and infighting plagued the Baath Party and another coup occurred in 1968, bringing Ahmad Hassan Bakr into power. The party instituted land reforms and tried to pacify the Kurdish nationalists in the north who often demanded independence from Iraq. They implement an agreement that permitted some degree of autonomy for the Kurds, but the Baathists did not allow them complete independence. The Baath Party was dominated by Sunni Muslims and Iraq's Shiite majority grew increasingly impatient with their lack of full representation in the country. In 1979, Shiite Islamic fundamentalists seized power next door in Iran and instigated Iraqi Shiites to demand a larger role in their political system. The then Iraqi vice president Saddam Hussein's harsh approach to the Shiite situation displeased Bakr. Political pressure forced Bakr to resign and Saddam became president in the summer of 1979. A ceremonial election was held and Saddam quickly executed twenty-one officials, including several members of the Revolutionary Command Council, the nation's major executive body.[6]

Less than a year after taking the presidency, Saddam invaded Iran, sparking the Iran-Iraq War that lasted from 1980 to 1988. The United

States provided Iraq with logistics and support during the war.[7] The Americans feared that an expanding Iran posed a greater threat to international stability as the country held U.S. hostages and was aggressively anti-American. European powers also aided Iraq's effort in the war. The conflict drained the resources of both nations and cost Iraq some $200 billion. When Iraqi troops returned from the battlefield in the late 1980s, they found themselves unemployed. Bloody labor disputes ensued as Iraq experienced an economic crisis trying to pay off the war debt. Part of the problem was an OPEC oil quota that restricted the amount of petroleum that Iraq could sell.

In 1990, Iraq accused Kuwait of exceeding that quota, thereby driving down the price of oil. Iraq argued that both the quota and falling prices made it nearly impossible to rebuild its economy. Saddam also believed that Kuwait was "stealing" oil from a disputed oil field on the Iraq-Kuwait border, and claimed that Kuwait was rightfully part of Iraq, artificially separated seventy years earlier by European imperialists. Ultimately, he threatened to attack Kuwait in retaliation. At least one Kuwaiti official stated that they ignored Saddam's threats because the United States supported Kuwait in spite of, or perhaps because of, its production of oil beyond the OPEC quota.[8]

Given that Iraq maintained friendly relations with the United States in the years preceding the Kuwait dispute, Saddam misunderstood U.S. intentions in the region. On August 2, 1990 Saddam invaded Kuwait. The United States led the call for a UN resolution against Iraq's invasion, which was approved by the body in 1990. In January 1991, the United States and its allies launched a bombing campaign and ground war called Operation Desert Storm. The allied effort successfully removed Iraqi troops from Kuwait, and a "cessation of hostilities" was announced on February 28, 1991.[9] Saddam remained in power and a series of UN resolutions were imposed to contain Iraq. Some observers now claim that then president George Bush, Sr., failed to finish the job by leaving Saddam in power. Bush Sr. and his national security adviser Brent Scowcroft gave an interesting explanation in 1998 as to why Saddam was not removed in 1991, one that appears to contain some useful lessons for the current occupation of Iraq:

> Trying to eliminate Saddam...would have incurred incalculable human and political costs...We would have been forced to occupy Baghdad, and, in effect, rule Iraq. The coalition would have instantly

collapsed...Under these circumstances, there was no viable "exit strategy"...going in and occupying Iraq, thus unilaterally exceeding the United Nations mandate, would have destroyed the precedent of international response to aggression that we hoped to establish. Had we gone the invasion route, the United States could conceivably still be an occupying power in a bitterly hostile land.[10]

The Bush Sr. administration avoided an occupation of Iraq as it was too risky and dangerous. Instead, a cease-fire arrangement was established under the UN Security Council Resolution (UNSC) 687 following the first U.S.-Iraq War in 1991. This measure ordered Iraq to return all property to Kuwait, accept the UN designated Iraq/Kuwait border, and dismantle its weapons program. An inspection team was formed, the UN Special Commission (UNSCOM), that worked to ensure Iraq's compliance by examining sites throughout the country. Another resolution, UNSC 688, was passed after Saddam ruthlessly suppressed a rebellion in the north; it imposed sanctions against Iraq, placing limits on imports and exports. The purpose of these sanctions was to prevent Saddam from building up a nuclear arsenal and from planning future invasions.[11] By the late 1990s, the UNSCOM inspectors declared that Iraq's nuclear arsenal was likely eliminated. However, the Iraqi regime was hardly cooperative, and a cat-and-mouse game between the regime and UN inspectors left unanswered questions regarding the country's biological and chemical weapons capacity.

Meanwhile, the Soviet Union had collapsed in 1991. The previous five decades of U.S. foreign policy was animated by the cold war conflict between the United States and the Soviets. With the winnowing of the Soviet Empire, the United States emerged as the world's remaining superpower. Many political commentators began calling for U.S. "primacy" or an American global presence, whereby the United States would serve as a global protector. In 1992, William Clinton defeated George H. Bush in the presidential race, despite some observers accusing Clinton of being too soft in international affairs. One such group, the Project for a New American Century (PNAC), directed its attention to Clinton's stance toward Iraq. The PNAC included both "neoconservative" and traditional conservative analysts, who urged him to remove Saddam Hussein from power. The neoconservatives, in particular, promoted an interventionist foreign policy with the goal of spreading democracy by way of defeating tyrannical regimes. In 1998, PNAC sent a letter to President Clinton demanding regime change in Iraq.[12] The letter was signed by several people who later assumed important positions in the George W. Bush administration, such as Donald Rumsfeld, (defense secretary, 2001–2006); Paul Wolfowitz (deputy secretary of defense, 2001–2005); John Bolton (U.S. ambassador to the UN, 2005–2006); and several others. Not all the PNAC analysts can be classified as neoconservative; Colonel Lawrence Wilkerson argues in chapter five that Vice President Cheney and Rumsfeld are "ultranationalists," who joined so-called neoconservatives such as Wolfowitz in the drumbeat for war against Iraq. The ascendancy of these policy-makers to official government posts under Bush, Jr., has led to a spirited debate over the degree to which they controlled U.S. foreign policy, particularly the decision to invade Iraq in March 2003.

The terrorist attacks against the World Trade Center and the Pentagon on September 11, 2001 renewed concerns regarding the U.S. role in international affairs. The United States charged that the Taliban government in Afghanistan was harboring Osama bin Laden, who was assumed to be the mastermind behind the 9/11 tragedy. On October 7, 2001 the United States attacked Afghanistan under the banner of Operation Enduring Freedom and quickly removed the Taliban regime. Instability and ongoing skirmishes continued in the years following the U.S./allied invasion of Afghanistan, while Osama bin Laden remained elusive.

As the conflict in Afghanistan slowly receded from public view, the Bush administration turned its attention to Iraq. The administration alleged that Saddam Hussein both aided bin Laden's Al Qaeda terrorist group and possessed weapons of mass destruction. In September 2002, the administration released its "National Security Strategy of the United States." The document articulated a U.S. foreign policy of U.S. global leadership, unilateralism, and preemptive war. This policy was dubbed the "Bush Doctrine." The administration also identified countries that it said posed a threat to the United States, labeled the "axis of evil," which was comprised of North Korea, Iran, and Iraq.

Critics immediately charged that the Bush administration was "hijacked" by the neoconservatives, who had earlier called for a unilateral, preemptive foreign policy as well as an attack on Iraq. Famed *Washington Post* journalist Bob Woodward reported that Donald Rumsfeld and Paul Wolfowitz, the two leading figures at the Defense Department at the time, advocated an attack on Iraq after the September 11 disaster, despite the lack of evidence of Saddam's role in the terrorist plot. Pentagon planners had allegedly been working on an invasion of Iraq before 9/11 and Rumsfeld sought to "take advantage of the opportunity offered by the terrorist attacks to go after Saddam."[13]

Bush went before the UN in September 2002 to warn of the danger that Iraq presented to the world. The next month Congress passed H.J. Resolution 114, "Authorization for Use of Military Force against Iraq Resolution of 2002." Section 2 of the resolution asserted support for diplomatic efforts, while section three authorized the President to use force against Iraq in accordance with the War Powers Act of 1973. In November 2002, the UN passed Resolution 1441, which reestablished weapons inspections by UNMOVIC (UN Monitoring, Verification and Inspection Commission) in Iraq under Hans Blix. It offered Iraq "a final opportunity to comply" with the inspection process. Section 4 of the UN Resolution 1441 specifies that Iraq's breach of the inspections would be "reported to the Security Council for assessment." In February 2003, then Secretary of State Colin Powell appeared before the UN to convince the body to enforce Resolution 1441 on the grounds that Iraq possessed weapons of mass destruction. It is worth noting that in February 2001 Powell acknowledged that Iraq "has not developed any significant capability with respect to weapons of mass destruction."[14] A second vote to authorize force was not undertaken. Many nations and UN inspectors were not convinced that Iraq posed an imminent threat as the Bush team charged.

On March 20, 2003 the United States launched Tomahawk missiles into Iraq from ships in the Red Sea, marking the start of Operation Iraqi Freedom, and beginning a debate over the legality of the war that persists today. Experts on international law claim that the U.S. attacks violated Article 2, Section 4 of the UN charter that states, "all members shall refrain from the threat of force" against another. The war's opponents also point to a July 23, 2002 document, dubbed the "Downing Street Memo," which was reprinted in the London *Sunday Times* newspaper. It revealed the minutes of a secret meeting among some of Britain's highest-ranking defense officials concerning their interactions with the Bush administration. One summary of a meeting with former CIA chief George Tenet before the war states that

[Sir Richard Dearlove, head of Britain's intelligence agency] reported on his recent talks in Washington...Military action was now seen as inevitable. Bush wanted to remove Saddam, through military action, justified by the conjunction of terrorism and WMD. But the intelligence and facts were being fixed around the policy.[15]

The Bush administration had invaded Iraq on the pretense that it held weapons of mass destruction, but the secret memo suggests that the United States had decided on war as the inspections were unfolding and it was still unclear if Iraq violated the resolutions and built an arsenal. Yet, supporters of the war argue that the Bush regime was authorized by Congress to attack Iraq and the rogue nation violated UN Resolution 1441. Hans Blix suggests in chapter five that the invasion was inconsistent with international law.

The Center for Public Integrity has claimed that key administration officials made "at least 935 false statements" regarding the threat of Iraq to the United States in the build up to war. These misleading statements include President Bush's March 2003 assertion that there was "no doubt that the Iraq regime continues to possess and conceal some of the most lethal weapons ever devised."[16] Significant doubts were raised by the International Atomic Energy Agency (IAEA), UN weapons inspectors and American policy-makers.[17]

Doubts over the necessity of war and the administration's trustworthiness were also aroused following claims that Saddam Hussein attempted to obtain nuclear material from an African nation. "Iraq recently sought significant quantities of uranium from Africa," Bush insisted in a 2003 presidential address, but this was later demonstrated to be false and was disputed privately by the CIA at the time of the announcement.[18] Former diplomat Joseph Wilson publicly debunked the President's assertion, and his wife's identity as a CIA operative was leaked to the press. Vice President Cheney's chief of staff, Lewis Libby, was convicted for obstruction of justice and perjury in this matter. Libby was sentenced to over two years in prison and fined approximately $250,000. President Bush commuted Libby's prison sentence, but not the fine.[19]

The administration's credibility was further eroded following Cheney's claim that Iraq was "the geographic base of terrorists who have had us under assault for many years, but most especially on 9/11." This remark strongly suggested that Iraq helped to facilitate the 9/11 assault, an assertion that Bush and Rumsfeld acknowledged was without sufficient evidence.[20] The official 9/11 Commission has documented that Saddam

Hussein could not credibly be connected to the terrorist attack on the United States.[21]

Misleading assertions that Iraq was involved with 9/11 are especially relevant to the present study insofar as it influenced the attitudes of American soldiers. A Zogby poll illustrated that 85 percent of U.S soldiers who served in Iraq believed that they were there "to retaliate for Saddam's role in the 9/11 attacks." Critics suggest that had the soldiers not been misled, many may not have supported the war effort. These observers point to the same poll that illustrates significant dissatisfaction among soldiers as U.S. objectives became increasingly unclear as the war dragged on. 29 percent of soldiers polled said that the United States should withdraw immediately; another 22 percent felt that the United States should depart Iraq within six months; and 21 percent believed the troops should leave somewhere between six and twelve months. In sum, "an overwhelming majority" of 72 percent of U.S. troops declared that the United States should withdraw within one year.[22]

Even if we allow for a wide margin of error, this poll suggests a significant portion of American soldiers favor withdrawal. Many of the antiwar veterans in chapter two emphatically pointed to this Zogby poll, some demanding that I remember to include it in this narrative. It seems that they wish to confirm that they are not isolated individuals. Their sense that the war is misguided is shared by at least some of their comrades. None of this information should nullify the voices in subsequent chapters who argue for staying the course. However, any viable debate over withdrawal can not gloss over these findings.

Iraqi citizens also appear to oppose a continued occupation.[23] One reason why Iraqis might resent the U.S. occupation is that the Americans established a Coalition Provisional Authority (CPA) in their country in 2003. First led by Jay Garner, it was turned over to L. Paul Bremer III in May 2003. The office created the appearance of U.S. imperial control over Iraq, with some people calling Bremer a "proconsul," a term used to describe colonial administrators in the Roman Empire. President Bush mistakenly declared that major combat operations in Iraq were complete in May 2003. The president's "Mission Accomplished" stance was undermined by bombings and roadside attacks that continued to devastate Iraq. The deteriorating conditions and American control over Iraq contributed to the population's dissatisfaction with the U.S. presence there.

Events seemed to turn for the better in June 2004 when the CPA yielded control to the Iraqi Interim Government. Iyad Allawi was designated prime minister. Supporters of the war pointed out that the long, arduous journey toward "democratizing" Iraq was underway. The administration's justification for war shifted from the danger of nuclear attacks to the humanitarian effort to build democracy. Talk of democratic elections in Iraq to form a new government seemed to confirm the Bush administration's lofty rhetoric about setting captives free and spreading liberty abroad. The Bush administration's plan for elections was not as democratic as it seemed on the surface. The Bush administration wished to postpone elections until after an Iraqi constitution was drafted. According to the *Washington Post,* the United States sought to appoint local leaders and opposed general elections where one person gets one vote.[24] By 2004, the occupation forces had already cancelled elections, which was "creating anger and resentment" among Iraqis.[25] The Iraqi people orchestrated a campaign of nonviolent demonstrations, demanding direct participation in elections. In January 2004, 100,000 Iraqis participated in a peaceful protest that called for a general election, the *Associated Press* reported.[26] After much tension, the occupation authority agreed to hold elections, but they were postponed until January 2005, when historic elections were held. *The Nation* news magazine reported that the, "Iraqis voted overwhelmingly to throw out the U.S.-installed government of Iyad Allawi, who refused to ask the United States to leave."[27] It was the will of the Iraqi people coupled with the U.S. ouster of Saddam Hussein that led to democratic elections, rather than U.S. goodwill alone. These elections led to the formation of the Iraqi Transitional Government that drafted a constitution in October 2005.[28]

A second, major election was conducted in December 2005. A 275 member council of representatives and the Permanent Government of Iraq were established. The Shiite United Iraqi Alliance (UIA) and the Kurdish Democratic Patriotic Alliance (DPAK) won most posts, while Sunnis generally boycotted the election. Eventually Kurdish leader Jalal Talabani gained the presidency and Nuri al-Maliki became prime minister as a member of the Islamic Dawa Party. The elections indicate the sectional strife in Iraq. Approximately 60 percent of the population is Shiite and 30–35 percent is Sunni Muslim. And, the ethnically and politically distinct Kurds hold a Sunni majority.

The elections are a salutary development but they have not stabilized Iraq. Road side bombings, U.S. skirmishes with insurgents, and factional violence plague the country. Fears of a civil war are daily pronounced in the media. At least twenty insurgent groups are believed to exist inside Iraq. The various groups hold grievances that include claims that the United States is "stealing" Iraq's oil and is responsible for skyrocketing unemployment. Other complaints are leveled at an Iraqi government that some see as a dupe of U.S. power.

The insurgent groups include the Islamic Army of Iraq, a Sunni group.[29] Moqtadar al-Sadr leads the Mahdi Army, a Shiite group that holds seats in the Iraqi Parliament. In June 2006, coalition forces killed Abu Musab al-Zarqawi, the leader of the Tawhid or "unity" resistance group. It was hoped that the Zarqawi's death would weaken the resistance movement, but it has continued. Other factions are former Baath soldiers, such as the Al Medina division and the Sunni Ansar-as Sunnah along the Syrian border. Smaller bands of resistance movements entail the Salafist group, and more secular "Nasserites, Communists, Socialists and National Resistance Brigades." According to the *American Conservative*, "many of these groups issued a joint call for liberation of Iraq from all foreign occupation and a free, democratic election." Camilo Mejía, a combat veteran turned peace activist, claims that in Iraq he confronted the "beginning of a widespread popular rebellion."[30] It is still unclear if Iraq is mired in a civil war or if the general population is in support of an uprising against the American occupiers. Sectarian strife rages between Sunni and Shiite factions in Iraq, which is further complicated by infighting among the Shiite groups. The demands for a separate Kurdistan in the North adds to these complications. This chaotic environment is where U.S. soldiers work to carry out Operation Iraqi Freedom.

On December 30, 2006, an explosive news report from Baghdad hit the Western world when Saddam Hussein was hanged for crimes against humanity. In early November 2006, Iraq's Special Tribunal (IST) sentenced Hussein to death for murdering an estimated 148 people in Dujail in retaliation for an assassination attempt on the Iraqi leader.

The sensational news of Hussein's death captured the attention of global news outlets. Few noticed a less dramatic story in the *Military Times* on December 29, 2006. It featured a poll of U.S. service members, which indicated dissatisfaction with President Bush's handling of the Iraq War. The year end poll of active duty service members, 66 percent of whom served at least one tour in Iraq, demonstrated that 42 percent of respondents expressed disapproval of Bush's command of the war, while only 35 percent indicated approval of the President's management of the war.[31] Normally the troops support the president when at war. This poll is interesting insofar as it points the military's frustration with the Bush administration. It does not mean that these soldiers oppose the war, but there is a clear dissatisfaction with Bush's handling of the war across political affiliations.

I have attempted to present a measured chronicle of the war, presenting perspectives of those who both oppose and support the continued U.S. presence in Iraq. I tried to respectfully and accurately portray their experiences and views, while attempting to offer the reader a fair account for which they can determine what they wish about the war. We should not, however, sacrifice accuracy on the altar of balance. A vast majority of Iraqi, U.S., and global citizens have expressed clear opposition to the U.S. war. In December 2006, the Congressionally sponsored Iraq Study Group, co-chaired by Republican James A. Baker III, released its much-heralded report, which acknowledged that the "majority of Americans are soured by the war." The situation in Iraq is "grave and deteriorating," the study continued. According to the Study Group, 3,000 Iraqis were killed each month with 180 attacks each day during 2006.[32] Meanwhile, the polls above show a similar, albeit less widespread, dissatisfaction with the Iraq invasion among U.S. soldiers.

Readers may be tempted to dismiss some of the analysis above as evidence of the author's bias. They might argue that the removal of Saddam Hussein is the first step in long process of developing democracy in Iraq. I will not quarrel with such criticism. Events are still unfolding and the final judgment on the Iraq War awaits future scholarship when all the evidence is in. In the meantime I invite readers to grapple with the testimony here with the aim of broadening the public dialogue regarding the U.S. invasion of Iraq.[33]

TWO

The New Winter Soldiers Redux:
The Patriotism of Antiwar GIs

You don't have to worry about soldiers not wanting to fight, as long as there is good reason for being at war.

—*Staff Sergeant Camilo Mejía*[1]

The army recruiter "only told me the great things" about the military, Michael Harmon says as he remembers enlisting in the service. Harmon, a veteran of Operation Iraqi Freedom, saw people "literally split open," and no longer trusts the U.S. government because the "whole war was a lie."

Not since the Vietnam War has the nation witnessed such passionate denunciations of war by its soldiers. Loose comparisons between the Vietnam War and the Iraq War are often misleading and inaccurate as the culture and geography of the two nations are worlds apart. Some basic similarities nonetheless remain among the two, disparate conflicts. One striking similarity is the open and public resistance among U.S. service members. In 1967, the Vietnam Veterans Against the War (VVAW) emerged when a half dozen soldiers marched in the Spring Mobilization in New York. Ron Kovic achieved national notoriety after the publication of *Born on the Fourth of July*, an autobiographical account that documented the horrors of war and how it often destroyed the young soldiers who proudly enlisted. Around the same time Tim O'Brien published an equally moving depiction of the conflict in *If I Die in a Combat Zone: Box Me up and Ship Me Out*.[2]

Like their Vietnam era counterparts, Iraq War veterans are also writing memoirs to document their experiences. These books include *The Road to Ar Ramadi: The Private Rebellion of Sergeant Camilo Mejía* by Camilo Mejía, who participated in an interview for this chapter. Other works include Anthony Swofford's *Jarhead: A Marine's Chronicle of the Gulf War and Other Battles* and Colby Buzzell's *My War: Killing Time in Iraq.*

Another phenomenon that begs a comparison to the Vietnam War is the appearance of Iraq Veterans against the War (IVAW). It first entered public view in July 2004 at the annual meeting of Veterans for Peace in Boston, Massachusetts. Earlier Mike Hoffman, the son of a steelworker from Allentown, Pennsylvania, who served in the Marine Corps, and Tim Goodrich, an Air Force veteran met at the "Dover to D.C." protests in March 2004. Shortly thereafter, they decided to contact other antiwar veterans, which quickly burgeoned into IVAW. The group claims 1,200 members and groups of Iraq War veterans are found at major antiwar demonstrations throughout the country.

A similarity that is subject to distortion and misrepresentation is the presence of Posttraumatic Stress Disorder (PTSD) among veterans of both wars. Sociologist Jerry Lembke has argued that the emphasis on stress disorders among Vietnam veterans has been used to portray the antiwar soldier as the "bad" veteran. He detailed how the media coupled stories of PTSD with coverage of significant GI protests to suggest that something was wrong with the soldier who turned against the war.[3] Questioning a war that was started on a faulty premise hardly constitutes a psychological problem. Combat stress impacts soldiers irrespective of their political views, and it does not convert the individual into a dysfunctional sociopath. In fact, this chapter will suggest that battlefield trauma can lead to positive social action, and a healthy attempt to restore the self among GIs who turn to activism as a form of patriotism.

Keeping in mind the misuses of PTSD in American culture, the U.S. Department of Veteran Affairs defines it as a "psychiatric disorder" and "stress reactions" that occur after "life threatening events such as military combat."[4] It is not a new phenomenon as PTSD has been documented in World War II, Korean War, and Gulf War veterans as well as in soldiers throughout the world. Some of the oppositional veterans who I interviewed spoke candidly about the syndrome. Naval Lieutenant Harvey Tharp reported that, "I now have bipolar disorder, which is very strange as I don't have a history of it in my family . . . If you have a tendency for it, a stressful event can trigger it. I have had mild PTSD symptoms, but nothing compared to some of my veteran friends." An army veteran, Herold Noel, exclaimed: "the soldier is angry... and might end up blowing some shit up or snapping." Fortunately, Herold adds that, "I am readjusting myself with some counseling."

A study in the *Journal of the American Medical Association* documents the frequency of PTSD in Iraq War veterans. The researchers conclude that there is a "strong relationship" between combat service in Iraq and mental health difficulties. For instance, approximately 19 percent of Operation Iraqi Freedom veterans reported mental health problems. The article cites a *New England Journal of Medicine* study that found 17 percent of Iraq War veterans "screened positive for PTSD, generalized anxiety or depression, prevalence nearly twice that observed among soldiers surveyed before deployment."[5] The military's own Mental Health Advisory Team (MHAT) acknowledged that roughly 20 percent of Operation Iraqi Freedom (2005–2007) soldiers "screened positive for a mental health problem."[6] The personal toll that war takes on the individual soldier deserves attention.

Robert Jay Lifton, a former air force psychiatrist and medical doctor who has done extensive work with combat participants, illustrated how combat distress can be transformed into political dissent as the highest form of patriotism. Lifton argued that an "animating guilt" can heal the veteran and maybe the nation as well. Veterans who worked to raise consciousness about war crimes also worked to heal themselves. He discovered that Vietnam veterans were capable of articulating their own misdeeds without slipping into a paralyzing sense of overall failure. These veterans accomplished this by accepting responsibility to resist the war and exposing its "grotesque details," while demanding that U.S. citizens and leaders take responsibility for the devastation that was inflicted on Southeast Asia. They illustrated "an impressive capacity to transform guilt feelings into expressions of responsibility in seeking to redirect their society toward a more humane path," Lifton concluded.[7]

This dynamic was often expressed by Operation Iraqi Freedom veterans whom I interviewed. Consider one Marine's reflection upon his tour in Iraq, whose testimony is not recorded in this text: "It was disgusting. I saw people carrying groceries get shot at... not real combat... I remember thinking over there 'are we allowed to do this?' The government just released us on this country, randomly killing people." But the war "made me reevaluate my opinion of the military. None of the romantic feelings were satisfied...It wasn't heroic...After being exposed to the hyper-macho [Marines], I really think it is the college students who actually voice their opposition to war who are the real heroes, especially in America because the country was founded on questioning things...The students who were shot at Kent State are more heroes than the Marines I knew."[8]

A sentiment that resembles an animating guilt, transforming destruction into social action, was voiced by Iraq War veteran Camilo Mejía. The army staff sergeant returned home after a tour in Iraq and then refused to redeploy on the grounds that he was a conscientious objector. Having served nearly a year in prison for his refusal to deploy to Iraq a second time, he surmised that, "I abused prisoners...I should have resisted my orders, and I should have fought for the dignity and preservation of life. I didn't because I was too afraid...I now know exactly what empowered me as I [entered prison]...I gained my freedom...freedom is not something physical...On that day I learned that there is no greater freedom than the freedom to follow one's conscience." He concluded that "it took the experience of war for me to see things in a broader perspective."[9]

Both of these accounts acknowledge that the battlefield caused an emotional strain, and one which was overcome through an appeal to morally engaged citizenship. What Lifton observed in Vietnam-era rebellious soldiers has again surfaced among Operation Iraqi Freedom veterans.

Richard Moser's comprehensive study of antiwar soldiers during the Vietnam War expanded Lifton's concept of animating guilt, and explored how oppositional veterans dealt with the country's cultural meltdown. In condensed form, Moser argued that the Frontier narrative of America as a beacon of freedom, spreading (or preserving) liberty across the globe, became untenable during the 1960s. No longer confident that the United States was governed by noble intentions, people en masse began to question U.S. values. The military resistance that emerged under these circumstances advanced "a new cultural form of immense historical importance—the figure of the new winter soldier." The Winter Soldier narrative draws on an alternative tradition of the citizen-soldier. Vietnam assaulted the glorification of weapons, war and the traditional warrior. Soldiers beset by battlefield horrors could no longer fall back on this heroic image for existential sustenance. They recovered instead an image of the citizen-soldier that rendered the battle for peace and social justice heroic. What these soldiers turned to was the "historically available enactment of the classic American-citizen soldier."[10] That is, they evoked the American Revolutionary image of the citizen-soldier who was suspicious of standing armies and insisted that the country adhere to its professed ideals.

The most dramatic expression of this recovery of an alternative warrior ideal was embodied in the January–February 1971 Winter Soldier hearings, a moniker derived from Thomas Paine's denunciation of summertime soldiers who deserted during the American Revolution when the conditions became too harsh. The true patriot, according to these Vietnam Veterans, was the one who spoke out against war and war crimes. An increasing number of such Winter Soldiers emerged and the veteran antiwar movement climaxed in 1971 as roughly two thousand VVAW [Vietnam Veterans against the War] members rallied on the streets of Washington, DC, for a series of protest actions.

It is no coincidence that the Iraq Veterans Against the War have turned to this "historically available enactment" of the citizen-soldier as they organized their own Winter Soldier hearing in Washington, DC, in March 2008. One of the main organizers of the new Winter Soldiers, Perry O'Brien, acknowledged that the 1971 hearings were an "inspiration." While the IVAW is modeled on the Vietnam veteran's hearings, they aim to create "our own tradition," articulating Moser's notion that dissenting soldiers strive to refashion the dominant image of the warrior. Discussing war crimes is important because there is "tremendous guilt about what we saw and did," O'Brien said, "in some sense we can live up to our moral responsibility by participation" in the Winter Soldier hearings and antiwar demonstrations. Inviting the public "to bear witness" has the potential for "healing" both the veteran and the nation.[11] O'Brien's remarks explicitly reflect both the reconstruction of the warrior from battlefield heroics to political engagement, while capturing Lifton's theory that an animating guilt propels many GI dissenters.

The veterans raised the specter of war crimes in 1971 and 2008, some having confessed that they participated in such horrors. These raw and honest declarations often encouraged other veterans to refuse orders, lest they partake in such transgressions. As military resistance blossomed in the Vietnam years, a massive draft resistance movement simultaneously spread across the nation. A less sensational case where war crimes were invoked to support a draft refusal during the Vietnam War concerns David Mitchell. In 1965, Mitchell called the draft an instrument of murder and refused to contribute to what he considered war crimes, noting that U.S.

conduct in Vietnam violated the Nuremberg Principles. The Nuremberg Principles were adopted by the International Military Tribunal following World War II as a standard in which the Nazis could be judged and punished accordingly. The principles outline crimes against peace, war crimes, and crimes against humanity. The tribunal deemed punishable aggressive wars, "ill-treatment of prisoners," and "wanton destruction of cities, towns, or villages." Images of the massacres at Ben Suc (1967) and My Lai (1968) brought macabre war crimes into American living rooms. Mitchell's invocation of the Nuremberg principles in 1965 was prescient. Even the conservative pundit William Buckley acknowledged that he was fortunate that he was not Mitchell's trial judge. "I could have scolded Mr. Mitchell along with the best of them," Buckley wrote, "But I'd have to cough and wheeze and clear my throat during that passage in my catechism at which I explained to Mr. Mitchell wherein the Nuremberg doctrine was obviously not at his disposal."[12]

Some of the volunteer soldiers during Operation Iraqi Freedom, although not subjected to the draft, have resurrected the Nuremberg Laws. In Hawaii, U.S. Army officer first lieutenant Ehren Watada emerged as someone who might loosely classify as Mitchell's counterpart. Of course, Mitchell's resistance arose from his draft refusal during Vietnam, while Watada volunteered for military service. Their stories might serve as a metaphor for the different nature of today's military resisters compared to the Vietnam era. Both men, however, are similar in claiming that their government committed war crimes and that international law prohibits them for partaking in such offenses. After refusing to deploy to Iraq, Watada faced a military court. In his testimony, Watada observed that

> It is my duty as a commissioned officer of the United States Army to speak out against grave injustices. My moral and legal obligation is to the Constitution not to those who would issue unlawful orders. I stand before you today because it is my job to serve and protect America's Soldiers, its people and innocent Iraqis who have no voice. It is my conclusion as an officer of the armed forces that the war in Iraq is not only morally wrong but a horrible breach of American law. Although I have tried to resign out of protest, I will be forced to participate in a war that is manifestly illegal. As the order to take part in an illegal act is ultimately unlawful as well, I must as an officer of honor and integrity, refuse that order. The war in Iraq violates our democratic system of checks and balances. It usurps international treaties and conventions

that by virtue of the Constitution become American law. The wholesale slaughter and mistreatment of Iraqis is not only a terrible moral injustice, but it is a contradiction to the Army's own Law of Land Warfare. My participation would make me party to War Crimes.[13]

Soldiers such as Watada and those in the Iraq Veterans Against the War are not seeking to avoid the draft or military service. They volunteered to serve. It was specific policy actions and the conduct of the Iraq War itself that led these young men and women to rethink their own presuppositions concerning war and peace. Naval Officer Harvey Tharp explained in his resignation that he accepted the rationale for the invasion and volunteered to extend his tour in Iraq. But he came to believe that U.S. invasion of Iraq was "unjustified and immoral," and certain "operations may...constitute offenses under the Laws of Armed Conflict."[14] And, the testimonies in this chapter begin with soldier Aidan Delgado's blunt description of abuses that he witnessed in Iraq. Delgado referred me to an official military survey of soldiers, which provides some ammunition for the soldiers who discuss battlefield misbehaviors. Less than half of the soldiers and Marines in the survey believed that non-combatants (civilians) "should be treated with dignity and respect." Yet, at the same time, only 17 percent of those surveyed felt that non-combatants should be treated as insurgents. 30 percent of Marines admitted to "insulting or cursing" at non-combatants.[15] The survey was conducted by the official organs of the U.S. military, so it is reasonable to assume that at least some of the soldiers' underestimated or did not report on the mistreatment of non-combatants. As Delgado reminds us, people behave differently under conditions of combat, and the presentation of these misdeeds are not meant to diminish the individual soldiers, but might be better understood as a commentary on war in general.

Recall that the Bush administration's march to war was met with global opposition, both by world leaders and citizens filling the streets in protest, such as the massive rallies on February 15, 2003. More and more veterans seem to be joining the ranks of this movement. In January 2006, two active duty military men, Jonathan Hutto and Liam Madden, generated a petition, Appeal for Redress, which stated: "As a patriotic American proud to serve the nation in uniform, I respectfully urge my political leaders in Congress to support the prompt withdrawal of all American military forces and bases from Iraq . Staying in Iraq will not work and is not worth the price. It is time for U.S. troops to come home." They delivered the petition to Congress on January 16, 2006 with over 1,000 signatures from active duty, active reserve and individual ready reserve personnel.[16] Congressman John Lewis of Georgia praised the soldier's courage.

The raw and emotionally charged testimony of these veterans may indeed help to decenter the administration's narrative of the Iraq War. In the lead up to war, U.S. newspapers often published stories about Iraq's deadly arsenal. Fears of Saddam Hussein unleashing weapons of mass destruction were serious and troublesome. In the course of the interviews veteran Michael Harmon, an articulate and passionate young man from Brooklyn, challenged this doomsday scenario and insisted it was the Bush administration, not Iraq, which threatened world peace. Harmon told me that Bush contemplated painting a drone in United Nations colors "to create an incident." I felt it was necessary to ask Harmon for clarification. Overblown rhetoric from the antiwar movement is no more tolerable than exaggerations out of Washington. The former soldier pointed me to a *New York Times* article that reported:

> A confidential memo about the meeting [between President Bush and British Prime Minister Tony Blair] written by Mr. Blair's top foreign policy adviser...shows that the president and prime minister acknowledged that no unconventional weapons had been found inside Iraq. Faced with the possibility of not finding any before the planned invasion, Mr. Bush talked about several ways to provoke a confrontation, including a proposal to paint a United States surveillance plane in the colors of the United Nations in hopes of drawing fire.[17]

The point is not to uncritically treat the veteran's testimony as the final arbiter on the war. It is an example, however, of how the narrators are capable of shaping, interpreting and contextualizing their experiences. Harmon's negative experience on the battlefield has led him to move into the realm of broader political interpretation, as he actively exercises an engaged citizenship through study and analysis of the war. In an important sense, the views of these veteran resisters are inseparable from the Bush administration's mistakes and occasional manipulations. The administration's misleading justifications for the invasion provide ample ammunition for these antiwar veterans. Any history of the war can not call itself complete without the inclusion of their voices.

In my experience with these oppositional veterans, I have for the most part discovered a group of generally well-informed resisters who are often acutely aware of opinion polls, administration strategy and world affairs. The following chapter introduces the reader to these voices.

We should not pit the voices in this chapter against those in chapter three. Readers are encouraged to understand the motives of the antiwar soldiers in this chapter as well as the pro-war soldiers in the next. Neither group should be reduced to a category of the "good" or "bad" veteran, but as patriotic individuals who are concerned about the future of their country, albeit from competing interpretations over the meaning of patriotism.

Specialist Aidan Delgado

"He was juggling a Kuwaiti skull."

Aidan was born in November 1981. He traveled widely as a youngster as his father was a Foreign Service Officer for the Agency of International Development and in his early years lived in Thailand and Senegal. Aidan attended middle school, high school and college in Egypt and speaks Arabic. After moving to the United States, Aidan joined the U.S. Army Reserve in 2001, and he watched the terrorist attack on the World Trade Center as he sat in the recruiter's office in Tampa, Florida on 9/11. Aidan served in the 320th Military Police Company based in St. Petersburg, Florida. His military occupational specialty was a mechanic and Aidan deployed in Iraq from April 2003 to April 2004. His unit first spent roughly six months in al Nasiriyah before assignment at the infamous Abu Ghraib prison. While in Iraq, and influenced by his studies of Buddhism, Aidan applied for conscientious objector (CO) status, which he successfully acquired and was honorably discharged in 2004. At Abu Ghraib, he witnessed the mistreatment of prisoners and interacted with soldiers who sometimes discussed their brutal treatment of Iraqis. Aidan has chronicled the harrowing details of his experience in The Sutras of Abu Ghraib: Notes from a Conscientious Objector in Iraq *(Beacon Press). He holds a bachelor's degree in Religion from the New College of Florida.*

Both my parents were Peace Corps volunteers in the Vietnam era, and were certainly patriots but not in the conventional sense. Both of them were very critical of U.S. foreign policy.

I was in the Tampa recruiting facility on 9/11, and someone said, "Hey come in, look what's on TV." We watched the attacks and it made me feel vindicated about my decision. I had spent my entire life overseas and I was not fitting in very well at college in the United States. I initially felt proud to be in the military. It was a means to participate in the American project more so than I had before.

My basic training was at Fort Knox, Kentucky, and it was a very gung ho place. There was a lot of anti-Arab and anti-Muslim sentiment. There were chants and songs, with phrases such as "Go set turbans on fire." I was sensitive to that kind of talk given that I grew up in the Muslim world. The Afghanistan invasion was underway, so I thought, well okay, maybe it is just the training environment and they are only doing it to work people up for combat.

Before I went to Iraq, I started to think about conscientious objection [CO]. It was a gradual process that set in after I was in Iraq for fourth months. When you see conflict first hand and the mistreatment of prisoners, it really hits you. It becomes a lot more difficult to say that I am not responsible for what's going on when you are close up. Even though I worked as a clerk, it became impossible to deny my responsibility.

I physically handed in my weapon. I went to the unit armory and they took it. They were completely unclear about what CO meant. I had read the regulations thoroughly and knew they couldn't make me carry a weapon if I didn't want to.

Although my CO application was eventually approved, it was not handled in accordance with the regulations. It was delayed inordinately. CO claims are supposed to be handled within ninety days, but mine took fifteen months. I can understand some of the delay as we were overseas in a combat situation, but they lost my application altogether. I have met a lot of COs and they all have experienced something similar. I pushed very hard to get the army to follow through on my application.

One of the problems with the CO process is that it far too academic. It is a white collar parachute for people who are good at writing essays and debating. In addition there is a place in the army for people who are willing to fight in some wars, but not others. I can't see why you couldn't have a separate division in the army for these selective objectors. You could have a separate division of the army for those who agreed to fight no matter what the circumstances. And, you could have something parallel to the National Guard, where people choose to fight for the conflict they support. I don't see why they need such a narrow door. The army could benefit from some people who are willing to serve sometimes along with those who serve no matter what. Selective conscientious objection would be a good thing, some European countries allow for it.

A lot of people in my unit didn't understand my beliefs as a Buddhist or on politics and they felt like I was standing in judgment of them. The vast majority of them isolated me and viewed me as a suspicious party. People wouldn't sit next to me or talk to me. I had a physical confrontation with one guy. He grabbed me in front of several people and proceeded to intimidate me out of being a CO. I felt threatened, but there was also a sense of having nothing to loose. They had taken my ballistic plates. They hated me, gave me the worst jobs, and withdrew my home leave. After a certain point, I felt liberated by my lack of status. There was nowhere else to go but to complete the process.

One of the major turning points was a day that I was at a mass grave site. There was a sergeant and he was juggling a Kuwaiti skull from a person who had been killed in the First Gulf War. This lackadaisical attitude toward human beings and Arabs in general really had a corrupting effect on the troops. They had become very different people that they were in civilian life. They were laughing and giggling over a skull because of the corrupting influence of war. That was one of the markers that we had reached a moral turning point.

This problem reoccurred at Abu Ghraib. I wasn't involved in the iconic abuse that you see on CNN. I was not a witness to the Lynndie England group, who were covered in the media.[18] Among my own unit there was plenty of misconduct. A number of prisoners were killed for throwing stones during a demonstration. Members of my unit took these prisoners and photographed them, while they desecrated the bodies. In fact, one of the guys stood over a dead prisoner with a plastic spoon as if to scoop out his brain. You can look at the photograph on my website, <http://www.aidandelgado.com>, if you thinking I am making this stuff up. I know it is horrifying.

At headquarters, I had access to the prisoner's records at Abu Ghraib. This is another thing that repulsed me. What the army was telling me and everyone else was that these were the most dangerous, violent criminals in Iraq. The truth was they were petty, nonviolent criminals. They were certainly not insurgents, which is what they started to say back in America when the scandal broke. Some people were arguing, "Oh, well, see we treated them badly, but these are hardcore terrorists, so it is okay." The reality was most of them were not terrorists or even violent.

There was certainly awareness among the Army bureaucracy it was going on well before the story broke. The military searched everybody's bag. A commander stood us all up in formation and said, and I am paraphrasing, "If you got anything you shouldn't have, destroy it; if you have any photos, destroy them. Don't write home about it. We don't air our dirty laundry in public, we are all family here." Their first response was to cover it up, and not to condemn the behavior but to condemn people who might talk about it.

I wasn't completely isolated. A sergeant was beginning to show repulsion at what was happening at Abu Ghraib. While he is still very much promilitary, he recognized that some sort of moral line was crossed and regrets what happened. That is becoming much more common. People look back on the detention operations and they know that it wasn't right. Because everyone around them was doing it, it seemed acceptable at the time.

After I came home, I had written a book about my experience and became known. It was very difficult for me, conservatives, pundits and soldiers had been sharply criticizing me. There was a moment when I ran into a guy from my unit who had been one of my staunchest enemies, we had nearly come to blows in Iraq. He told me that he had left the army on a psychological discharge. He shook my hand, and said something to the effect of "I see your point. I see where you were coming from back then and I am sorry for how we treated you." It was wonderful. For me, it was like coming around full circle. I think with a lot of soldiers when given enough time to reflect they change their views.

The Left has won the intellectual argument over the war. But there is a very strong rhetorical argument, usually from the conservative side, that links ending the war with weakness or this notion that we are surrendering to the terrorists. Also, the most pernicious thing is that they say if you're against the war, then you're against the soldiers. We soldiers and peace activists know that is not the truth. But the argument has a lot of traction with American people. The challenge of the peace movement is to reinvent itself and to get away from this myth that peaceniks spat on soldiers, which in fact, probably never happened even in the Vietnam War. I wish people would read Jerry Lembke's *Spitting Image*, which debunks this myth. I've heard people repeating that old chestnut about spitting on soldiers. This whole idea that we are a perpetual third column looking to undermine America is totally untrue. Most of the people I meet at peace demonstrations are first time activists as a result of this war.

I consider myself patriotic. The country has deviated from its true ideals. If we treasure the idea of America, we have to stop it from becoming something that we are not proud of. In that case, obedience to the government is a disservice to the country. It is our patriotic duty when we see the country going awry to correct it, to work toward restoring its ideals. The Winter Soldier hearings by the Iraq vets in 2008 are an example of this patriotism. But the problem I have with the Vietnam War Winter Soldiers was that it was used to discredit John Kerry. The 2008 Winter Soldiers is a reminder to people that we are still fighting a war. We can talk about progress or adding troops and it is like rearranging deck chairs on the Titanic. Iraq is in chaos. Dissent is patriotic.

Sergeant Aaron Hughes

"Vietnam did not change until the veterans spoke out."

Aaron joined the U.S. Army National Guard in 2000 with the aim of helping victims of natural disasters. Aaron's father, a Lutheran minister, was generally supportive of his decision to enter the National Guard in part because Aaron's grandfather served in the U.S. Marine Corps. Aaron's parents divorced when he was twelve years old. He was raised by his mother, an inner city school teacher in Illinois, who also worked evenings at a local shopping mall. Aaron says that in joining the military he was hoping to find some independence from his parents; it offered the opportunity that he could take care of himself. Issues of finding his manhood also figured in Aaron's decision. While an industrial design student at the University of Illinois, his National Guard unit was activated on January 30, 2003. He served as a team leader and convoy commander with the 1244th Transportation Company Army National Guard from North Riverside, Illinois. On April 17, 2003 Sergeant Hughes and his unit were deployed to Kuwait, where they provided combat support services by way of transporting supplies from Kuwaiti ports and camps to U.S. military sites in Iraq. This service continued for one year, three months and seven days as Aaron's unit received three extensions. Aaron's company returned to its home base on July 24, 2004 in Riverside, Illinois. He was formally discharged from active duty on September 9, 2004 and from the reserves in June 2006. In the Spring of 2005, Aaron retuned to the University of Illinois as an undergraduate majoring in painting. Aaron is working on a painting project, Dust Memories, *which is a collection of paintings, drawings and collages that convey Aaron's ambiguous and tense time during his combat support service in Kuwait and Iraq. He recalls the days of dust in his mouth, on his face and in his hair. Aaron hopes to one day publish a book of these drawings that will help people to understand the complexity of war.*

The great floods of 1993 in the Midwest really made a big impact on me. The damage and hearing that something like fifty people died left a mark on me, so I joined the National Guard to help people if there was a tornado or something. I never thought they would call the National Guard to foreign wars, unless there was another World War II. I went to basic training and was a good solider, graduating at the top of my class. It definitely changed the way I think, but I am not sure of the exact changes. Maybe it was the feeling of being part of a community there, the feeling that you were doing something important. But it was also kind of hypocritical. The Army promoted values of loyalty, dignity and selfless service, but you are really being trained to kill people.

I went to drill in January 2003, and we had a big meeting. Everyone was talking about Iraq and one commander told us "We're not going anywhere. But, have your ducks in order just in case." I returned home from school on the evening of January 30 planning to attend a basketball game and my platoon sergeant called. He said we are deploying and that I must report within forty-eight hours. I went to the basketball game with my friends and got trashed.

We first went to Fort McCoy, Wisconsin for three months, which was an ordeal in itself. Our trucks were not the best and we were probably the least prepared to go anywhere. We were also the only inner-city, ethnically diverse transportation unit in Illinois. Some guys wondered if that was the reason why we were activated, and I don't know if that had anything to do with our deployment. Some of us felt that our unit had been shafted. We did not have tools or even an extra spare tire for some of the trucks. When we left, we still did not have all our equipment; I did not get my DCU's [Desert Camouflage Uniform] or plates for my armor vest. Eventually we received fifteen plates for over one hundred people and we didn't even use them. It was strange, you know, who the fuck do you give the fifteen plates to?

When we first arrived in Kuwait in April, we changed battalions maybe three times and it took our unit a long time to get our trucks because our boat broke down in the Mediterranean. We operated out of Truckville in Arifjan from April 2003 to August 2004.

We would pick up supplies at Kuwati ports and bring it to Iraq. We lived in tents the whole time, but supposedly there are no more tents there. They weren't army tents, they were set up by contractors and they had false bottoms. Everything was covered with dust, and then the rainy season hit and a couple of tents were washed away. We had really old trucks and it was always really hot on our missions, not only from the desert heat but our over-heating trucks.

The drives were long and it felt like 200 degrees in the truck and we could not at first drink the water because we didn't get coolers. The water was hotter than coffee, we kept it cold by putting it in socks and hanging it out the window. We ended up buying ice and coolers from Iraqis. Our trucks were 818s, some of the oldest. I don't remember who it was, but someone commented "These have to be the oldest trucks in the theater. I can't believe they are here." He thought it was great, maybe in a nostalgic way. I was thinking "No you don't understand, they are falling apart as we drive."

I can only remember one time that I thought I was going to die. As I look back, there are many times that should have been scary but they were at the time considered normal. We got lost in Fallujah one night, way up west of Baghdad. We had just been extended. Because we were extended we had turned in our little black boxes that allowed us to set our radio frequency in line with other military radios in the area. When the Marines took command in that region, they changed radio communications from single channel to frequency hop. Our commander was arguing with the Marines to give us a black box, but it wasn't authorized since we didn't have the proper security clearance as we were truck drivers.

Regardless, on this mission we were trying to find, if I remember the name correctly, a Camp Ridgewood. Our command was lost and sent a scout down a road that ran across a road block set up by armed insurgents. They didn't shoot at us, it was amazing. Maybe they couldn't believe that we were there, so far lost. We were lucky, if we got hit there was nothing we could do, we couldn't call anybody.

Earlier in the deployment I remember our command had a briefing with information such as if you see anyone with a gun, shoot them as they are insurgents. But there were so many mixed signals, we at one point hooked up with MPs [military police] who knew more about the local areas (southern Iraq). We were on a mission and the MP's Humvee broke down; so I was pulling rear security. There was an Iraqi guy walking up behind me with an AK47, I immediately flipped my weapon on fire and turned to him, and as I am doing this an MP screamed, "No." I guess he was an Iraqi policeman, and I was supposed to know this? It was complicated and confusing, a lot of miscommunication.

Other times we would break down in the desert and people would suddenly appear. Old women and kids begging for food and water, some of them looked like they were four years old. We were not supposed to give them anything. One time a women came up to me asking for food, and I had some MRE's [meal ready to eat] in my truck and handed it to her, and an officer came over, screaming "What the hell are you doing?" I said, "Feeding the hungry, sir." He did not saying anything after that. I was lucky he didn't give me an article.

The trips were very long and sometimes you would find hundreds of kids in the street. You know, they were just kids, they wanted food. I don't know sometimes the kids played chicken with the trucks. Some guys carried rocks on the trucks because kids would throw rocks at us and they would throw them right back. A couple of occasions, once, I mean, it would get really backed up. Some kids were run over. I remember some British Military Police just standing there looking at them, not knowing what to do. It was surreal. I don't know, I guess shit happens. We were a convoy of hundred trucks. They would jump on the truck and grab stuff; my buddy lost his backpack.

We had gotten there when President Bush said the war was over. I had this truck and was thinking what I could do with it. I was so naïve, imagining that I would be bringing water, food, generators and supplies to Iraqi people who just got the crap kicked out of them. Instead, I was hauling air conditioners and SUVs for contractors. I thought I was there to help kids and then if they are in the road it was okay to hit them as if they didn't matter. The job was to get the supplies from point A to point B. There has been progress as the roads I drove on were being rebuilt, but it seemed that the same people stood on the side of those roads for a year begging for food and water. I remember my NCO [noncommissioned officer] started crying, saying "What? They're still here." The southern part of Iraq is probably the poorest, it was neglected by Saddam Hussein because he feared an uprising and preferred that the people starve. We didn't change any of that.

It seemed that our lives, too, didn't matter. We never got our plates [body armor], till the end of our time there. You see the contractors with all these sophisticated gadgets and fancy trucks. Our mechanics were cutting scrap metal and adding it to our trucks. When a transmission went, we would just strip that truck and use the parts for other trucks, but then we would be down a truck. This is the best Army in the world and we didn't have the supplies. It is about money, the whole contractor issue. I try to tell my closest friends and they still believe the war is altruistic. But I am now thoroughly convinced that this war is happening because people are making money. I think it is sick that people are even making money on this shit.

Our missions included third party nationalists, who are mostly poor people from the third world who came for work. They were hired by contractors and the Kuwaiti authority They were treated like they were nothing. We would make them stand outside the camp because we didn't trust them. They would plead with us "Let us in. Let us in." They were almost like indentured servants. We stood over them with weapons, these people were contracted to work with us and we had to escort them to the bathroom, they had no freedoms. I hear that Halliburton and KBR [Kellogg, Brown, and Root] subcontracted all these companies and the poor people on the bottom are forgotten. If you are on the top, it is a long way to see those on the bottom. I don't think the administration even thinks about this. [Former] Defense Secretary Rumsfeld didn't visit these people. He did visit the troops and a soldier challenged him about the equipment problems, and his answer was to suck it up.[19] What does he know about sucking it up? Bush and Rumsfeld talk about supporting the troops, when the troops are getting crap.

I got a little army handbook about Iraq; it provides a timeline. If I remember correctly, it says: 1993, UN clear out WMD; it documents that Iraq was largely disarmed. This was one of the handbooks that the army gave to us, but I guess most people don't read them. But, the administration changed its reasons for going to war. They argued that it was to bring democracy to Iraq. I don't think there has ever been in history a democracy that has come through an authoritative movement. A lot of politicians talk about building democracy, but when I was there that was not our purpose. Our purpose was sustaining ourselves, building camps and a shell around ourselves and basically establishing our presence. I did not see us going out educating people about choices and the democratic process, it was more about building an infrastructure and bases. If you say that you want to build a free market in Iraq based on capitalism, it is a different thing than democracy. Maybe that is what is happening. So, I guess it all depends on how you want to use the word "democracy." Historically, the United States has used the military to support dictatorships, which help the corporate infrastructure grow.

The United States has to leave Iraq: people are right; the shit is going to hit the fan. Look, we fucked up. We are not changing the political, economic and social structure in Iraq. We need to leave. I am not trying to tell people what to do or push my political agenda. In fact, I produced some art to convey my feelings about the war with the aim of complicating the understanding of the war, which can not be understood through slogans. I want to share the personal aspect of the war; it is far more complex than a political ideology.

Veterans need to tell their stories. The media and the government are not going to tell us, Vietnam did not change until the veterans spoke out. Veterans deserve the space to share their experience. There are parades with fire engines and people declaring the local veteran a hero. It is an easy thing to embrace if you have been pushed down your whole life, but the reality is far more complex.

Specialist Michael Harmon

"The whole war was a lie."

A Brooklyn native, Michael graduated high school with "little direction" and the army seemed like a reasonable option at the time, especially since he was a New Yorker who witnessed the 9/11 tragedy. He enlisted in army in May 2002 to serve as what the recruiter described as a "health care specialist," or what he later learned was a combat medic. Michael served as a medic at the rank of specialist in the U.S. Army 167th Armor Regiment, 4th Infantry Division and was deployed to Iraq in April 2003 and returned home in April 2004. His regiment was stationed in Al-Rashidia, which is approximately ten miles from Baghdad. Worried that the army might involuntarily extend his contract through "stop-loss" and send him back to Iraq, he began drinking heavily and told his superiors that he could not return to the combat zone. Shortly thereafter, he was honorably discharged in 2004. He is a college student studying respiratory therapy, and an active member of Iraq Veterans against the War.

I was born and raised in Brooklyn, New York. I was not sure what I was going to do after high school and I took a year off. I met with an army recruiter, who only told me the great things about the milit: joined. As a New Yorker, I was also affected by 9/11 and felt th the Army made sense. I was shipped to Fort Benning, Georg 2002 for basic training, then to Texas for medical training.

On Martin Luther King Day in 2003, we were told that we were going to war against Iraq. I did not see any tie between Iraq and 9/11. I had my doubts about Bush, although I voted for him in the 2000 election. I was a fresh, young inexperienced soldier and I did what I was told. My division originally planned to invade through Turkey, but they refused to allow the U.S. entry for the invasion.

After arriving in Iraq, I remember my first taste of combat. I was driving in a Humvee smoking a cigarette and all of a sudden I heard machine gun fire, small arms fire and RPGs [rocket propelled grenades] exploding around us. We returned fire. Another day we were doing vehicle checks and my sergeant and I were enjoying an MRE [meal ready to eat]. We didn't get to eat all that much. We were limited to one MRE and two bottles of water a day. The scout Humvee was fired on and it had a Javelin [portable anti-tank weapon] inside, so it exploded. I remember one guy who was literally split open. It was crazy. It was surreal. After such scenes, I would smoke five cigarettes in a row. It felt like I was watching a movie; it was pretty scary and sick. Things like hearing wounded guys scream "I want to see my kids. I want to see my wife" really affected me. I saw shot children and dead children as well as dead soldiers.

A turning point for me was one day when I saw a pudgy, little girl. She was maybe two years old. She had those cute pudgy legs, and when I looked at her I saw that she had a bullet wound on her leg. An IED exploded and soldiers started firing all over the place in response. The baby got hit. The baby looked at me—she wasn't even crying, but looking at me and it might sound nuts, but it seemed as if she was saying to me, "Why, why do I have a bullet in my leg?" I thought this is ridiculous. This is enough.

While I was there stuck doing this, I thought I might as well try to help whoever I can. I offered medical services to my fellow soldiers and they appreciated it. This kept me going.

I knew a first sergeant who in my opinion was really scared, he wouldn't leave the base. He used the generator for himself while the soldiers had no lights. My Captain, however, was decent and treated us fairly.

I talked with the Iraqi people. They wanted to know what we were doing there. One Iraqi said, "Fuck America." But, we were in his country; he had a right to say it. They were glad Saddam was gone, but they didn't want us there. Poverty in Iraq was unbelievable.

I don't trust my government anymore. The whole war was a lie—based on the false WMD claim. I just read a news story about Tony Blair and George Bush having a meeting where Bush made it clear that he was going to war no matter what. Bush proposed painting a spy plane in UN's colors to create an incident where Saddam might fire on it. More and more evidence is coming out against Bush. The whole Bush regime can't be trusted. And, a poll showed that over 70 percent of U.S. soldiers want the United States to leave Iraq.

The United States should withdraw from Iraq immediately. Iraqi polls show that the violence will be less if we leave. The division between the Shiites and Sunnis is largely because of the invasion. Remember Bush divided the United States, saying "you are either with us, or with the terrorists." He drew a massive rift in this country and he drew a massive rift in Iraq. When I was there early on, I didn't see this Sunni/Shiite tension. Before the invasion, they were a sovereign country and Bush can't explain that. Another thing Bush says is that he wants democracy. But when it doesn't go his way, he has a fit. For example, Hamas was elected by their people, then Bush said oh no this is not allowed. He is a terrible leader, who is out for "white" America. By this I mean rich, corporate America: Halliburton and the oil companies. He is not looking out for the average person.

Soldiers who return from war are starting to question it. It takes a while to process what happened. When soldiers first return, they are very angry. People should notice this and ask why are these people coming back messed up? Why support something that is destroying soldiers and families in Iraq? I ask people directly: "How would you feel if your child was just blown up?" You can say "support the troops" all you want, and put yellow ribbons on your gas guzzling SUV to feel better about yourself. I say let's wake up.

People have accused me of being a traitor for saying these things. I am not a traitor. I was a soldier who served in Iraq and I say immediate withdrawal is the way to support the troops.

When I returned home, I did not know what was wrong with me. Your body is so pumped up after being on high alert for so long; you no longer know how to relax. I didn't shower or shave. I was diagnosed with PTSD and took pills, which did not help. There was talk of redeployment after I just returned. I had about a year and a half left on my contract and it was made clear to me that I was going to get stop-loss [service extended beyond discharge date]. I told the military to let me out. There was a fight, they gave me a field grade Article 15 [nonjudicial punishment] and stripped my rank. I told them I will not do it any more. They let me go. I guess they didn't want a problem soldier infecting the ranks.

Lieutenant Harvey Tharp

"I was able to use Halliburton's greed to my advantage."

Harvey grew up in the suburbs of Cincinnati in a working-class family; his father was maintenance mechanic and his mother worked as a secretary. Harvey dropped out of high school and eventually earned a diploma so that he could enlist in the U.S. Air Force in 1994. He served for four years as Arabic translator, making several trips to Saudi Arabia. Harvey was part of Operation Southern Watch in the early 1990s, a surveillance operation to ensure that Iraq adhered to United Nations Resolutions following the 1991 Gulf War. Harvey worked in Signals Intelligence, flying aboard RC-135 Reconnaissance aircraft. He was honorably discharged from the U.S. Air Force in 1997 and attended law school at Ohio State. He was commissioned as a Naval Lieutenant in 2000 and served as a Judge Advocate (lawyer) in New Orleans and Hawaii. While serving as a judge advocate, he was deployed to Iraq in 2003, and worked on the reconstruction project in Kirkuk from October 2003 to April 2004.

I was an Arabic translator in the air force. Later, in December 2002, when I was in the Navy they had anyone with Arabic knowledge take a test to assess their competency in Arabic. They hadn't change the test since I had first been in the military, so I must have taken the same exam ten times. I retook the test in 2002 and I just put in all the same answers again and aced the test, even though I hadn't studied Arabic for three years. I really did not know Arabic, but the records showed that I was fluent. I thought I would go to war immediately; the military was really short on anyone who spoke Arabic.

Around this time, the United States established the Coalitional Provisional Authority (CPA), but it didn't have any presence outside of Baghdad. They came up with some plan to manage the outside provinces, but they didn't have the people. They wanted people from the State

Department, but the CPA didn't have the armored cars, security details, communications and everything else needed for the State people to work in these nineteen provinces. Most of the Foreign Services officers were already working elsewhere, so the CPA turned to the navy and requested anyone who spoke Arabic. They took me, a lawyer. They were thrilled to have me. I was supposed to be a translator.

When I first got the call to go to Iraq, I was extremely nervous about it. I never thought the Iraq War was a good war. I don't know anything about insurgencies. I spent nine years in the military and they had been good to me, so the thought of not going never entered my mind. Well, I thought, I've been tapped and now it's time to go.

I spent three days at the Republican Palace where the CPA briefed us and then sent us out. There were so many different problems: getting people paid on time and getting the ministries restated, etcetera. I was in charge of reconstruction projects in Kirkuk. I made sure contracts were signed and I hired Iraqis to work. Jobs were very hard to come by so naturally the Iraqis that I hired were delighted. I was paying them on the Halliburton pay scale and I think they made more money than the local mayor. You know, we were in theory the Imperial Pro-Council Office for Kirkuk.

I really didn't have a unit so these Iraqis served as my emotional support group. We had this incredibly feisty, brave Sunni woman, Sannah, and she became one of my closest friends in Iraq. Also a Christian engineer who headed the project assessment named Raed. One day we got in Raed's car and went to his house. I wasn't supposed to leave the base without two vehicles and two shooters per vehicle and here we were sneaking off to his house for lunch so that I could meet his family. I didn't have body armor but I finally purchased it myself through bulletproofme.com

I was able to use Halliburton's greed to my advantage and employ twenty-four Iraqis. They were always bringing in cases of candy bars and potato chips when there was only a few of us in the office. We gave the snacks away to our employees. The idea was to buy and spend as much as you can. They sent candy bars and potato chips, but I didn't have a radio for my car or a memory stick for my computer.

It started to dawn on me that our presence in Iraq was part of the problem. I came to think I will not kill someone for the power and glory of some old men. One of the most striking things that I remember was that a bunch of senior British generals complained that the Americans mistreated Iraqis. The U.S. generals seemed to care little for the Iraqi people. This all didn't gel for me while I was in Iraq. But, every night the army would shoot off mortars and one night there was a Kurdish man who told how his son had been killed in one of these assaults.

While it is an outrage that Bush claimed Iraq had WMD, just about every war the United States fought was started on a false pretense. The WMD claim was just a bad lie. I returned home and was almost certainly going to be sent back to Iraq. I put in my resignation as I could not justify killing Iraqis. Some of the actions of the U.S. military violated the laws of war and armed conflict. We bombed urban areas. When you bombed the so-called Al Qaeda safe house, there is a high likelihood that you will kill civilians in the process. I resigned and they let me go. I suppose that they didn't want to get into a public pissing match with me.

I now have bipolar disorder, which is very strange as I don't have a history of it in my family. It usually manifests itself in people sixteen to twenty-four and I am thirty-four years old. If you have a tendency for it, a stressful event can trigger it. I have had mild PTSD symptoms, nothing compared to some of my veteran friends. I lucked out and got a good doctor in the Veterans Administration. I have been back for a few years now, and I am not sure how bad it is now. Polls are showing that almost three out of four soldiers are repudiating the mission. This made it through the news cycle, but I keep repeating it as it is important that people understand this.

Let's put aside the Iraq vets for a moment. You see Veterans of Foreign Wars or American Legion veterans and for them to keep the demons at bay they have to believe that what they did, and what the U.S. government ordered them to do, was necessary and right. Now, we are in a losing situation and we have to have the debate over the war. I am not trying to demoralize the average soldier; they are in the same position I was in when I was there. They have to believe in the war to keep going. There is a breakdown in morale that worries me.

Corporal Adam Charles Kokesh

"Kindly, go fuck yourself."

Adam graduated from the Native American Prep school in Santa Fe, New Mexico in the spring of 2000. He holds a bachelor's degree from Claremont McKenna College in California. When he was seventeen, Kokesh joined the Marine Corps Reserves through the delayed entry program in 1999. His reserve unit was November Battery, 5th Battalion, 14th Marines, an artillery battery of 155mm Howitzers. Adam served in Fallujah, Iraq from February to September 2004 as part of as Marine Corps Civil Affairs team. In Iraq, he was assigned to Team 10, First Regiment Detachment, a moving tactical team that patrolled an area west of Baghdad. The area included Abu Ghraib, Al Karma, and Al-Fallujah. Part of his duties included helping to establish the Fallujah Liaison Team facility (FLT) to serve as a Civil Military Operations Center (CMOC).

He was twice activated as a reservist, extending his service beyond his six year obligation, and was discharged on November 16, 2006 into the Individual Ready Reserve. A self-described libertarian and economic conservative, Corporal Kokesh is a member of Iraq Veterans Against the War. On March 19, 2007, he participated in Operation First Casualty, a protest designed to illustrate the truth about the war. As part of the demonstration, Corporal Kokesh wore military camouflage gear. The next day the Washington Post *ran a story about the protest with a photograph of Kokesh from the protest.[20] Although Kokesh appeared in a camouflage uniform without his name or the Marine Corps logo, the Marine Corps sent him a notice concerning the appropriate use of military uniforms. Kokesh replied with a strongly worded letter that concluded "Kindly, go fuck yourself." He was summoned to hearing at the Marine Corps Mobilization Command in Kansas City, Missouri, on June 4, 2007. The board recommended that his honorable discharge be changed to a general discharge.*

In 2007, Kokesh moved to Washington, DC, to pursue a master's degree in Political Management at George Washington University.

I joined the Marines out of patriotism. I wanted to be part of the national defense and put my life on the line for my country. To me, it means something to defend your country and to put your life on the line for the nation's defense. At the military entrance processing center, a couple of noncommissioned officers laughed at me when I told them I joined out of patriotism. I suppose it was something that most Marines didn't come out and say. Every since I was fourteen years old, I wanted to be in the Marines. I went to "Devil Pups," which is a two-week junior boot camp program. We learned how to march in formation, got yelled a little bit and we saw a lot of cool military demonstrations. It was hard, but I had a blast. I still love the Marine Corps, it is a great institution. As long as it is necessary for the United States to have a defense, the Marine Corps is an essential part of it. Marines risk their lives to defend the country and I am proud to be a Marine.

I volunteered to go to Iraq as part of a Civil Affairs Group. You know, I didn't want to be the one Marine who didn't go to Iraq. I was against the war before it started, but I thought it was still a noble effort to clean up Iraq. I wasn't convinced by all the false intelligence. I went to the occupation, not the war. I respected Bush at the time for trying to clean up the mess he created in Iraq. But, now I know that is a fallacy and I don't give him any credit.

In Iraq, I was part of a civil affairs team that worked to establish the FLT. Only in the Marine Corps do they call a facility a team, so we helped to set up a liaison facility. My job was to run a check point at the facility. Any Iraqi could come up to my check point and say they wanted to work with us. My job was to frisk them and make sure they were okay to enter. It was chaotic at times as I don't think that culturally Iraqi's are accustomed to waiting in line the way we are in the United States. I was proud because I helped to keep it orderly. One day there were about two hundred ICDCs [Iraqi Civil Defense Corps] and IPs [Iraqi Police] lined up at my check point. It was progress and I felt good that I was able to run my check point in an orderly way.

Things were not always orderly. I was at the first battle of Fajullah. Our facility got shot at and bombarded constantly. We had rockets landing outside and around our facility. There was an explosion near me; it went off on the other side of a berm [raised fortification] that was put up only a week or two before. It saved my life. I thought, well, I am not dead. Another Marine was not so lucky. As he walked out to that check point, a rocket exploded and threw him forward, breaking his ribs. I was so disengaged; I was always real cool under fire, not because I am cool. I dealt with it by being cool. You develop something to keep you stable to get through situations. Everybody in my unit was pretty cool under fire.

As for politics, I have a personal theory about Operation Phantom Fury or the invasion of Fallujah in November 2004. There's no way that I could prove it and it is just my opinion. The attack occurred on November 6 or 7, right after the presidential elections. It was close between Bush and Kerry and the news of a bunch of Marines killed in Fallujah could have cost the president. It could be as simple as Rove [President Bush's chief of staff] saying to Rumsfeld [then Secretary of Defense] "Hey man, why don't you give the ICDC a little more time to be effective." It seems like they delayed the attack on Fallujah for the purpose of the election, but I can't prove it.

After Iraq, I was sent to Camp Pendleton, California. They gave me a readjustment class, where they defined Posttraumatic Stress Disorder [PTSD] and reassured us that it's normal to feel stressed. There was some group counseling, but it wasn't really that helpful. I went to some group counseling with Iraq Veterans Against the War, and it was a lot more effective. It was better because I was there on my own, as opposed to being ordered to go. You share and you feel comfortable being emotional; it is not with guys that you have to work with the next day. The classes were run by military chaplains and officers. Guys who want to get emotional and have important stories to tell are probably not going to do it in that environment. Those classes caused me more stress. Being with other veterans who cared was more effective.

I joined Iraq Veterans against the War because I have a moral imperative to speak out. My experiences as someone who served don't support whatever it is that we are pretending the current mission is. Whether the weapons of mass destruction story was a deliberate lie or a mistake, it is clear that we can't trust the government. You need to find other sources for information. Veterans are a good source, but many of us are being intimidated to prevent us from speaking out. My story is only a very small part, but I do think it can help to shift the debate or to help other soldiers speak out.

There are people who accuse soldiers who speak out as destroying the troop's morale. But compared to having the military extend a soldier's enlistment by twelve months or more, it is nothing. I didn't even know there was a peace movement when I was in Iraq. It is time for the people to stop this war; and the people include the soldiers by refusing to fight. This is how we got out of Vietnam. Nixon was forced to remove the ground troops from Vietnam because the soldiers knew it was bullshit and refused to fight. There are a number of things civilians can do: they can support GIs who refuse to fight or people can block ports where war materials are being shipped out. Yes, I am talking about civil disobedience and risking arrest. Remember it was Thomas Jefferson who said dissent was the highest form of patriotism.

Sergeant Kelly Doughtery

"The U.S. invaded Iraq to control the oil resources."

Kelly grew up on Canon City, Colorado, a small town with roughly 13,000 residents. She joined the Colorado National Guard in 1996 as a

seventeen-year-old senior in high school. Her primary motivation for enlist-
ing was the money offered to help pay her college tuition; and she eventually
earned a bachelor's degree in biology from the University of Colorado. In
1999, she was activated and served in Hungary as a convoy for troops mov-
ing into Bosnia. Having been trained as a medic, she was again activated
in January 2003, but would end up serving with the Colorado National
Guard 220th Military Police Company. With this change in her military
occupation, Kelly first went to Kuwait before a March 2003 deployment to
Nassiryah, Iraq. She spent ten months in Iraq and eventually received an
honorable discharge in August 2004. Kelly is one of the founders and the
executive director of Iraq Veterans against the War. Her father, a Vietnam
Veteran who initially discouraged her from joining the military, is also active
in the antiwar movement.

I was in high school when I joined the National Guard, although the military was such a foreign idea to me. I really did not have a good conception
of what was going on in the world at the time. My stepfather suggested the
National Guard as his son had a good experience with it. When I told my
father that I was joining the National Guard, he was very much opposed,
saying that they'll turn you into a robot. He served in the navy during
Vietnam, and he never really talk about it. My mom saw it as a way for me
to gain some discipline, get college money, and some training.

I enlisted as a medic, but in the area of Colorado that I was in, the
Guard was over strength in medics. There were three of us who were in
as medics from 1996 until 1999, when we were deployed to the Balkans.
Our sergeant told us we should enroll in a military police (MP) training
course as it would be helpful for the deployment and promotion. So, we
went for the military police training. When I got back from the Balkans,
my name was on a roster as an MP and I was upset. I found out later
that even though the Colorado Guard unit had enough medics, they still
were accepting them. I therefore transferred back into the medic unit until
2003, when again I was put into the military police.

I was starting my final semester of college, and I got a call from an
officer in the Colorado National Guard headquarters. I did not call her
back. Then my sergeant from the medical unit called. He said, "I am
really sorry to tell us this, but you have been transferred to the 220th
MPs, and they have been activated." I was told the day before the unit was
activated for Iraq. I was really shocked and was in denial. I thought that I
would just go and explain that I can't be an MP.

I was totally against going into Iraq. I was not all that political. But, I knew about the sanctions against Iraq and the horrible conditions that it left the country in. I definitely did not trust President Bush. There was plenty of information out there to know that what the administration was saying was false. I knew the Iraq–Al Qaeda connection and WMD talk was bullshit. Iraq had nothing to do with 9/11, but that was the mindset that they were encouraging to get people ready for war. The first thing I heard when I walked into the National Guard Army after being activated was a speech about how Iraq was behind 9/11. I was late, and I couldn't walk into drill formation. I just stood there and my sergeant pulled me into formation.

I soon talked to my first sergeant and explained about how I was a medic and shouldn't be deployed as an MP. I told him that I was totally against the war. He said, "I know the unit screwed you over, but we need people." When I talked to my platoon leader, he said, "You know, I have my skepticisms about the war. But you can't go AWOL, you'll get a court martial."

When the war started, my unit was in Kuwait. There were sirens for several days with and we hid in concrete bunkers when they went off. The anticipation of war was scarier than actually going into Iraq. Fighting a war was never really my thing. We went in right after the whole Jessica Lynch story. There were rumors flying around in the military about how the Iraqis were publicly executing prisoners of war, which wasn't true.

We didn't really know what to expect. It was strange to go from Kuwait, which was really opulent with people driving Mercedes and woman carrying Gucci handbags, into southern Iraq, which was poor and barren. As we crossed the border, there were huge concrete barricades and a spray painted message, "Watch out for children in the road." There were barefoot little kids in rags begging for water and MREs. As we moved north, it was so arid, dry and flat. There aren't many people in southern Iraq. There are Bedouins and goat herders. The landscape stayed the same until we arrived at our airbase outside Nassiriyah. Nothing was set up, it was very confusing. We had to put up tents.

Early on the people were hospitable. The Iraqis would wave at us, but others would make rude gestures. The rude gestures came only after we were there for a while. As the months went on, we started to patrol north of Nassiriyah, which was more populated. Some Iraqis said, "Go Bush." Some would say, "Go Saddam." The truth is that you never really know what they think. Maybe they were being nice because we had guns.

One day there was an accident with two semi-trucks, and there was a huge traffic nightmare. We went with the Iraqi police, but they didn't really do anything. There was a huge crowd. It was dark and there weren't enough of us to control the crowd. They were throwing rocks and bottles at us. I was scared. I was pushing people back with my rifle and hitting people. It was not a good situation.

After this incident, my fellow soldiers started to respect me. I remember one person saying, "Hey, Sergeant Doughtery I heard you were hajji beating last night. I never thought you could take care of yourself." It was a pretty messed up thing to say. I did not enjoy having to hit people and wonder if I might have to shoot someone. I didn't want to be in a situation where I might have to hurt people. And it was avoidable. If it wasn't for the sanctions and our occupation, the Iraqis probably wouldn't be so poor and running up to our trucks begging for food. I did not want to feed into that mentality that celebrated pushing people around. I understood it—the soldiers were told that they are heroes helping people. Then they encountered angry and hostile Iraqis, and under the circumstances, a soldier might start to hate the Iraqis. I don't agree with it. But I could understand the feeling.

Another problem concerns something I read that noted that contractors were complaining that they were driving empty trucks. They would travel north and back south because private contractors got paid by the number of trucks they had on the road. It made sense when I read it. I saw many empty trucks or big flat bed trucks with one pallet on it.

The trucks would break down and we were called out to guard them. But, they would end up abandoning the vehicle any way, so it was a waste of time. We were not supposed to leave anything behind and were told to burn vehicles in the road. Once there was a refrigerator truck, filled with food and we burned that. It seemed so absurd. We did it in front of the Iraqi people. I felt ashamed. The Iraqi people were pissed, wondering what we were doing. They were watching us as if to ask, "Why are you burning food that we can eat?" If the American people knew what we were actually doing over there, it would bother them. It made no sense--we were guarding a truck, then destroying it a few hours later. And it is not just me: many of the soldiers were upset about this because it was insensible.

I don't know how often it happens, but kids would get run over. My unit drove onto a scene where a transportation unit drove over a little boy and three donkeys. The convoy apparently didn't stop at all, they just kept going. Two people I know were drivers in transportation units, one drove over a little kid who jumped on truck to grab an MRE and slipped into the tires. Another one mentioned that he ran over a kid. People get run over all the time and you are basically told not to stop. My unit did not have an experience like that, but it happens all the time.

We had nonlethal ammunition for crowd control. When it was issued to us, we were informed that it could be deadly, so you should use the same restraint that you would with any weapon. It was not a joke. In one situation, two teams went out to protect two broken down fuel tankers. I was with one team and we kept the crowd back. My gunner never fired a shot. The other team, their gunner was shooting into the crowd. That crowd started getting very agitated. Someone in the crowd likely had a gun. It wasn't necessary to use that level of force. My team wasn't and we had the situation under control. We felt that the person shooting into the crowd randomly was really out of control. We wanted to report him, but decided not to.

When we were getting ready to leave Iraq, we had extra nonlethal ammo [ammunition]. We couldn't take it back with us. That day, one guy drove through the market, dropped smoke grenades and starting firing wildly into the market place like a drive by.

I think the United States invaded Iraq to control the oil resources and have a presence in the Middle East. Our economy is driven by oil. I think the people who initiated the war did not anticipate how difficult it would be to install a government favorable to the U.S. Bush announced an oil sharing deal as if it was great for Iraq, but it would give something like 70 percent of the revenues to U.S. oil companies. The Basra oil workers fought against it.

My dad joined Veterans for Peace (VFP) and went on a delegation to Iraq while I was deployed. I did not get to see him though. When I got back home, my dad encouraged me to go to the VFP convention in Boston during the summer of 2004. I looked at the program online and I saw one panel featuring veterans from Iraq. I was surprised because my name was on the list to speak! I was not sure what I would say and felt overwhelmed. I met the Iraq vets, and they asked me to join a press conference and talk to a reporter. They had been hatching an idea to create a separate organization, Iraq Veterans for War. Folks like Dave Cline from VFP and others were supportive. They asked me to join. Then, we held an event at Faneuil Hall. There were less than ten of us, and now we have grown into an organization of over 1,000. I convinced my friend Elizabeth Spradlin to join. She was against the war, but didn't want to join a group—I think here are many soldiers like this, who are reluctant to join but do not support the war.

In the beginning of IVAW, there was a lot more pro-war sentiment, but that has changed. But, I find that most people who disagree with me still say they respect my opinion. There has been a resurgence of groups like Gathering of Eagles. It seems like they have made it their mission to rail against IVAW. They say they love the troops and that we are demoralizing the troops. But we are the troops, don't they love us too? They perpetuate the urban legend that Vietnam veterans came home and got spit on and were called baby killers. I can only speak to my experience now, but the only time I've ever heard of a vet getting spit on was by rightwingers spitting on an antiwar vet. My friend Tina was spit at by one of these people.

Staff Sergeant Andrew Sapp

"We need to get closer to a social revolution."

Andrew was born in Kansas City, Missouri and joined the U.S. Navy in 1976 about a year after he graduated high school, having served as an electrician's mate for six years. Andrew subsequently moved to Connecticut to earn a Bachelor's degree from Yale University; and then moved on to acquire a Masters of Education degree from the University of Massachusetts. He is currently a high school English teacher in Massachusetts. He entered the U.S. Army Reserves in 1994, the National Guard in 1999, and has accumulated over nineteen years of military service. His National Guard Unit was activated in June 2004. In November 2004, he arrived in Kuwait as a member of the National Guard 272 Chemical Company from Reading, Massachusetts. From January to October 2005, Andrew served at the Forward Operating Base Summerall in Iraq, which is roughly forty-five miles north of Tikrit. It is also near the town of Baiji that sits toward the northern end of the Sunni Triangle. While in Iraq, Andrew held the rank of staff sergeant and squad leader. He was honorably discharged from active duty in November 2005 and is on the board of Iraq Veterans against the War (IVAW). Andrew lives in Billerica, Massachusetts, and is married with three children.

My family has some relationship with someone who served in the military back to the Revolutionary War. My father served in the armed services during World War II and he later volunteered to go to Korea. I grew up in the shadow of World War II and the patriotic idealization of the military. We were living in southern Idaho when I went to high school. At the time, it wasn't possible for me to go to college. It was a rural area, which was not terribly prosperous and there were few opportunities. I joined the navy and they trained me as an electrician and I spent six years on active duty. I actually enjoyed a lot about the Navy and thought about making a career out of it. I left the Navy in 1982 because my wife and I wanted to start a family. I worked for several years on the water front as an electrician. Finally, I cashed in my GI Bill and went to college and became a teacher. Teacher's salaries being what they are, I joined the Army Reserve and they made me a chemical operations specialist. I could have re-enlisted in the officer corps as I had a master's degree, but I didn't want to be part of that world. My wife and I moved to Massachusetts as there were teaching jobs available, and I entered the National Guard to stay in my military occupational specialty as there were no Reserve chemical companies in the area at the time.

I enjoyed the military. I enjoyed the people. Here I had a degree from Yale, studied at Harvard, and I taught classic British literature. I had no contact with the working class background that I came from. I was a fish out of water. The military helped me to stay in touch with real people. I could talk in a way that felt natural, and joke around in a regular, comfortable way. Just being around the other soldiers was enjoyable.

The first time that I really saw how people in positions of power manipulated and used the military to follow their venal and petty agenda was when I was in the Navy during the Reagan years. The constant saber rattling with the Soviet Union seemed to disrupt the balance of power that was keeping a nuclear nightmare in check.

By the time 9/11 rolled around, I was in the National Guard. No one really dreamed that we'd be in a war where the Guard was called out. Maybe we would do some home land stuff; rescue kitten's stuck in water. Initially, however, we thought we might get called up to protect water reservoirs or help with the clean up at ground zero. After weeks went by, we weren't called and we all relaxed. In early 2002, a lot of things started to happen in the National Guard: money and new equipment starting coming in. A motor sergeant told me he had an order to get all vehicles in the

Massachusetts Guard in order for shipment to active duty. He told me, "You better stand by; something big is going to happen." Five months later the Bush administration started all that nonsense about aluminum tubes and chemical weapons. I was trained as a chemical operations specialist, and so much of what they were saying rang hollow. Right from the start I said to myself that this administration is lying to the American people.

I never hid my politics and there were opportunities when I said that this was all bogus. Honestly most of the soldiers weren't interested in politics. It was more like they wanted to go because of the excitement and adventure. I did not see any point in arguing with people because we were going to go regardless. They felt that they were doing something good for the country and let them believe what they want. It made no sense, from the point of view of morale and unit cohesion, to undermine their beliefs. In fact, it would have put all of us in more danger.

My wife and I discussed how I might get out of this. I didn't want to go off and do something that I didn't believe in. But the truth of it is that you don't really deploy for God, country and apple pie. You deploy for the people in your unit.

My unit eventually deployed to Kuwait, and then we arrived in Iraq. We were tasked under an active duty unit, which was largely incompetent. The arrogance of the active duty officers and senior NCOs [noncommissioned officer] was sometimes appalling. The lower ranking troops were okay. I supervised both active duty and Guard soldiers, so I got to experience first-hand not only the arrogance of the leadership, but also got to see the disaffection and frustration of the regular soldiers.

The only construction I saw was what the Iraqis were doing themselves. I didn't see any organized reconstruction. The base was near Baiji, which has the largest oil refinery in Iraq. This might give us a clue as to why we were there. The only thing that I saw that was different from the time I arrived to the time that I left was the railroad that led to the oil refinery in Baiji was repaired. Again it was the Iraqis who did the work.

When I first got there, the towers were mortared and shot at regularly. In May and June 2005 there was a lull. From June onward, the IEDs [improvised explosive devices] really picked up. It was amazing because the guard tower overlooked the roads and they still were able to place them there. The guys in the tower weren't slacking, I guess these insurgents were that good.

I was not favorably disposed to going to Iraq beforehand and nothing I saw when I was there convinced me that I was wrong. I was angry. Part of it was that the active duty unit gave us all the shit work and they broke up our unit. Keeping a platoon together and keeping a squad together is vital for morale. With it broken up, there was no one to talk to. By August, I was really starting to have some issues. One day I was in the guard tower shooting the shit with a active duty sergeant and we got along very well. All of a sudden the horizon just lit up. A moment later the ground shook like an earthquake, the tower rocked back and forth. We both stopped and froze and I said "That can't be good." About ten minutes later the artillery on our base started firing out; helicopter gun ships came in; then I heard that we had F16s overhead.

What happened was that one of our patrols, a group that was with the Pennsylvania National Guard, had been ambushed. The next day I learned that it was a set up. The patrol was lured into an alley way and the first Humvee hit an IED. They were able to jump out. But as they tried to back out of the alley, a second Humvee was hit. This was the explosion that I heard from the guard tower. The bomb was probably intended for a tank because it obliterated the Humvee, only the chassie [frame] was left, the rest was burned, twisted metal. There were five guys in the Humvee. The gunner was blown out of the vehicle but survived. The four other guys, well, were quite literally blown to pieces. They had to pick them out of trees.

It was all very sobering and serious. I went down to the chow hall before my shift started. They had two big TVs, one was playing ESPN and the other was the news. All of a sudden I saw on the TV, "Explosion in Baiji." Sure enough, it was the attack and there was a crater where the Humvee was destroyed. It showed about eight or nine kids, ones like the students I teach in the high school. They were jumping around celebrating. One of the kids had a piece of uniform with burned flesh on it. This made it on the news before the families were contacted. At that point, I was so full of rage and hatred toward Iraqis. I really just wanted to go out and kill someone, I wanted to hurt people. I just wished that they would call in an air strike and level the whole place. Look, I am not that kind of a person.

It was a turning point for me, it has stayed with me. The anger took a long time for me to get under control; it shifted gradually from the Iraqis to the people who put us there. My wife became involved with Military Families Speak Out soon after I deployed. When I was in Iraq, she emailed me and told me about these veterans who formed Iraq Veterans against the War. I said that's for me and I joined.

I never made an issue of my politics when I was in Iraq. I didn't push it on anyone. But the longer we were there; more and more soldiers came to me with criticisms of the war. I would never go out and solicit it. And, I would say forty or more soldiers told me that at the very least they were having doubts about the war. Some of them really spoke nastily about President Bush and the military. One of the reasons, I think, that they would confide in me is that I was "safe." Especially the lower-ranking, active-duty guys would catch hell if they raised any questions.

When I first went into the military, it was 1976. Vietnam had done serious damage to the military. Never again were we going to allow ourselves to be used like we were in Vietnam. We were not going to allow politicians to wreck the military. And here I was in Iraq and it was the same thing all over again. I remember talking to one of the older guys who served in Vietnam while I was in Iraq, and he said to me: "This is Vietnam, the only difference is that it was jungle over there and desert here." We are pawns in a game.

My experience was that the troops on the ground, even up the chain of command, generally didn't look too favorably on the contractors, especially when we had to train them so that they could do our jobs for maybe three times the pay.

The Pentagon and State Department pay big private contractors, who hire third party nationals. The base I was at had Sri Lankan workers. They were wonderful guys, they worked twelve hour days. They were kept in a kind of de facto slavery. I would stop short of saying that this war was just to transfer public funds into the private coffers of these companies. But it is certainly a factor. The privatization of the military is a terrible rip off. The war is being contracted out and huge amounts of money are going to private companies. I know that oil is another major factor. We can quibble over controlling the supply and surplus, rather than the actual oil drilling. I don't know any of that. But the oil refinery outside our base certainly had something to do with why we were there. You don't have to be a cynic to know that oil is a factor as to why the United States is in Iraq.

Look at how the Bush administration has used the military and how it has manipulated the law. You have men and women going back for their third, fourth, and fifth tour in Iraq. While the administration wraps itself in the American flag and tells the people to support the troops, it resisted increasing veteran's benefits. You have people in the administration who did everything that they can to avoid military service, or we might say honorable military service. We have a president who manipulated his way into the National Guard and didn't complete his obligation. If that was me, they would have come after me. We have a vice president who had something like five deferments. And these are people who claim to support and understand the military. These people are hypocrites through and through.

Polls are showing that 60 percent of the Iraqi people believe it is morally okay to kill an American. That sort of tells you that we shouldn't be there. All this talk that the United States can't cut and run is jingoistic nonsense. The infrastructure is so entrenched it would take at least six months to pull out. The United States should seriously engage, rather than pretending to, the players in the region. The Saudis, Turks, Iranians, Syrians, the Arab League, should come in and take over some of the security operations. Any westerner is toxic in Iraq and rightfully so. If you can bring in security forces that are more palatable to the Iraqi people, it should help to stabilize the country. If Iraq can not remain as a unified country, at least it might fragment in a way with the least amount of violence in way that harms the fewest Iraqis. As long as the U.S. is there it will continue to be a target. The Sunni-Shiite split will continue. Now, the Kurds are waiting to make their move. When I was in Iraq, I read an intelligence report. It was after the elections, and the governor's of each area were supposed to swear to uphold the central government of Baghdad. Well, the governor for the Kurdish region swore to uphold Kurdistan but he refuse to say anything about Baghdad.

Unless we are going to commit one million soldiers, this mess is going to continue. Probably 600,000 Iraqis are dead; I never believe the U.S. government figures. The *Lancet*[21] study is probably accurate. It is human suffering at epic proportions and the United States is responsible. We have to atone. We have to gain a better understanding of what happens to people who live through war--not only vets and families but the Iraqis too. I came home with PTSD. Let's say one third of soldiers have PTSD; it is human suffering on a great scale. America is in denial about the gravity of the suffering of the Iraqi people. We understand the monetary cost of the war, but the human cost is greater. Maybe if people understood this more directly, they would demand that leaders put an end to it.

My wife and I are losing faith in the country. I grew up in the Vietnam years, when the jingoistic slogan "love it or leave it," was thrown at people who criticized the war. I may have internalized it; I am wondering if I still love my country and have thought about moving to Canada. The system that led us into Iraq has not changed. If it does not change, we will have another Iraq, just like we are having another Vietnam. Sooner or later it is going to lead to the destruction of this country. If we are capable of doing this to twenty million people who were never a threat, we deserve to be condemned. We are beholden to late capitalist society; the voices of millions of people seem to matter less than a few CEOs. For all the rhetoric out of Washington, it is not a representative government; it is one that wants to keep workers quiet. It is more like a feudal structure masked as capitalism. The values that I grew up believing in are traded in by our leaders. I grew up in the shadow of President Eisenhower, whose farewell address warned about the military-industrial complex. By the time Eisenhower left Washington he had moved further away from militarism and closer to pacifism.

The people who experience war first hand can realize just how brutal people can be toward one another. If a political system allows or encourages this brutality it does not deserve to exist, something new needs to take its place. We need to get closer to a social revolution to change this system.

Staff Sergeant Camilo Mejía

"There is no greater freedom than the freedom to follow one's conscience."

Camilo was born on August 28, 1975 in Managua, Nicaragua. His father, Carlos Mejía Godoy, was the official poet/songwriter of the revolutionary Sandinista movement during the 1980s in Nicaragua. Godoy composed the popular "Peasant's Mass" or "Missa Campesina." Camilo holds dual citizenship in Nicaragua and Costa Rica, and is a legal, permanent U.S. resident. His parent's separated when he was very young. Camilo eventually moved to Miami with his brother and mother, Maritza Castillo, in 1994. Over his parent's objections, Camilo joined the U.S. Army in 1995 when he was nineteen. He served eight years in the military: three and a half on active duty as a Bradley driver and the remainder in the National Guard as a squad leader. Camilo's contractual obligation would have ended in May 2003, but the stop-loss program extended his service, and he remains on appellate leave.

He was deployed in Iraq from April 2003 to September 2003 as a staff sergeant with Charlie Company, Florida National Guard's First Battalion, 124th Regiment. His unit patrolled the turbulent Ar Ramadi region of the Sunni Triangle. In September 2003, Mejía was granted two weeks leave and returned home to Florida, where he decided that he would go underground or AWOL (Absent Without Leave). Camilo surrendered in March 2004 and declared himself a conscientious objector. A military tribunal convicted him for desertion in May 2004. Since that time desertions "have risen sharply," the New York Times *reported, as there were at least 3,196 desertions in 2006 alone according to U.S. Army figures. In Mejía's case, the Army punished him with a bad conduct discharge, his rank was stripped to private and he was sentenced to a year in a military prison at Fort Still, Oklahoma. Amnesty International declared Camilo a prisoner of conscience, having concluded that Mejía is a "genuine conscientious objector whose objection to war evolved in response to witnessing human rights violations in Iraq."[22] He was released early from prison for good behavior on February 15, 2005 and has since become an outspoken critic of the Iraq War, with media sources calling him the "poster child" of veterans' antiwar movement. He has appeared on CBS's* Sixty Minutes *and chronicled his military service in a powerful book titled,* Road from Ar Ramadi: The Private Rebellion of Staff Sergeant Camilo Mejía. *Camilo completed a Bachelor's Degree at the University of Miami and plans to attend graduate school.*

My dad had a radio show in Nicaragua in the 1970s. He created a character that poked fun at the military dictatorship under Somoza, which ruled the country for over forty years. The regime threatened him with fines and jail, but my dad was so popular they didn't want it to backfire and he got away with a lot of stuff. My mom wasn't politically involved till she met my dad, then she started to interact with the leadership of the Sandinista movement. She did surveys for them, trying to find out what were the needs of the people. I suppose she was trying to make the connection between what the people needed and what the Sandinistas were fighting for.

At one point, there was a really successful action by the Sandinistas. They took hostages from a party hosted by one of Somoza's closest friends.

At first, they got all their demands met, but it led to very strong repression by the dictatorship. It also contributed to the break up in the Sandinista leadership because some were arguing for a more combative stance. They wanted to continue actions, such as the hostage taking and bringing the fight to the cities. Others were saying let's try to work more on the periphery. So this split—and the repression from Somoza that became quite crude—left many lower-ranking Sandinista operatives without any guidance. My mom was one of them. She and my dad were not getting along at the time, so she decided to go to the United States. I was only one year old at this time. We lasted less than a year in the States and went to Costa Rica, where my mom was from. She worked with the Sandinistas who were operating in Costa Rica. She gained a more prominent role, facilitating command meetings and running safe houses. Meanwhile my dad went into exile to Spain. This is now July 1979 and the Sandinistas overthrew the Somoza regime and took control of the government. We all went back to Nicaragua. My mom was in the army and worked in the security agency. My dad was doing his music and radio program. By this time he became famous, he was sort of the international culture ambassador of the Nicaraguan social revolution.

As a child, I can't say that I had a real political conscience. It's like when you grow up in the United States you don't really have a concept of capitalism, you just live it. For us, it was socialism. But Nicaragua wasn't really entirely socialist; I went to a private Catholic school. We didn't think, "Oh this is socialism against capitalism." But, in school we sang socialist songs and learned about Lenin and Castro. You know, people in the United States don't have a genuine understanding of the Founding Fathers. People uncritically accept that they are heroes. But they were slaveholders; George Washington wanted to serve in the British Army before he became a revolutionary. People just follow the image without thinking too deeply about it. In Nicaragua, we did the same with Marx, Lenin, Trotsky, and Fidel. We were taught to admire them. But, I wasn't really politically aware.

In Nicaraguan culture, the United States was seen as the big monster and Reagan was the face of it. My dad wrote the Sandinista anthem and part of the lyrics say "We struggle against the Yankee, an enemy of humanity." I think that was a pretty prevalent feeling among the Nicaraguan people. The Yankees were our enemy, not necessarily American citizens, but the U.S. government and military. I remember helicopters flying over, people would say it is the "black bird," but we never saw it because it was so fast. It symbolizes the sort of the dark, invisible presence of U.S. imperialism. At the same time, the Nicaraguan revolution was dream come true for so many people. People from all over the world came to participate and learn from it, including U.S. citizens. The Nicaraguan people did not hold hostility against American citizens.

The Sandinistas lost the election in 1991. My mom was left without a job, so we went back to Costa Rica for a couple of years. My grandma is a longtime naturalized American, so she got my mom her green card. My brother and I got it automatically because we were minors. We came back to the United States in 1994 and been here ever since. I went from being a privileged child of the revolution to being working-class. It was the first time I had to work for a living. I was sweeping parking lots, flipping burgers, wondering where my college tuition would come from. I didn't have financial stability. This was my mind frame when I joined the military. I wasn't thinking about the Sandinistas or imperialism. I was working for minimum wage and wondering if I'd have money for tuition. At the same time, I was really lost. I didn't have a sense of belonging anywhere. I moved from Nicaragua to Costa Rica to Florida. It was a really an unstable life. I had attended community college for a couple semesters and I didn't have a circle of friends at nineteen years old. I didn't have anything. I didn't know what my future would be. I craved a sense of belonging and financial stability. The army seemed to provide that. I suppose these are the same reasons why many people join the army. It really had nothing to do with politics for me.

I went to basic training in Fort Benning, Georgia, where they have the School of Americas. This is ironic because a lot of the people who were involved in attacking the Nicaraguan social revolution were trained there.[23] Boot camp was hard; it was horrible—you have a huge dude screaming an inch away from your face all the time and you have all these grown men shitting their pants. Well, really big kids, but we were afraid of the drill sergeants. The training was all about killing. But I just blocked it out, I didn't even think about it. I did my bayonet, rifle, and warfare training and just concentrated on the methodology. I coped and adapted pretty well, but you would see privates crying in the latrines at night. At the time that I was in boot camp, I wasn't a pacifist or a conscientious objector. I believed in the military. I believed that the United States could go overseas and fight a good war.

But, the politics of the Iraq war bothered me a lot. North Korea claimed to have weapons of mass destruction, not Iraq. The majority of the alleged 9/11 hijackers were from Saudi Arabia, not Iraq. Why are we going after Iraq? Everything around the war seemed liked a huge lie. I didn't want to go to war. But the majority of the people in my unit were pro-war; not necessarily because they believed in the mission or that they hated Saddam, but basically because we were infantry men and were trained to go out there and "kick ass." There was a sense of unresolved business for the ones who never went to combat. It was their big chance to go and shoot shit up, and blow shit up and kill people; they could prove themselves as infantrymen.

Even though I now believe that this war was in the planning for a long time, in early 2003 my unit wasn't sure if we were going to go to war. The media kind of did its job. We heard about millions of people protesting the war and the weapons inspectors saying that they didn't find weapons. We also heard news that the UN Security Council did not authorize war. To us grunts on the ground, it wasn't clear if we were going to have a war, although it was already decided in the White House. There was a joke in my unit based on John Lennon's song "Give Peace a Chance"; except they were saying "Give War a Chance." I felt completely the opposite. I was older than most of them. I didn't want to see anyone go home in a body bag. I didn't need to prove myself as an infantryman. I kept all my thoughts to myself. But I needed to do something to send a signal home.

My unit was in Jordan before we went to Iraq. With my daughter on my mind and the possibility of me dying, I wanted to let her know that I was against the war. One day I wrote a sign that said "Give Peace a Chance." During watch duty I unfolded it and my friend took a picture of me holding it. I felt like it was an act of sedition, like a dark secret. I destroyed the paper after the photo was taken.

When we left Jordan to go to Iraq, we didn't get orders to go there. Usually there is a manifest: You do a head count, follow a packing list, there's a whole structure. We were told in two in the morning to pack our shit. We arrived with no food and no orders. Nothing. We went to other companies asking for food and water because we had nothing when we first arrived in Iraq. Finally, we got orders for a mission in al Assad. As we were leaving, we looked like a gypsy caravan; we had this huge convoy from Jordan to Iraq of old, dilapidated deuces [supply truck] and five tons.

I don't know if the army was getting ready to throw this shit away and someone in my unit said we'll take it. It was like a circus.

When we finally arrived at al Assad, we entered a huge Iraqi air base with large concrete structures for fighter jets that looked like sand dunes. The United States had bombed the place, but all the damage was to the bunkers. The jets were in the desert; they fooled us. I didn't know if I should feel like an idiot for my military. All the jets were in the desert, so we bombed all the bunkers and the jets were fine, except for one.

Anyway, we went to the main base in al Assad, which the army was just starting to take over. There was an improvised shitter [bathroom], a wooden shack with a barrel cut in half. There was also a concrete structure where they held prisoners. Each area was enclosed in concertina wire. The prisoners—called enemy combatants—were barefoot, hooded and bound with plastic ties. We were told you're here to run this camp. We were instructed to keep the enemy combatants on sleep deprivation. We asked, "How do you know these guys are combatants?" We were told the spooks [untraceable personnel, ranging from perhaps intelligence operatives to contractors] decide. The spooks were not wearing military attire, and they had names like Bear and Rabbit. I don't know who they were: civilian contractors, Special Forces, CIA, who knows. Bear was really big, kinda fat, who wore wrap-around sunglasses. He had a huge beard and looked like a bear. He was an expert in weapons and god knows what else.

So, our job was to keep them sleep deprived. The way we did that was to yell at them, tell them constantly to get up and down. But sometimes yelling didn't work because they were so tired. Someone would then hit the wall with a huge sledge hammer. The structure was circular and had a huge echo. The prisoners were hooded, so when they hit the wall with a sledge hammer it sounded like a huge explosion. It scared the hell out of the prisoners. When that didn't work, they produced a .9 millimeter pistol and put it to their head and cocked it. There was no bullet in it, but they made it seem like they were going to get shot in the head. The person you were doing it to would cry and scream. There was one guy who had not obeyed. They put him in a chamber where you had to stand because it was so narrow. A soldier would remain there and hit the wall with a stick, causing a cranking noise to disturb the prisoner. They would let prisoners sleep for thirty seconds then wake them up to destroy their sense of time and space: Totally fuck up their minds. This is how they got them ready for interrogation.

Later we were assigned to ar Ramadi, the first time where I actually fired at a human being and he died. I don't want to say killed. We were all firing on him because he had a grenade. It is one of those experiences that stuck with me. People say "You joined the military, you were an infantry man and you knew what you were getting into." But nothing could be farther from the truth. It doesn't matter what training you received, nothing prepares you for when you, you know, when you shoot at a person. I don't know; it is hard to describe, nothing prepares you for it. You don't know what it does to you when you fire a rifle at a human being.

What happened that day was that my unit was really tired. There was a sand storm, and then an ambush, and our base was attacked by RPGs [rocket propelled grenades]. We got a call to go to the Mayor's Building, what we'd call city hall. There was a political protest against the occupation. I remember they had "No Bush! Yes Saddam!" signs. They wanted the occupiers to leave. We went into the building, which we had used as a base for operations in Ramadi. The protestors were pissed and started throwing grenades. We were in a walled off building and they threw a black bag over the wall. The bag was smoking, and then it exploded. So, we took positions on the roof top. We were given orders to open up on anyone who threw a grenade. You could tell when someone was going to throw a grenade because it got quiet and everyone moved to one side of the street. It was amazing how they got out of the way to avoid getting killed, but not too far away. They still wanted to see the grenade explode. It is hard to explain; it was strange.

This one time, everyone started to move to one side of the street. A young man came out of the crowd. We were on a second floor balcony and I watched him. He was really young, you know I don't remember his face or expression, but I remember he was maybe sixteen. He was swinging his arm. He had something in his hand. Just as he got ready to throw it, we opened up on him, I remember seeing him fall. I remember him being dragged in his own blood by town men after we fired on him.

After this, the rifle fire came from the crowd and we called in helicopters to disperse the crowd. In the end, there were four dead Iraqis and a couple of wounded. After that, we did a quick extraction. We went into a home and someone recognized one of the grenade throwers and we basically kidnapped him. They arrested a couple of young kids. When I went on patrol after this incident, it seemed like everyone was carrying a friggin' black bag in the marketplace or city. And there were kids everywhere. Your mind is totally fucked because now you can't trust kids. You are so jumpy. There are explosions, and grenades and kids. You're out there with your finger on the trigger. Imagine when you can't trust kids. It was really fucked up, it fucks you up.[24]

But I had the opportunity to become really close with the manager of a propane station, Mohammad. The Iraqi people had a sense of unity. At patrol points, you stop people on the streets and you hold them while you search. People stood there on the side of the road waiting, and they would hug and smoke a cigarette together. There was this familiarity and warmth among people. It made me realize a lot of the things that we say about Iraqis are not true. Some people say that they are tribal savages that want to kill each other, but I saw so much warmth among the people. I was assigned to the al Hadithah dam, where the workers would share food with us. They shared their dinner with us. I always said yes, and people in my unit would say, "How could you? It is hajji [ethnic slur for an Iraqi] food." Their hospitality extended to us, the occupiers. It is not that they wanted us there; it is just that they were able to see our humanity. We see them as horrible Muslims and degrade them as hajjis. I read the Koran with them and learned that they were cool with Jesus and Mary. It was different from everything I was told about Muslims.

What I saw in Iraq looked like a popular rebellion. The "enemy" was so elusive. It is not face-to-face combat; they are like ghosts who disappear into the towns and cities. You can't do that without the support of the people. It takes time to set up an IED; they do it on a street corner, where people can see them. When the attack takes place, they run through alleyways and homes, all of which requires the support of the people.

The theory behind our Operation Shutdown was that there were people from Syria and outside ar Ramadi, who were coming in to fuck shit up. To me this was completely dumb. It's like saying if the United States was occupied we would need to bring in Canadians. I had been there two months and I knew that it was locals who were coordinating attacks on us. One time they blew up a Humvee from the 3rd regiment and one soldier lost his leg and another lost part of his leg. The commander was furious, so we sealed off the city. The fighters were already inside the city. This notion that it was just people from outside was wrong. But the Intel said we were fighting Al Qaeda and foreign fighters. From what I saw, it was people in the neighborhoods where we were patrolling who were fighting us. They knew the alley ways; they knew the roads and homes to get away.

To escape the way they did requires the support of the people. They just disappeared. Again, I think it is more a rebellion than a civil war.

There was a story in the *New York Times* about Shiites driving Sunnis out of neighborhoods. It described a grandma who called the police, and the U.S. military intercepted Shiites who were evicting Sunnis. The guys were from one of the ministries in the Iraqi government that is under U.S. control. They were using their official identification to kick people out of neighborhoods. The next day the grandma was shot in the head. The story was reported as Shia driving out the Sunnis, but in reality you have a government entity here under the supervision of the United States that is driving people out.[25]

In September 2003, I was given leave for a couple of weeks. My green card was expiring and I asked for leave to go home and resolve it. My status as a non-U.S. citizen made me ineligible for the stop-loss that extended my service, which made my whole deployment illegal. I wanted to clear that all that up legally. Then I realized it is not just about the legality of my personal deployment, but about the illegality of the war and the killing of civilians. I had a lot of guilt because I was a squad leader. I didn't want to be called a coward and a traitor if I refused to return. When the time came for me to report back, I kept saying I'll go the next day. It was like a hurricane inside me. After some time, I realized I wasn't going back. I didn't have the moral courage at the time to say I am taking a moral stance here.

I went underground. I had learned about conscientious objectors (CO), but I said I am not a CO. I had been in combat, fired my weapon. COs are supposed to be against violence and killing. I thought I couldn't be a CO because I killed people and I was a grunt on the ground, but a counselor from the GI Rights hotline said I should read the regulations because I sounded like a conscientious objector. I kept thinking, "How could I be a CO after I did all these things in Iraq?" It took awhile for me to realize that there's no more compelling and powerful argument against war than war itself. It is not what you have done, but what you are willing or unwilling to do after experiencing these things. What we did in Al Assad, what the military did in Abu Ghraib, these are war crimes. And, it is a pattern, it is systemic; it is chronic and it is spread out like a cancer. It is not just isolated individuals and this raises it to the level of a crime against humanity. The way we used our weapons was a war crime: we were using light anti-armor weapons against buildings where people lived. We were conducting missions by mosques, hospitals and schools. We were blowing the shit out of neighborhoods; basically violating the rules of warfare. We were instigating fire fights in heavily populated areas with complete disregard for the lives of Iraqis. The whole war itself violated the UN Charter.

While underground, I found an attorney and started working on a CO claim. It was an exploration and discovery for me; my application was sixty-five pages long. I learned about myself; it was like therapy. I knew that I never wanted to grab a weapon and fire on someone again. I was done with the military; I was done with violence; I was done with war. I didn't want to hurt a human being again in my life. The experience of war is so overwhelming; you can never cease to understand how it changes you.

My sense is that a lot of people in the military feel that their duties to the military and their duty to their conscience are in complete disagreement. But they might be afraid to act on their conscience because they could go to jail or be called cowards. But you really can't be free unless you follow your heart. I have no regret for taking a stand against this war and against killing. There is no greater freedom than the freedom to follow your conscience.

From Bunker Hill to Baghdad: We Will Continue the Mission

Some people are not comfortable in life if they are not part of something bigger—if they are not part of a team. Being in the military is like that. I think it is a place where people come to seek order and to be part of something special...I see an [a]rmy of soldiers who want to better themselves. I see an eagerness in their eyes and their desire and motivation..."
— *U.S. Army Brigadier General Jim Chambers*[1]

The sincerity of the antiwar soldiers who understand patriotism as being true to one's conscience and engaging in political dissent is matched by the pro-war soldiers' commitment to a different definition of patriotism. The following testimonies preserve the memory of those soldiers who defend the war for both ideological and personal reasons. Interviewees in this chapter capture the ways in which soldiers attempt to facilitate positive change in the middle of a combat situation.

Some of the soldiers whom I interviewed asked that I not refer to them as pro-war. No one is pro-war, they insisted, having argued that war was an unfortunate necessity. The term pro-war here is not employed in a derogatory sense as if these soldiers favor any and all wars. It is used for brevity to indicate that the following interviewees generally support the Iraq intervention and/or the war on terrorism. Designations such as "pro-victory" were preferred by some but not all of the soldiers in this chapter, and so the labels pro-war and pro-victory are used interchangeably here to indicate support for Operation Iraqi Freedom.

Several books have appeared that document the experiences of American generals and combat soldiers in Iraq, expressive of traditional notions of patriotism. These include Tommy Franks' *American Soldier* (2004); General Anthony Zinni and Tony Koltz's *The Battle for Peace: A Frontline Vision of America's Power and Purpose* (2006); Major Chuck Lawson's *Heroes among Us: Firsthand Accounts of Combat from America's Most Decorated Warriors in Iraq and Afghanistan* (2008); Jay Mann's *The Green Berets: Action in Iraq* (2007); Milo Afong's *Hogs in the Shadows: Combat Stories from Iraq*; and others. The present work differs insofar as it does not simply present war stories, but explores the soldiers' interactions with family members, impressions of their antiwar counterparts as well as their service accomplishments.

Many soldiers remain fully committed to the mission in Iraq. Narrators in this section defend the invasion of Iraq from a variety of perspectives. These service members generally maintain that the removal of Saddam Hussein was an admirable achievement that will facilitate positive changes in the region. For example, they suggest that the openness of Libya in regard to weapons of mass destruction [WMD] was in part the result of the Iraq invasion. Others view the elections in Iraq as a small, but significant step on the long road to democracy. Several interviewees emphasized the long-term prospects of democratic change, while others highlighted individual actions that provided Iraqi citizens with medical care, food, and shelter.

In addition to these acts of positive change, veterans in this chapter back the mission because they view Iraq as an arena for terrorists. The United States must therefore confront, or contain, this threat overseas so that it does not spread to the continental United States. Confronting terrorism abroad, these soldiers often argued, would make Americans safer at home. They embrace the Bush Doctrine's assertion that "our best defense is a good offense." A few of the interviewees conceded that this offensive approach has not been as successful as anticipated, but the new military strategy implemented in 2007 provided optimism for greater success, if not triumph, in Iraq.

Pro-victory veterans' organizations have been formed to facilitate this success. Vets for Freedom and Vets for Victory are two outspoken examples with members appearing frequently in the print and television media.

The present author contacted Vets for Victory, a group that works against "defeatist opinion," for an interview. One of its representatives believed that my antiwar preferences would compromise its mission to foster support for victory and declined to participate. It was a congenial exchange and I regret that I was unable to engage the group in discussion, yet I respect their decision.

Another organizing effort from pro-victory soldiers unfolded during the fall of 2006. Lieutenant Jason Nichols and Staff Sergeant David Thul, both of whom served in Iraq, teamed up with Vietnam Veteran Larry Vandergriff to launch the Appeal for Courage. The Appeal for Courage states

> As an American currently serving my nation in uniform, I respectfully urge my political leaders in Congress to fully support our mission in Iraq and halt any calls for retreat. I also respectfully urge my political leaders to actively oppose media efforts which embolden my enemy while demoralizing American support at home. The War in Iraq is a necessary and just effort to bring freedom to the Middle East and protect America from further attack.[2]

One reason for the soldiers' action was to counter the antiwar, "An Appeal for Redress," which urged Congress to support "the prompt withdrawal" of U.S. forces. Another reason concerns Senator Harry Reid's suggestion that the Iraq War was lost. After hearing the senator's remark, Lieutenant Nichols wrote to conservative reporter Michelle Malkin and complained that such "words are killing us."[3] The Appeal for Courage was circulated in conservative media outlets and gained some momentum. Its co-author, Lieutenant Nichols, welcomed my interview request. Nichols explained that calls for withdrawal only hindered the troop's ability to do the job that they were trained to perform. He stressed his disagreement with antiwar veterans and activists, but recognized and respected their right to dissent.

In January 2007, President Bush acknowledged the nation's dissatisfaction with the war, while presenting a new course for victory. "The situation in Iraq was unacceptable to the American people," the President conceded as he pledged that a new strategy would lead to a triumph. Bush noted that the jubilation over the 2005 Iraqi elections was "overwhelmed by political" fissures. Critics had charged that the 2005 celebrations were premature, not unlike Bush's earlier declaration in May 2003 that the mission was accomplished. Known as "the surge," the president outlined plans for an additional 20,000 U.S. troops in Iraq, primarily around Baghdad and Anbar province. By June 2007, an additional 28,000 U.S. troops were deployed, increasing the presence to some 160,000. The troops would accompany Iraqi forces to both build local security and empower the Iraqi forces to eventually subsume security operations. The Iraqi government would simultaneously appoint military commanders in the Baghdad area. A significant percentage of the forces, Bush announced, would target Al Qaeda in Anbar province.[4]

The new strategy, known as the "surge," has indeed offered renewed hope for those veterans committed to the mission. One curious supporter of the troop escalation was retired major general John Batiste. Earlier he called for Rumsfeld's resignation and announced in a television advertisement that "I left the army in protest" because the President has "placed our nation in peril."[5] Batiste, now embracing the President's plan, penned an article with the Executive Director of Vets for Freedom, Pete Hegseth, in the *Washington Post*. The two Iraq War veterans argued that the nation must "rally behind" five basic principles. Since these principles capture many of the "pro-victory" veterans' perspective, it makes sense to list them here. The first tenet is that the United States must battle "worldwide Islamic extremism" in a "long war" that requires decades of commitment. Second, Iraq is a "staging ground" for this extremism, and one that could slip under the control of Syria or Iran, a situation that must be halted, the authors imply. Third, General Petraeus's counterinsurgency operations during the surge indicate progress. Coupled with diplomatic measures, the escalation will result in greater security. Fourth, Iran must be contained and prohibited from acquiring nuclear weapons. And finally, the military needs to be strengthened. The authors' conclude that "American veterans—young and old—are resolved to support and defend the Constitution from enemies, foreign and domestic. This commitment, and nothing less, should compel us to stand together, in and out of uniform."[6]

Journalist Dahr Jamail, who has spent considerable time in Iraq, has questioned the surge's success. The Iraqi Red Crescent claimed that "Iraqis displaced from homes quadrupled" during the surge; and the United Nations High Commissioner for Refugees [UNHCR] reported that some 2.3 millions Iraqis have fled the country. Jamail agreed that sectarian violence decreased, but Baghdad remained divided across sectional factions, with neighborhood's enclosed by cement walls. In the year of the surge, Jamail noted, U.S.-coalition troop casualties were at its highest for a single year. General Petraeus countered such reports, having argued that, "Since the 'surge of offensives'…attacks and civilian deaths have decreased by 60 percent." It is still too early to assess the full impact of the latest strategy, but the President's new vision has offered hope to soldiers and veterans committed to staying the course in Iraq. Hoping to inspire these soldiers Petraeus insisted that, "Our nation's men and women in uniform must rank with the finest soldiers, Sailors, Airmen and Marines in our country's history."[7]

The following accounts should be explored and understood as individual viewpoints, not simply as a vague category under the label pro-war. Occasionally people in the peace movement speak of the brainwashed, pro-war soldier. I encountered veterans, who while fully behind the mission, do not blindly adhere to the administration line. Major Brian Bresnahan, who is associated with the Veterans for Freedom, was thoughtful and hardly one-dimensional. He suggested that I consult Michael Gordon and Bernard Trainor's *Cobra II: The Inside Story of the Invasion and Occupation of Iraq*. The authors' previous book had received an endorsement from Dick Cheney. Gordon and Trainor nonetheless acknowledged that "U.S. troops and the Iraqis themselves have paid an unnecessarily high price," and outlined "five grievous errors" of the administration, while lamenting the "chaos, suffering and a future that is still vexed." Yet, they hold a "hope" for an "outcome that would justify" the "sacrifice" of American forces.[8] Captain James McCormick, a highly decorated veteran who backs the war, referred me to other soldiers who offered a different perspective. One of the soldier's whom McCormick put me in touch with had told me that he believed that the United States should be expanding its role in Afghanistan and should never have entered Iraq. The point here is that those soldiers who aggressively embrace victory offer multilayered perspectives beyond the easy stereotypes of the soldier as a programmed killing machine.

The title for this chapter is a quotation from Captain McCormick. He sent a letter to President Bush to express his support for the intervention. The army officer wrote, "If needed, all of us would return and continue the mission. It's a just and much needed fight. Please know that many of us still live by the code of honor that so many soldiers before us had, from Bunker Hill to Baghdad."

Captain James L. McCormick

"It really is a sense of honor; it is the right thing to do."

McCormick was born and raised in West Virginia. He enlisted the Army National Guard while still in high school in 1985; then entered active duty and fought with the 24th Infantry Division during Operation Desert Storm in 1991 where he earned his first Purple Heart and Bronze Star Medal with V (for Valor). After leaving active duty, he earned a bachelor's degree in Business Management from West Virginia State College and became a commissioned officer in the National Guard in 2002. While a Second Lieutenant, McCormick volunteered for Operation Iraqi Freedom from February 2004 to October 2005, with the 1487th Transportation Company. During the Al Sadr, Easter weekend, in April 2004, McCormick's gun truck crew fought its way through four ambushes and defended the south wall at the airport against a determined enemy attack. After the uprising, he was recruited to form the 518th Combat Gun Truck Company, which was organized to defend convoys traveling through Kuwait. McCormick earned two more Purple Hearts and two Bronze Stars with Vs as a result of his combat duty in Iraq. He has been recommended for the Distinguished Service Cross and Silver Star Medal for actions leading the defense of BIAP [Baghdad International Airport] against Madhi Army Shiite Militia and in another desperate gun battle with insurgents on the night of the Iraqi national elections. Wounded several times in battle, he sent a letter to President Bush expressing his wish to return to Iraq and continue the mission. President Bush visited Morgantown, West Virginia, on July 2, 2005, where he praised McCormick and presented him with a Presidential Coin.[9] *Captain McCormick is the Commander of the 1487th Transportation Company of the Ohio National Guard and lives in Scott Depot, West Virginia. He is married with six children.*

My father served in Vietnam and his father served in World War II. Patriotism was always strong in my community, even during a time when it wasn't cool, so I joined the National Guard when I was in high school.

I wanted to go to Iraq. I put my name on the volunteer list three times before they finally called me. I didn't know what I was getting into. They sent me with a transportation unit, but I had been trained as an infantryman. Before I left, I started to research convey operations, and that's when I learned that it was one of the most dangerous jobs to do over there. But

I always felt honored to go. It was a chance for me to pass on my combat knowledge to other soldiers.

I was going through a divorce at the time of my deployment to Iraq, so I had little family support. It was not a good time for me. I had four children; the two youngest were only four and five years old and really didn't understand what was happening. My two older boys were very upset and cried. I sat them down and told them, "[t]his is important; it is something that I have got to do." Eventually they came to understand and now they are very proud. It was very hard to tell them that and it was hard to leave. It was tough on my kids. Their mother was in the [National] Guard too and also deployed. My kids did not get the proper care while we were gone. There were other battles going on, other than the one in Iraq.

I deployed to Iraq with the 1st Platoon of the 1487th Transportation Company. Some of these guys, like myself, had combat experience in Desert Storm in 1991. Some of my soldiers had the belief that we were going into a Desert Storm situation, we would just drive trucks and that would be it, but I told them that this was going to be very different. We trained very hard at Camp Atterbury, Indiana, and it was snowing at the time. I will never forget thinking, "God, what a place to go to train for the desert." Lots of things were going through my mind as I left for Iraq. But, I am a small, insignificant piece in a larger puzzle and I had a duty and obligation.

After an eighteen hour flight, we landed in Kuwait City, which was very industrialized. It looked nothing like the Kuwait of 1991 when the Iraqis just destroyed that area. We drove to our base, Camp Navistar, which sits on the Kuwait-Iraq border at Abdali. We were the last station before you cross the border into Iraq. I remembered seeing tracer fire and wondering what was happening. It was celebratory gun fire, the Iraqis like to fire their weapons into the air.

On our very first mission, we were on a route between Fallujah and Ramadi and got hit by a roadside bomb. Everybody was just in shock and stopped. I said, "What the fuck are you doing, you have to keep moving." On our next mission, we got hit again around the same area. One soldier was wounded, we were getting hit by small arms fire, and it was the first time I realized that we are going to lose people if we keep taking hits like this every time we go out. I thought, "To hell with this, we are going back and we are going to kill these guys like infantrymen." I remember seeing two insurgents shooting at us from a building. We pointed our vehicle at them, mounted with a SAW [Squad Automatic Weapon], and we nailed them. Some soldiers were shocked by that. They said, "God, I can't believe you killed those guys." It was not a good moment.

We went back to that spot on March 22nd and got hit hard again. There were Iraqis on a bridge shooting down on us. This was just outside Fallujah, and they had a good ambush. I'd have to give the insurgents some credit. This time we kept moving. We didn't have the .50 caliber machine gun at this point. I told my driver to go to the top of the bridge and the insurgents were in shock. We took fire from below too. We got into a long gun battle. I was calling on the radio and got shot in the leg [by a ricochet]. Suddenly six Humvees pulled up, and it was a convoy with [Marine Corps] General [John] Kelly. I didn't know it was him as he was not wearing any rank, but a captain was saying "Yes sir" to him, so I knew he was a high-ranking officer. I was standing there, and General Kelly was asking me what was going on. I was impressed by his courage, standing there with only a pistol on the bridge. I felt sick to my stomach. I had been shot before, so I knew what it was, but so much was going on. General Kelly put his hand on my shoulder and said, "You've been shot. I am going to call you a medevac [air evacuation for injured]." I refused. I went back to base camp and got patched up. I have a quarter-sized scar on my leg. There were some people who were scared during the fight. Very few of them were willing to accept the fact that if they didn't fight back, they were going to die. You can't just be a transportation driver; you have to be a combat soldier too.

On the next mission, I had to stay back at the main camp because I was injured. On April 5, 2004, [beginning of the Al Sadr Uprising] a sergeant [from another company] came and said, "Get your gun truck. We need to take you on a mission." I thought that this was going to be bad, so I went to get a .50 caliber machine gun. The 201st Field Artillery from West Virginia was at our base camp. This is no joke—we borrowed a .50 caliber from them. It was at the time of Fallujah and battles up north and we were headed to Baghdad. We cut a hole in the top of our Humvee and mounted the .50 caliber to it. We had no armor, and put Kevlar jackets over the doors. We loaded up all the ammo we could. I manned the .50 cal[iber] and people said to me, "You're an officer, you're not supposed to do that." I hand picked a few soldiers who I trusted and respected, and we rolled out.

Things were fine until we got into Baghdad. There were two ways into Baghdad International Airport: Route Irish, which was closed, so we took Route Tampa, which was wide open but allowed us to see very well. There were some kids throwing rocks at us, but that was a common thing. We kept driving. Our gun truck floated around the convoy, kind of like a hawk looking for prey. We wanted to give the enemy notice that we were there. Our vehicle was painted with tiger stripes, so that it would actually stand out to the enemy. The guys jokingly called it "Zebra," but I told them, "You don't see Zebras fighting, do you?" Anyway, that's what we called it. If we made a positive effect on the enemy and let them know we are not going to take their crap, they would remember our vehicle. The message was: If you attack this convoy, you're going to get shot. If you identify your vehicle, the enemy will recognize you as the guy that shot them up last time. You have to go into that animalistic thinking. You weren't allowed to just kill anyone, there are rules of engagement. If you let people just do what they want to do, there will be anarchy. There are people who have no scruples. Because they are pissed off, they'll shoot a farmer. Look at Blackwater, well, I don't want to say too much about them, but you hire people to do a job that the military could do better. The military does a great job.

So were driving toward the turn for Baghdad Airport, when suddenly an IED went off. I remember hearing, "Contact Left! Contact Left!" Then there was machine gun fire. "Contact Right! Contact Right! Hell, Contact everywhere! Get in the gate!" Right when we slowed down to make the turn, we realized it was an ambush. I remember hearing on the radio the driver from the lead Humvee gun truck saying "Oh my God, Oh my God save us, they're all dead!" We pulled up to the turn off point, where they were hammering us. I started cranking off rounds with the .50 caliber machine gun and it drew a lot of attention. A bullet came in and fragments shattered my hand. I was bleeding all over the place, but I tried to keep firing. I reached down to pick up some more ammo. My guys were fighting their tails off. As I was trying to load the ammo, I remember seeing a guy pointing a weapon at me from about 170 meters away. Suddenly something slammed into my chest. He shot me! I fell to the bottom of the vehicle, the .50 cal [machinegun] was pointing straight up in the air. I had my vest on, and the bullet was lodged in my Sapi [Small Arms Protective Inserts] plate. My driver saw the blood from the hand wound and thought I was dead. I lost track of time but remember thinking I am going to kill every one of these sons of bitches. I was scared. I got up and the guy who shot me wasn't even paying attention to me. I squeezed off a ten-round burst of the .50 caliber, and I remember seeing his rifle falling to the road. Shit I remember it well. I remember thinking, where is the rest of the convoy? They stopped and went into a box formation. We kept calling for help; our vehicle had four flat tires.

The fire fight continued and I recall at some point reaching down to grab more ammo. I looked up and standing there were two insurgents. I had no time to reload, so I fired a flare at them; and then my men and I started shooting at them. I distinctly remember seeing a piece of scalp. Yes, human scalp. There was a pool of blood, it was very disgusting.

Things started to settle down. There were eighteen confirmed killed in that battle, we lost no trucks, no cargo. You know, just one of those eighteen insurgents could have been a key leader who orchestrated a terrorist attack in New York or Los Angeles. It was our claim to fame; we were awarded Bronze Stars for this. The doctor told me you've been wounded twice in two weeks and should go home. I thought about how my soldiers looked at me. I started thinking, "If we leave, who is going to protect them?" It is not a heroic type thing. How could I leave these people? They needed me.

Out of this experience the 518th Combat Gun Truck Company was created. We never lost any military cargo to the enemy and we were in seventy-three engagements. The enemy always lost all of them. I don't know any football team that has a record like this. I don't mean to be boast, but we did it with Guardsman, Reservists and some active duty guys and with broken down Humvees. The story of the 518 has to be told.

You hear people saying that we shouldn't be in Iraq. We need to be there to stop terrorism. All the terrorists have decided to congregate in Iraq. How is eliminating this threat in Iraq a bad thing? Whether this war is about oil, I don't know and I don't care. The soldiers I fought with, that was what it was about. The truth is that we are all fighting for each other, fighting for the soldier next to you. We are establishing a democracy in a country that has been living under oppression for years.

I wrote a letter to President Bush, commander in chief. I wanted to let him know that not everyone felt that the war was a disaster. I was angry from hearing all the negative things. There are some of us who live by a code of honor. I meant it when I wrote "From Bunker Hill to Baghdad." There is a long history of living, not just saying it, but actually going out to die for your cause. I get chills just talking about it. After the letter, I received a call from the White House, I couldn't believe it. The person on the other end said, "[t]he President was so impressed by what you wrote he wants to invite you to Morgantown for one of his speeches." I was so impressed. The President actually gave a crap about what I had to say. It was an invitation-only event. I handed my ticket to them. They stopped and said, "[o]h, you're the one the President wants to talk to." I went to a back room. The former governor of Virginia was there and a Congressman. Amongst all these people, someone walked up to me and said, "[t]he President wants to speak with you." They pulled me into a back room with the President; I am not joking you. The President walked in and asked, "How are you doing McCormick?" He said he knew what I had done and was proud of me. As the President shook my hand, someone handed me a presidential coin of excellence. I really cherish that coin, it means a lot to me. The President also mentioned me in his Fourth of July speech.

I am going to stay in the military until this war is over. It really is a sense of honor; it is the right thing to do.

Lieutenant Colonel Thomas Sisinyak

"You signed up for this. You have a responsibility to fight."

Sisinyak is a 1983 graduate of The Citadel, the military college of South Carolina. He has been in the U.S. Army Reserve since 1985. He was the Commander of 812th Transportation Battalion out of Charlotte, North Carolina. He led the battalion for a tour in Iraq from February 2004 to October 2004 and for most of the time was stationed at Camp Navistar on the Kuwait-Iraq border, which is south of Basra. He is studying for a master's degree in Strategic Studies at the U.S. Army War College and lives in North Carolina.

My father was a career army officer, who retired as a Two Star General. I had aspirations to follow in my father's footsteps. I decided to keep one foot in the military, and one foot out. We moved around a lot when I was young, and it is not the easiest way to raise a family, because the family must endure numerous relocations so I went into the Reserves.

No one was shocked when we learned that we were being activated, although it was a very nervous time. We're citizen-soldiers, who train on the weekends. You train and wonder if you would ever go to war. Then, when you find out that you are going to war, you start to wonder: Am I ready? So there was the fear of the unknown. You have confidence in your training, but you never had a chance to test it.

The soldiers and their families were anxious. Most of the soldiers were able to settle down as the army has made great strides since Desert Storm with support groups. Problems still existed; soldiers left with financial problems, and military salaries often represented a drastic pay cut. There was also husband-wife issues, all the life issues still go on in the rear while the soldiers are deployed. But the army has a solid support structure in place and we were able to address the problems as they came up.

It was difficult to adjust to Iraqi culture, and the extreme temperatures. It was hard to fathom how people could work in such heat. Adjusting to the situation was like trying to drink from a fire hose, there was so much to learn and get a handle on. Everything happened so quickly.

We encountered insurgents on a daily basis. The convoys took on some small arms fire, rockets and IEDs on a regular basis. The amazing thing is that the Battalion did not lose any soldiers. I had many, many Purple Hearts and Bronze Stars to award. There were significant fire fights, but no one was killed. There is no rhyme or reason to that. I would like to say that we were trained and ready to fight, and I believe that to an extent, but there was a lot of luck involved. McCormick and 518th [see the testimony from McCormick in this chapter] was just a military phenomenon in itself, and I am not going to try to take any credit for that. My proudest accomplishment was bringing them all back home.

We were a Transportation unit, and were somewhat vulnerable. It was dangerous in the aspect that our equipment was not protected properly from IEDs, rockets, and so on. We were slow moving, soft targets and the enemy knew it. We had trucks, with thin skins—like commercial trucks.

There was the incident with the soldier complaining to Secretary Rumsfeld about "hillbilly" armor. I question this comment, it made the army look less than prepared. I don't know if they took him seriously at the time. But eventually somebody listened. We got a lot of attention; all kinds of dignitaries came over to see the "hillbilly armor." Executives from the Humvee company spoke to us about the ballistic steel for vehicles.

In March of 2004 the Iraqi's began to ambush our convoys. One of my commanders in the 172nd out of Omaha, Nebraska, came up with the idea that maybe we can build some armor to put on these trucks and Humvees, and hopefully save lives. We decided that quarter-inch ballistic steel was needed. We brought the idea to a general. He had steel sent in from stateside and we bolted it on to the trucks. It is a good news success story. The Reserves did not have the proper equipment, but by thinking out of the box we were able to protect our soldiers. The army has since developed equipment based on our early efforts and the voice of the soldier. The new MRAP [mine resistant ambush protected] vehicle is an extension of our efforts to focus on soldier protection.

Operation Iraqi Freedom and Afghanistan has placed a tremendous strain on the Reserves and National Guard, and we have to fix that. The challenge is to create a future force that is capable of providing the proper support around the globe. How we posture the military to fight the war on terrorism is a large question that needs to be worked on.

But we have to make certain that the soldiers understand the mission. Soldiers are going to be soldiers. They want to understand why they are doing whatever it is they are doing. I am from the old school, where you don't ask, you just execute. My personal opinion is that the younger generation questions things. I feel it is necessary to keep them informed, and made a point to get in front of the soldiers to explain what was happening. Soldiers would hear that they would be sent home on a certain date. But that date would come and go, and they were still in the theater. They were extended. A lot of soldiers, mostly the young ones, wanted to know why they were not going home. We owed them an answer. We had to explain to them the bigger perspective. A majority of them accepted it. They certainly didn't like it, but it gave them an answer that they could bring back to their families, who were all up in arms because we had to keep the soldiers longer than expected.

Soldiers absolutely have the right to speak out. But, it is very frustrating to see soldiers who turn against the war. I always say, "You signed up for this. You have a responsibility to fight the global war on terrorism." The military has made great strides to take care of soldiers in the last couple of decades. It is not perfect, but there are wars and there are going to be more wars, so we have to listen to and support our chain of command.

Our efforts in Iraq will not be realized for decades. There are differences of opinions on exit strategies. My personal opinion is that we are still uncertain on how to tackle this monster. I certainly don't have the answer. But, the mission dictates that the U.S. presence is necessary. The most important thing is to take care of the soldiers.

Sergeant Vincent Micco

"The man reached over and kissed me on the cheek."

Born and raised in Bergen County, New Jersey, Micco is the son of an Italian immigrant. He remembers coming home from school each day to find his father reading the encyclopedia before beginning his nightshift working in a warehouse so as to better integrate into American society. Sergeant Micco served in the U.S. Army Reserves, Bravo Company, 325th Military Intelligence Battalion for nearly a decade before being summoned for active duty on February 2003. His tour in Iraq lasted one year, from March 2003 to March 2004, where he worked in counterintelligence in the Sunni Triangle. He was awarded the Army Commendation Medal and Global War on Terrorism Expeditionary Medal. After returning from Iraq, he ran for Congress in the 9th District of New Jersey. Micco is the 3rd vice president of the Republican Club of Rutherford, NJ, and a member of Vets for Freedom. He works as a mortgage banker and is married with four children.

I joined the Army Reserve in September 1995. My dad is an immigrant from Italy and ever since I was a little boy he always instilled in me a love for this country and that inspired me. I wanted a kick in the butt that comes with military service too; I wanted the rite of passage of basic training and to experience the rigors military life. I always wanted to serve and joining the Reserve was a compromise. I had a young son and I didn't want to go off into the regular army and leave since his mom and I had then recently split up. I began to feel like a lot of my dreams, like joining the military, were going to be tough now. I have since reconciled with my wife and we are now happily married with four children.

I went to basic training in Fort Jackson, South Carolina. It seemed tough but if I had to do it again today, knowing how much more of a mental game it is than physical, it would be a lot easier. I took everything so seriously then. I remember our NBC (Nuclear, Chemical, Biological) training, which required us to go through the dreaded gas chamber. This exercise was designed to get us comfortable with our protective masks. They bring you and your squad into a room, where they released CS [tear gas] grenades. You go in with your gas mask on and they order you to take it off. You have to stay in a certain amount of time before your line can exit. If anyone panics, they stop the line, and drag the person to the back. You have to wait while this is going on. My eyes, skin, and throat were stinging. My lungs kind of locked up. When I got out of the chamber, I let out the loudest and longest belch! It was a mental game meant to build up our confidence in our equipment and ourselves.

I had an exceptional senior drill sergeant, Staff Sergeant Jannone, who was an Italian-American too. He was regularly awarded the noncommissioned officer of the month. He led by example and brought out qualities in me that have made me proud. He spoke to us in an inspiring way about his military career, and brought out good qualities in a lot of us. To me it was important the way he talked to us since they yelled at us all the time, and I was wondering, "Shouldn't they be nicer to us. Didn't I volunteer to help my country?" When he talked to us, it made us feel much better about what we were doing.

My Reserve unit is a Military Intelligence unit, where I spent six years training one weekend a month. I spent most of the last two years of my eight year enlistment in what they call the IRR [Individual Ready Reserve], which meant I didn't have to go to drills any more but remained a member of the Army Reserve. After 9/11 I began to feel compelled to stay in the military and eventually started going to drills again, even though I didn't need to. After I had been back for a couple of drills, we got word that we were going to be deployed.

In early February 2003, I was a squad leader and I got a call at the mortgage company where I worked. It was a Friday afternoon. My sales manager had just left for the day and he said, "Vinny, don't forget the sales meeting on Monday morning, don't be late." An hour later, I got the call from my unit telling me to contact everyone in my squad and tell them to get ready to report at 0800 Monday morning, we're going across the pond. I guessed I wasn't going to make the sales meeting at work on Monday morning.

It was not a complete surprise. The previous month our company commander gave us a candid assessment about the prospect of being deployed. I went home and told my wife. She started to cry and said, "What happens if you get killed?" I feel like there is a GI Joe inside every guy, and mine was pretty excited. I didn't want to show that excitement but I just kept upbeat and positive. My family saw that I was not disturbed or afraid. It all happened so fast. My mom was terrified, and she was terrified for every day that I was deployed. Inside, I felt that it was a privilege to be going.

Our battalion first went to Connecticut, then Fort Dix. We got all our shots, including anthrax and smallpox vaccine. On March 17, we flew out of McGuire Air Force base to Kuwait. I remember the painful good-bye to my wife and to my kids. By the end of the month, I was one of a handful of counterintelligence agents in the 325th who were scooped up and tasked out to the 519th Military Intelligence Battalion Tactical HUMNIT [Human Intelligence] Operations Section: it's known as THOPS. We were disappointed at first to leave our own unit and felt like we were being sold off. But I later learned that someone had spoken fondly of my abilities, and as a result, was tasked out to this really good, hard-charging active duty unit.

In early April, we crossed the berm, as they say, with the 519th into Iraq and at first it was scary. We drove for hours through the desert and small towns. Every where we went children ran up to the side of the road to wave at us. It is one of the warmest memories that I have. The first night was tense. You didn't want to get up and venture off into the dessert and go pee. There could be mines, anything. It was pretty cold and I remem-ber lots of wild dogs howling. Convoys were the most dangerous activity. Being shelled by mortars every night in Balad was tough. The earth would shake and they'd get louder and louder, which meant they were getting closer. I would get up and pace back and forth until my heartbeat would slow down and I'd go back to sleep.

My job was a counterintelligence agent so I made friends with the locals who might become informants for us. They would tell us about attacks that bad guys were planning against us; or those who were selling weapons out of their home to use against us; or that the local preacher at the Mosque was preaching jihad against the Coalition. You have to weed out who is coming to you because they just want a reward from those whose stories can be corroborated. I would tell the people who gave us good intelligence, "Listen, I realize how much you risked to tell us and what could happen to you. I just want to say how grateful we are as Americans." They would interrupt and say, "No, you don't need to thank us; we need to thank you, thank you for getting rid of Saddam."

On some missions, the whole thing was almost gentlemanly. We would search their vehicles before meeting. They weren't allowed to bring any weapons in. I had an informant one day and I watched him getting searched. After he was in, we talked and he said, "You gotta tell your secu-rity guys to be more careful, I forgot I had this pistol hidden in my car." It was laughable.

In Baghdad's Green Zone we set up a schoolhouse for Iraqi intelligence operatives. At the time there were five political parties in Iraq that were hammering out the Interim Constitution, we nicknamed them The Party of Five. Each of these parties had an intelligence unit and we would liaise with them. I acted as the liaison to the PUK [Patriotic Union of Kurdistan], and they were very good. But other parties, such as SCIRI [Supreme Council for Islamic Revolution in Iraq], weren't helpful. It was no secret that they were aligned with the Badr core and the Iranians. They were not useful, and never provided any intelligence. Call me biased but I felt like the Kurds provided the most information. Besides the PUK and KDP [Kurdish Democratic Party] and SCIRI, there was also the INC [Iraqi National Congress] and INA [Iraqi National Assembly]. We didn't really engage the other Shiite parties.

Sometimes informants would bring Intel that resulted in a command sanctioned raid. We would take rides with the 1st Armored Division at three in the morning to follow up on the information and search houses. Assault teams would go into houses and round up the mature males and I'd question them. I remember one time we went into this person's house. A woman was pointing to her husband and screaming to us and my Arabic interpreter informed me that she was saying, "Go easy on him. He was held by the Iranians." Apparently when Iran and Iraq had their war in the 1980s, this fellow was captured by the Iranians and they were especially cruel to him. I made believe that I was paying her no mind, so that I didn't show that her husband and teenage son were going to get sympathy. We brought them back to our compound. I questioned the husband and son for a long time. I made an assessment that they were of no intelligence value and that they should be released. I was then told to escort them back to their home. We put bags over their heads, so they wouldn't be able to see inside our compound and bound their hands. When we got to their home, I took off the bags and cut off their plastic cuffs. The man reached over and kissed me on the cheek and said something like "God bless you." It was gratifying because I know he came away thinking their treatment by an American was better than what the Iranians did.

I remember another mission in which the Blackhawks flew us out to Al Qaim, a remote area in the western desert of Iraq, near the Syrian border. We had arrived soon after U.S. forces raided targeted houses of mujahideen. Our mission was to screen the detainees for intelligence value.

The "target packet," prepared by the CIA, had listed several PIRs [Priority Intelligence Requirements], which meant we'd do full blown interrogations beyond screenings. I got a hands-on education in interrogation that day. By the next day we had forty-one detainees ready to be loaded onto two large Chinook helicopters for their transport to Abu Ghraib. During the flight to Abu Ghraib, the detainees, blindfolded and cuffed, were vomiting all over themselves and the helicopter floor because the pilot was flying up and down, parallel to the terrain features, called "nap of the earth," as opposed to flying in a straight horizontal line. We felt compassion for them and began giving them water from our canteens and whatever little aid we could offer.

On other occasions we'd be sent to the local CASH [Core Ambulatory Surgical Hospital] to interrogate injured "hajjis" as we nicknamed them, after they'd recovered enough from their injuries to be questioned. In the course of their activities against the coalition, the bad guys would manage to get shot by a local QRF [Quick Reaction Force] and so were taken to the CASH for medical treatment. "Hajjis" had their own special wing in the CASH, segregated from the rest of the patients. Whenever we'd push the curtain aside and walked down the middle of rows of enemy personnel laid out on hospital beds, they would prop themselves up nervously wondering who these armed soldiers were. After a while we had these visits choreographed like a scene out of *The Godfather*. Without making any eye contact, I would walk in first and grab a folding partition from the back and we'd all close in on our target's bed at the exact same moment. My teammates would surround the bed, looking as serious as a heart attack, while I'd methodically unfold the partition around the bed. At the last moment, I'd visually scan around the room giving everyone who made eye contact a ferocious look. Who knows if these little charades had any psychological impact on hardcore Saddam loyalists, whose own interrogation techniques under the former regime were unspeakably cruel. A seasoned interrogator from the CIF [Core Interrogation Facility] once commented that it doesn't take long for these detainees to realize that we're not going to physically torture them. At that point, the game is pretty much over.

My father owns an Italian restaurant and he would send sixty pound packages with goodies for me and my battle buddies. All of us who received packages in the mail would pack our goodies into the cargo pockets of our uniforms to give the Iraqi kids when we went on convoys. I still think about the kids and how they loved us and how the soldiers loved them right back. When they are old enough to run the country, I am convinced the United States is going to have the greatest allies. This one particular family in Baghdad always wanted us to stop in and have coffee and a flat Arabic bread that they made. I remember sitting in the living room and the TV went on and the Iraqi kids started singing a rap song that is popular in the states. They knew every word and they had their favorite American singers. Change isn't going to happen over night, but I have a great deal of hope for the generations to come.

For us to just cut and run would embolden the insurgents. They are only 1 percent of the population but they are vicious. If we prematurely left, we would be perceived as weak.

I am proud of the experiences, memories and friendships that I gained in the military. I'll remember the 130-degree weather, the sandstorms, and the danger and, no matter how smart I think I am sometimes, I realize that I am dependent on God. It's His favor upon our military and our nation that give us victory.

Lieutenant Jason Nichols

"It is not supporting the troops by keeping them from doing the job that they volunteered to do."

Lieutenant Nichols is a United States Naval Information Professional for the Multi-National Force in Iraq (MNF-I), a position in which he manages information technology. Nichols grew up in Ocala, Florida, and his mother worked both as a waitress and as a trainer for racing horses, so the family moved around a good deal. He attended high school in Arkansas, where he enlisted in the navy in 1993. Nichols was awarded an NROTC scholarship while enlisted as a Nuclear Machinist Mate and was commissioned in 1998 after completing his undergraduate degree. Upon graduation, he served on the USS La Jolla, *a fast moving submarine based out of Pearl Harbor, Hawaii, and he did deployments in the Mediterranean and Pacific. Later he served as an NROTC instructor at Florida State, where he also received a master's degree in Computer Science. Nichols left the navy for one year in 2004 and reentered following his request to go to Iraq. He deployed to Iraq in February 2006 for a tour that lasted roughly one year. Nichols drafted an "Appeal for Courage" in response to the "An Appeal for Redress," which was a soldiers' appeal to end the U.S. occupation in Iraq. Nichols's statement instead advised Congress to support the war.*

I was tense, but motivated as I deployed to Iraq. My first impression was that it was greener than I thought it was: I had expected to see nothing but desert. I was also surprised it was not as hot as I had imagined.

I worked in the Green Zone in Iraq and there is a popular misconception that it is safe. But it is actually dangerous inside the Green Zone, which surprised me. When I first got there, we received lots of incoming. There were several mortar and rocket attacks. There were one or two a day for a couple of minutes; some days there might have been five or six. It certainly makes you cautious, but the attacks seemed more like an act of desperation by the insurgents. I am a bit of a history buff, so I knew that there would be some danger and was not completely caught off guard by the hostilities. More recently, however, the attacks have slowed down, which indicates that we are making progress.

I worked with Iraqis who had technical skills, such as civil engineers, so they were probably better educated than the average Iraqi. Many of them spoke English. I traveled around a lot in my life and I found the Iraqis are pretty much like anyone else. They seemed like friendly and respectful people.

One day, I was surfing the web before I deployed to Iraq and I found the Appeal for Redress and it bothered me. It wasn't accurate; it gave the impression that the military was opposed to the war in Iraq. I thought I could make my own counterappeal. After reading the Appeal for Redress Web site, I started the Appeal for Courage Web site the same evening. I had to do some navy training so I was delayed in getting it online. A Staff Sergeant Thul e-mailed me and we started to work together on the site, I read his blog and he was a good writer. I received some negative e-mails in response to my actions. Some air force lawyer tried to send my boss a letter of warning, saying that I should not be doing this because it violated the Hatch Act. The Act limits federal employees pushing politics in a federal work place. He interpreted our Appeal as a petition, but the Act does not apply to the military, it was designed for federal, civilian employees.

I had read scholar Andrew Bacevich's article in the *Atlantic Monthly* where he argued that soldiers should not get involved in politics. He recently wrote an article in *Stars and Stripes* to which I wrote a reply, though it wasn't printed.[10] I quoted George Washington, who said, "When we assume the Soldier, we did not lay aside the Citizen." War is being improperly politicized by many citizens and politicians. It is incumbent upon the military to make a response. On an individual basis, soldiers have the right to express their political opinion. There is also a whistle blowers act that allows us to file grievances.

The antiwar soldiers are, for example, allowed to speak out. I think their arguments are wrong, but as long as they follow the guidelines, then I don't have a problem with it. The position I don't support is the slogan, "Support Our Troops, Bring Them Home." It is a contradiction, it is like saying "Support our astronauts, keep them out of space" or "Support our firefighters, keep them away from fire." It is not supporting the troops by keeping them from doing the job that they volunteered to do.

I think there is no alternative but military force to face the threat. The opposition who says that we don't need military solutions is unrealistic. They are trying to treat the war on terror as a law enforcement problem. Well, it is a lot more than a law enforcement problem. We need to get at the source. The religious extremists use the poverty in the region to manipulate followers; it is a weapon for the extremism. The only way to combat this is to spread freedom, and this involves military force.

We have created a fairly stable, although not fully established, democracy in Afghanistan. If we stay in Iraq, we will have an Islamic democracy there. The surge has helped a great deal. The change from when I first went to Iraq to today is like night and day. The insurgent attacks are down. We have secured Baghdad, which means we have a good shot at securing the country.

The central goal of the Appeal for Courage is to communicate to Congress that the troops support the war and we want to stay and finish the job. Of course, I can only speak for myself and perhaps those who signed the petition. You have to make your own judgment as to what the majority of soldiers think. I spent a lot of time with soldiers and I get the feeling that they support the war. Certainly there are soldiers out there who oppose it, but they are a minority. I am not concerned about the antiwar movement; it is not significant enough to have an impact on the war.

Colonel William V. Wenger (Ret.)

"They want you, your family and everyone you know who is not a Muslim dead."

Wenger entered the ROTC while an undergraduate at the University of California-Santa Barbara, where he earned a bachelor's degree in History and Anthropology in 1969. He has served in the Army Rangers, Airborne, Special Forces, Infantry, Armor and Military Intelligence in a career that has spanned over three decades with some ten years on active duty. Most recently he volunteered, after retirement, to serve in Operation Enduring Freedom (Afghanistan) and Operation Iraqi Freedom. Prior to retirement, Colonel Wenger was commander of the California Army National Guard. His duties in Iraq included service as chief of policy for the Multinational Force-Iraq for General Casey and Ambassador Negroponte, and later, for the second half of his tour, Chief of Border Security for then Lieutenant General Petraeus. He spent a year in Iraq, from June 2004 to June 2005. In 2007 he again volunteered to return to active duty and combat where he served as branch chief for Counter Improvised Explosive Devices in Kandahar, Afghanistan, for Regional Command, South, as well as branch chief for Combined Joint Task Force Paladin (South), 82nd Airborne Division from March to August 2007. Colonel Wenger is a graduate of and later taught at the U.S. Army War College. He holds master's degrees from California State University-Long Beach, Pepperdine University and American Military University. He is also a special reserve officer for the Los Angeles Police Department (LAPD) where he teaches leadership. Wenger is married with four grown children. He is currently national commander (Interim) of the Iraq War Veterans Organization. He holds numerous military awards, decorations, and orders of knighthood. Although Wenger was a high-ranking officer in Iraq who dealt with policy issues, he spent significant time in the field. As such, he is included in this chapter on combat veterans.

My family moved to California in 1951. My father wanted me to attend the military academy at West Point, but I was adamantly opposed to any involvement with the military. I had a college roommate at the University of California at Santa Barbara in ROTC who enjoyed it and encouraged me to give it a try. I did, and I found that I liked the challenge and the camaraderie. My father served in the National Guard, the Army Reserve and later the air force. When he could not make a living as a chemical engineer during the Great Depression, he decided to go back to medical school. He eventually landed on Omaha Beach as a regular Army medical officer during World War II. He was also at the Battle of the Bulge. After World War II, he transferred to the Air Force and spent more than thirty years as a Reserve flight surgeon. So, his experience with the military probably had some influence on my decision. I also have a long heritage of family members serving in the military. We had family members who served in the Revolutionary War, on both sides of the Civil War, in World War I, and World War II.

I spent well over thirty years in the military, but the only time I was shot at before Operation Iraqi Freedom was during the 1992 Los Angeles Riots. I commanded the California National Guard's Battalion Task Force, the first deployed in Los Angeles during the riots. We were fired on by criminals with automatic weapons and drive by shooters, and fortunately none of my people were hit, nor did they have to discharge a weapon. My task force was spread out over 350 square miles. My troops diffused many volatile situations and disarmed and turned over to the police many trouble makers. The junior leaders performed superbly, and as a result the battalion task force was later awarded the first ever Army Superior Unit Award for operational excellence.

After thirty-two years of military service, I was retired at the onset of the War on Terrorism. I was highly desirous to serve and contribute and realized there was a significant need for experienced folks, so I volunteered to return to active duty in 2004. I spent a year in Iraq. A year or so after I returned home, I received a call from a friend serving in Kabul, Afghanistan asking if I would consider serving again in combat with him. I was again thinking of volunteering. My wife said, "...Oh no, I don't want you to do that. You have done more than enough." We thought it over for a few days, and she said, "I know what this means to you, so if you really want to do it, go ahead." She was supportive but frightened. As for most families, there is a significant sacrifice on their part; and I really admired my family and other military families for what they do to contribute to our country. They are true patriots. My children were supportive of my tour in Iraq, but not Afghanistan because they suspected that I would not come back. They thought I was pushing the envelope a little too much at my age. But they remained supportive and wrote to me to keep up my morale.

When I first deployed to Iraq, I knew I made the right decision. While there is always some apprehension, I was excited to hit the ground in Baghdad and get to work. Oddly enough there was less anxiety and concern when I went to Afghanistan, even though I intentionally selected an Infantry assignment as far forward as I could get. There was much less angst going back the second time. Afghanistan is much different from Iraq, it is so abysmally poor, there's almost no infrastructure or market economy. More than half of Afghanistan's income comes from opium poppy. Over 90 percent of the world's poppy crop comes from the country. During the time I was there, Afghanistan saw an increase of over 50 percent in the production of poppy. I was on combat reconnaissance with a Special Forces A Team along with Afghan Army in Mizan District, Zabul Province searching for Taliban IED cell leaders and arresting Afghans who cultivated poppy. But I actually felt very sorry for these poor folks. For the average person in Afghanistan, seventy dollars a month is a good living. A person cultivating poppy can make twenty-five dollars a day. So, what is the farmer going to do to support his family? He's going to choose the crop that makes the most money.

My main task in Afghanistan, however, was in Counter Improvised Explosive Devices. I was attacked by IED's, both in Iraq and Afghanistan, but fortunately was not injured. None of the men in my immediate operations were killed, but some were seriously injured. We had some Afghans patrolling with us who unfortunately lost limbs. They would have died had it not been for the extraordinary and very rapid action of coalition medevac choppers and our exceptional medical personnel. The Army mobilization training was generally excellent, and we felt well prepared to cope with this environment.

For the first six months that I was in Iraq, I was chief of policy for Ambassador John Negroponte and General Casey. In that capacity, my staff section and I were the linkage between the Multinational Force-Iraq and the Embassy, so I spent as much time in the State Department as I did in the military, trying to work out a symbiotic relationship between the two entities. Ambassador Negroponte and General Casey had a good working relationship, but the two departments did not because the operating culture of each was so very different. Over time, the ability to work together productively improved. A major goal on which I worked was to disband the Iraqi militias.

Iraq is historically a relatively primitive and very tribal society. You can't blame these people for wanting these tribal militias as they provided a level of security for their communities and businesses that the Iraqi Army and the coalition at the time did not. I met often with militia groups and they were very cordial and polite. However, they absolutely refused to disband their militias. They might agree to disperse some of their people into the Iraqi Army into unified units thus allowing the exiting leadership to retain control, but they would not relinquish their command over forces.

Some of it was window dressing to comply with some of the demands of the Iraqi government. A lot business was conducted with money under the table. The Iraqi and all Arab cultures are built on bribery, and it was sometimes hard to stomach for a westerner.

During my second six months in Iraq, I wanted to get out to the field more. I went to Lieutenant General Petraeus and volunteered to work for him training the Iraqi police because of my civilian police experience. General Petraeus assigned me chief of border security for Iraq. Petraeus is a soldier's soldier and a true Renaissance man. He does everything so very well. First of all, Petraeus really cares about the troops. He is an extremely bright individual, who is extraordinarily politically astute. He is an intellectual, and a life long student of military history, especially counterinsurgency. He worked very well with the Iraqis. I can tell you on a personal level General Petraeus is extremely demanding and very quick and bright. So, before you brief him you must have your ducks in a row. You know he is going to pick apart what you are telling him. He always asked very probing, detailed questions to get at the heart of an issue. You must demonstrate to him that you are competent, and that you were willing to get out in the field. In both Iraq and Afghanistan I fought to get out into the field (not always easy for a Colonel) because you can't lead from inside a FOB [Forward Operating Base], and he respected this hands-on pro-active approach. The best accolade that I received from him was that he asked me not once, but several times, to stay in Iraq and work with him. I will always treasure the fact he asked me to stay. I am still in touch with him.

I was eager to get out into the field. I was responsible for about 450 forts, seven academies for training Iraqi police, and various maintenance facilities. In Mosul, General Petraeus had enormous success in reaching out to Iraqi communities. As for news articles that criticized Petraeus when he was commanding general of the 101st Airborne Division in Mosul for appointing Iraqis who later turned out to be insurgents, inevitably such things are going to happen on rare occasions.

I had personal experience with this problem. I was on an ambush patrol to capture insurgents in Al Walheed, who were coming from Syria. In the depth of the desert at night, we worked with the Iraqi Special Border Police (The Desert Wolves) to try and catch some of these infiltrators and smugglers. I was working aside a very fine Iraqi lieutenant who I thought was smart and doing a good job. Nonetheless, we did not have much success that night in terms of catching insurgents. I later returned to brief the Iraqi Brigadier General Saber, who I advised. He asked how it went. I said, "It was well executed and the Lieutenant did an excellent job." He said, "You know that Lieutenant you like? Well, he's an insurgent! He's in jail!" Well, that's why we didn't have any success that night; it is often very hard to determine who your Iraqi friends are. We constantly played a delicate head game as we dealt with the Iraqis to figure out if they are telling us the truth and what were their true motivations. There were people being found in the Iraqi governmental ministries who were subversives. It made it extremely difficult to make progress. But, I feel that I earned the trust, friendship and respect of many of the Iraqis with whom I worked, advised and trained. I spent many a night on the border with Iraqi forces. If they wanted to take me out, they could have easily done it. I owe my life to my comrades in arms, the loyal Iraq soldiers and police.

I also faced Iraqi prisoners who were being interrogated in holding pens. I never held animosity toward most of these folks who were just ordinary Iraqis caught up in a corrupt and poverty stricken economy. We knew for a fact that you could get an Iraqi to plant an IED for $150, or detonate one for $250. Al Qaeda took advantage of the extreme poverty and lack to prospects of the Iraqi people.

Combat situations are odd, and you eventually become inured to the danger. I can't tell you how many times we were mortared and rocketed in both Iraq and Afghanistan. I remember people on their first tour racing to the bunkers. I would say, "If the damn thing is going to hit you, it is going to hit you. It doesn't do any good to worry about it." Little by little you get used to it. A friend of mine was severely wounded in a rocket attack on the night of the January 2005 Iraqi elections. He wrote me after returning to the States and said something like, "You don't realize how much danger you are in until you are home safe."

There are times I had the equivalent of a flashback—I am reluctant to use that phrase. In my civilian life, I am a real estate property manager. One day I was inspecting an abandoned neighborhood of buildings in Los Angeles projected to be converted to schools. I had been home from Iraq about a month. As I walked down the street lined with old warehouse buildings, I stopped and thought to myself, "What am I doing walking down this open street with no body armor and no weapon?" The scene was so reminiscent of Iraq. Then I thought, "Hey, this may be a dangerous area of LA, but at least it is nowhere near as dangerous as Baghdad, or Al Anbar."

As for antiwar sentiment in the United States, the American people need more patience. We can't change this part of the world overnight. It is going to take decades to bring the Muslim world out of the seventh century and into the twenty-first. To build the infrastructure and market economy to permit these people stand on their own is going to take a long time. Yet, we can not expect them to build a country that is a mirror image of the United States. We need to give them the ability to rebuild and stand on their own, on their own terms which is going to take a long time. General Petraeus often quoted to us the knowledge of the brilliant insurgent advisor and fighter, T.E. Lawrence. One of General Petraeus' favorite quotes of Lawrence's was:

> Do not try to do too much with your own hands. Better the Arabs do it tolerably than that you do it perfectly. It is their war, and you are to help them, not to win it for them. Actually, also, under the very odd conditions of Arabia, your practical work will not be as good as, perhaps, you think it is.

I am incensed by politicians who depict the war as a failure because they condemn the war on terrorism for political reasons. They are rational men and women ignoring the facts of increasing, but generally slow success out of personal political motives. Such action, to me, is treason. This is a fight that must be prosecuted to victory. It is not just for the safety and security of Iraq and Afghanistan. We are directly threatened by terrorism, and have had many attacks since 9/11 thwarted by the FBI, law enforcement, and military. What most people don't realize is that we are facing an insidious enemy that is far worse than imperial Germany in World War I, or even Nazi Germany. These religious zealots, who are willing to kill their own children to further their cause, don't simply want to control your life and your government. They want you, your family and everyone you know who is not a Muslim dead.

Specialist Jennifer Sardam

"It was almost a personal quest for me."

Specialist Sardam grew up on an eighteen acre farm near the small town of Lexington, Alabama. In the middle of her seventh grade year at Lexington High School (called a "high school," although it included grades kindergarten through twelfth), she moved with her family to live in Jacksonville, Florida. At nineteen, when she was working as a drive-thru cashier at a Krystal's burger joint in Orange Park, Florida, a local U.S. Army recruiter stopped by. He was on a mission to enlist Sardam's friend, Ann, who was preparing to take the Armed Services Vocational Aptitude Battery, or ASVAB. Sardam, upon asking some questions of the sergeant, saw the army as an opportunity to help her achieve her own long-standing dreams of traveling abroad and attaining a college education.

Sardam was soon on her way, after signing on with the Army through a delayed enlistment program in June 1991, and shipping off to Basic Combat Training in September of that same year. Sardam served as an active duty soldier from 1991 to December 1995. She worked as a signal support systems specialist on Fort Richardson, Alaska; and also as a signal support systems specialist with the 101st Airborne Division at Fort Campbell, Kentucky.

Sardam was in the National Guard from July 1998 (following a three-year pause in service, during which she returned to civilian life in Jacksonville—from 1995 to 1998—and worked in various secretarial jobs and attended Jones College) to August 2000. That August, was when she reentered active duty with the 1st Infantry Division, Public Affairs Office, which is located in Wuerzburg, Germany. There she worked as both a print journalist and assistant magazine editor until 2003.

Sardam left Germany at the end of her active duty enlistment and moved to Casper, Wyoming. She wanted to remain connected to the camaraderie of military service, so she joined a detachment of the 111th Press Camp based in Laramie under the Wyoming Army National Guard. She remained there from September 2003 to October 2006. During the time that she was a member of the press camp in Wyoming, she worked for brief stints in Korea and Munich, Germany, and spent a month covering Hurricane Katrina relief operations in New Orleans. She was later selected as part of a four-person team to serve six months in Qatar. While based in Qatar, she and her team members interviewed soldiers, sailors, airmen and Marines, traveling to locations such as Iraq, Kuwait and Afghanistan.

I was born in Florence, Alabama, and my family later moved to Jacksonville, Florida. My father and grandfather had been in the Navy, but I joined the military because I had always been a person with big dreams. I wanted to go to college and I wanted to see the world. I wasn't seeing it very much at the time. Right after high school, I was working in the drive-thru at a fast food burger place. I was looking for a vehicle to carry me somewhere else. My dad wasn't around at the time I joined, but my stepfather was supportive, and although my mom was a bit worried, she was supportive.

My family members and friends expressed their surprise. I remember them saying they thought I was "The last person to join the military." I had never even considered doing so until that day I met the recruiter at the fast food chain where I was working.

I went to basic training in September 1991, at Fort Jackson, South Carolina. I was scared to death because I was not the type of person you would except to join the Army. I was quiet and book smart. I remember sitting terrified in my bunk bed on the first night, asking myself, "What did I get myself into?" Doing pushups was at first very difficult for me, but I made it through. My experience with the military was a good one. I enjoyed the feeling of camaraderie.

I deployed to Iraq as a member of a four-person team of the ESGR [Employer Support of the Guard and Reserve], when I was still a member of the Wyoming National Guard. I applied for a position on the team and was selected to interview soldiers in and around the combat zone from all branches of the military. I should say that I do not speak for the ESGR and my comments here are my own.

On the way over to Kuwait, our flight made a stopover in Bangor, Maine. We got off the plane in a little quiet airport. It was late at night. I thought the place would be mostly deserted. All of a sudden a string of people greeted us, clapping and cheering us on. Gosh, there was a line of veterans and older people. One lady hugged me really tight and patted me on my back. They were handing us cell phones with free minutes of talk time, telling us to use them to call home. It almost felt like an episode of the *Twilight Zone*. It was so amazing and unexpected. They provided cookies and refreshments. It made me feel good to know that America was supporting us.

Later, I would tell the story of this moment to others, and when I arrived at my station, I looked up this organization, which I discovered was known as The Maine Troop Greeters. I sent an email, trying to put into words how thankful I was for their generosity toward us that night.

On the day we departed for Iraq, I was excited for some reason. It was almost a personal quest for me. I had always been so scared of so much in my life, and I decided that I was going to face this. I was nervous, but I was more excited than anything else as I realized that I was participating in a cause that was larger than who I was. We entered Iraq during the evening and it was pitch black. I remember a large green flare or something going off. Some of us didn't know what was going on. I thought then that maybe we were being attacked, and I later learned that it was one of our own flares, a routine action, and not anything from the enemy. The next day or so, I remember seeing the Al-Faw Palace, which was magnificent and gave me a sense of the rich cultural history of Iraq.

I got off of the helicopter for an hour at Abu Ghraib, the U.S. detention facility in Iraq. It was the hottest place I had ever been in my life—like Death Valley. I was dripping with sweat and taking photos for an assignment. I could see the prisoners inside the facility, but I did not photograph them. It was scary being right there alongside them, wondering how many were dangerous, separated only by fence wire.

My general sense in speaking with many soldiers in the locations I visited was that morale is good. When I was there, we were all pretty well taken care of. Medical treatment was satisfactory, and the dining facilities were amazingly stocked.

I recall meeting one soldier from the New Mexico Army National Guard who had been through the thick of things. He had experienced a firefight and members of his team had gone down. When we spoke, he kept asking, "Why not me, why those guys?" I really respected him for what he'd been through. He had a wife and a little girl at home and talked about them often.

I had a feeling that the soldiers I met really cared about what they were doing. Some of them were upset that they didn't get more support from the American people. The phrase that I kept hearing was that soldiers and Marines go to war and America goes shopping.

In my opinion, the United States has done a lot of good in Iraq, but we can't be there forever. At some point, the Iraqis have got to take over as a people. I think many Iraqis are glad that we opened up things for them, and that they are able to have freedoms such as voting. A lot of positive changes have come about, but they do need to take on more autonomy at some point. Politicians talk about getting us out of there immediately, and I think those are nice words, but that maybe they don't realize the sheer logistical nightmare that will need to take place for this to happen. There are too many things that need to be put in place, such as a stable infrastructure, before the Iraqis can do their thing. It is going to take some time.

The war is not about oil. I thought so at first, because of what I kept hearing in the media. But, my opinion now, from what I saw when I was over there, is that we are helping a people who are seeking freedom. Getting rid of Saddam has done a heck of a lot of good. The most frustrating thing is the infrastructure (electricity, etc.); it is broken because the insurgents keep destroying it.

Major Brian Bresnahan

"You know who the bad guys are, don't you?"

Bresnahan grew up in Plattsmouth, Nebraska, a small town near Omaha with about 7,000 residents. He holds a bachelor's degree in Natural Resources from the University of Nebraska, where he earned a full NROTC scholarship. Bresnahan was commissioned in the U.S. Marine Corps as a First Lieutenant in 1992, and served on active duty until 1996. He was dispatched to both Somalia and Bosnia in this time period. He remained in the Marine Corps Reserves until he was activated to serve in Iraq from February 2004 to September 2004 as a member of the 3rd Battalion, 24th Marines. His infantry unit was charged with security at Camp Taquddum, which is approximately eight miles west of Fallujah. He currently writes weekly columns for Nebraska's York News-Times, Polk County News, Grand Island Independent, Kearney Hub, *and occasionally at other Nebraska newspapers and* Military.com .

All Marine officers go through The Basic School in Quantico, Virginia. The platoon commander asks everyone why they became Marines. I told him that ever since I was a kid I always wanted to be a Marine. I remember in elementary school reading about Guadalcanal and Iwo Jima, all the epic battles of the Marines in World War II. I wish I could explain it. He said, "Don't worry, 80 percent of the guys who sit at my desk tell me the same exact thing." My mother was mad that I was even considering entering as an enlisted Marine. When the recruiter came to our house, she treated the sergeant like dirt. When I was awarded the NROTC scholarship, she then thought it was okay for me to be a Marine officer. I didn't care—I wanted to be a Marine either way.

The warning order that we were going to Iraq came at the Marine Corps Ball in November 2003. My wife thought, "This is a great night to hear that." It wasn't a big public announcement; everybody was just talking about it. She was nervous. But she is a good woman who understands me and what I believe. She was afraid because we had been through two deployments before. She knew how tough it was and that weighed on her, but she is terrific and there was no conflict between us. My older son was worried. I told him "I need to go away. There are bad guys that I need to fight." He understood that and was okay.

We hit Kuwait at night. I woke up in the morning and it was just desert. If you've been to one desert, you've been to them all. It was as flat as a pancake. Being from Nebraska, I was used to areas that are flat. I felt that some of the guys couldn't fathom what we were getting into. We had a heart-to-heart talk the night before launching into Iraq. I did some yelling. I told them it was serious shit we're getting into. I was not trying to push the panic button or scare anybody. I needed to tell them that "Tomorrow is game time" and they didn't have their game faces on. I think it helped. We crossed into Iraq that morning in the dark. It was the first time they were near a combat situation, and they were awesome.

On that first convoy into Iraq (I think it was our third day) we were going through a town. It was like being on a boulevard, with lanes on both sides of a median and buildings on each side. We had been on an MSR [major supply route] before, but as we got off the main road onto a clover leaf to enter the town we were hit with an IED. We then proceeded into the town. As we were going down the boulevard I looked to the left and there was no one in sight. I looked to the right and there were people peeking around the corner. Before you could say, "Shit," there was a big boom. We got hit by an IED. I told my driver to punch it and others did too, but there were two ways back out of town and the convoy started to split on their way out. In one of the vehicles behind us, the kid just froze. He stopped in the middle of town. Part of the convoy already went to the left to get out and another straight—headed toward what was called the "grinder" because there were so many attacks in that area. I was trying to get the guys who had incorrectly gone straight out of town to come back. I was afraid for the guys who were stuck in town, and I was afraid for the guys going toward the grinder. But we couldn't get the kid to move and the convoy commander kind of lost it. Finally, I told him to get off the radio and raised one of the air officers in the back of the convoy on the radio. He got the back part of the convoy going again and a chief warrant officer who was with the part of the convoy that had incorrectly gone straight got them turned around and headed back. That was the time I was most afraid, with the kid stuck there getting hammered, anything could have happened.

One of the things I did in Iraq was to handle what we call solatia payments. It is compensation to Iraqis for various incidents involving our troops. You may have read about it in the media, where Iraqis receive condolence payments if we injure someone or damage property. I dealt with issues such as if we hit somebody's car or if our boats ran through fishing nets, we would work with the Iraqis to pay them back for the property. One day a bunch of fishermen showed up at the base, saying that they wanted money to replace their fishing nets. It was our job to deal with them and the executive officer asked me specifically to do it. I studied quite a bit before I went over—some language, and the Arab mentality beyond some of the cultural information they throw at you before you go.

I started to get to know a lot of the Iraqi locals. One incident really stands out. Four guys from one of the villages showed up: a sheik, his brother, and two sons. They wanted us to help them with getting water and electricity. There was HUMNIT [intelligence team] there. They had gone into that village a week before with an Army unit and got shot up. One of the Marines had died. They had no patience for these guys who showed up. We were asking them, "If you want us to help, we need to know who the bad guys are?" We could not go back in and get hit again without knowing who we were fighting. The sheik was insisting that he didn't know.

His son was sitting on the back bench staring at the ceiling shaking his head. He'd look at me and roll his eyes. It was obvious that what his dad and uncle were saying was just bullshit. Finally, I said, "Okay, everybody out." I kicked everybody out, except for my interpreter, guardian angel, and the son who was shaking his head. I looked at him and in English I said to him "You know who the bad guys are, don't you?" He nodded his head up and down with a big smile. In English again, I asked, "Who are they?" He just started rattling off names, what they looked like, where they hang out, everything. He came by to talk all the time. I consider him a friend. I keep a picture of him on my refrigerator at home.

What had happened is Al Qaeda showed up in the village. The sheik's son was threatened by Al Qaeda, they demanded that he fight for them, and he refused. They broke his son's arm. Our troops started to get the bad guys then and the guy who told us the original names recruited other informants. We got new information all the time. Al Qaeda was screwing up their neighborhoods and they didn't want them there. Getting to know the Iraqi people was something. They would invite us into their homes and try to feed us, give us gifts, even if they were poor. These are the things that really stood out for me.

The first couple months that I was in Iraq, the Iraqis didn't want anything to do with us. When that first guy told us who the bad guys were, it seemed around that time when things started to change. It was gradual, of course. You have to understand the Islamic Arab mentality: everything happens because of God's will. If Al Qaeda comes to my village, it's God's will. To see change from that viewpoint, and people taking action against it, was incredible.

In April 2004, we were on the outskirts of Fallujah. We were on Route Michigan, which goes all the way from the Syrian border through Fallujah into Baghdad. Our job was to set up vehicle checkpoints to check everyone coming in and out of the area. All the bad guys were trying to come into Fallujah from Syria. One day we had two patrols go out and set up blockades on Route Michigan. The first one was just four Humvees, and they got ambushed. I was in the Combat Operations Center. Here was a kid screaming on the radio that they got hit, and they had injuries. So we redirected the other platoon over to the fight. The captain with that group started a counterattack and an air officer with them called in air support. They shot up a lot of bad guys. One kid got shot in the head and lost his eye. We got about fifteen insurgents, but didn't get them all. The next morning, the same Captain led a patrol and captured another group of them sitting behind a house eating.

I had a chance to talk to one of our kids who got hurt in the firefight. You could just see that thousand yard stare. One firefight and he had it already. He was sitting there smoking a cigarette outside the battalion aid station. He was just staring straight ahead, probably trying to register what just happened. I just made sure he was okay.

I think the main issue of the war had been the lack of political will here. Many people, especially politicians, don't understand what were up against with the bad guys. They can't grasp what a defeat by Al Qaeda will mean, how dangerous it is.

If you face them on the street, you understand that if you backed down all it did was increase their confidence. There was a captain who I served with. He wouldn't wear his helmet at times on patrols and at checkpoints. The message he sent to everyone was "I do not fear you. I am the biggest baddest mother here. I will prove it to anyone I need to." It was a message to the bad guys that I am not going to take your crap. In Arab culture, if you back down it is a weakness. And weakness was not pitied. It was exploited, which was a cultural not religious thing. The fanatics, Al Qaeda, they take that concept of weakness to the tenth degree.

Winning isn't necessarily about increasing the troops. It is more about the strategy and tactics they employ. I reflect on it now, and there are some things we knew to do in terms of counterinsurgency that we didn't get to do. The troops started doing it in 2007, and it's working.

From Fallujah in 2004 to when General Patreaus took over, we didn't seem to employ all these strategies. In military terms, we needed a counteroffensive which General Petraeus brought us, along with a change in tactics and strategy. One of the biggest changes on the ground has been to move people off the major FOBs and push them out into the neighborhoods. The new strategy has the troops live with the Iraqis, share their risks and hardships, and be part of the neighborhood so that people will begin to trust them. This has opened the way to the Iraqis telling us who the bad guys are and giving us actionable intelligence. This is what's changing. Other high-ranking officers and diplomats are also meeting with different entities in Iraq to build trust. I have a lot of faith in this approach. The training of Iraqis has also taken place. They are more competent and capable. They won't be at the level of U.S. Marines, but they are much better now.

I don't necessarily agree with everything that the President does. I have some disagreement with his domestic policies. But, the President understands the threat we face from Al Qaeda and is doing the right thing staying strong in the fight. So I have faith in him and the fact that other politicians like Nebraska senator Ben Nelson also understand the danger of Al Qaeda and the danger of cutting and running. He says we should not put a hard timeline on withdrawal. He knows that it will also embolden Iran.

If you want to fault anybody, look at the whole intelligence community. They screwed the pooch on WMD, they screwed the pooch on the Intel for our forces that assaulted into Iraq. There are a whole lot of different intelligence agencies. You can read *Cobra II* on the details of what went wrong.[11] I don't fault the President for that. The things that went wrong can be traced back to the intelligence community.

If you want to know my opinion of antiwar soldiers, I'd have to say that I have all the respect in the world for them. They went and had a different set of experiences and so came to a different set of conclusions. That's fine, and you know why? Because they still ponyed up, they went through the shit. They just came back with a different view. Now, as for the antiwar movement people in the streets, I have an issue with them. A lot of them are politically driven. There are some loony, kooky people out there. I remember seeing Code Pink activists hanging out in the halls in Congress yelling at representatives. I have no respect for that, but the guys who fought and feel differently from me, I have no quarrel with them.

One thing we all need to do together is to care for the veterans. IEDs have taken a lot of limbs, caused a lot of traumatic brain injury, and we need to improve the VA health care system to handle those things. Anything we can to do fund it and make it more efficient is worthwhile. It needs to get more attention. I don't care if it's a guy who is pro-war or antiwar; we need to make sure the vets get the care they need. There are issues of PTSD, and it is so hard to gauge how it affects people. The system needs to take care of them. Some vets end up homeless and we need to help them. Groups such as Iraq and Afghanistan Veterans of America and the Wounded Warriors Project[12] are doing good work. If there is something that needs to be touched on more, it is helping the veterans.

FOUR

The Sacrifice of Military Families

The impact of war is not limited to the battlefield. The families of soldiers also make great sacrifices when one of their members is engaged in combat. Sleepless nights, loved ones missing at holidays, a parent left alone to raise children, and the torment of wondering whether the knock on the door is a military officer in full dress bearing the bad news of the death of a loved one are among the anxieties that military families face. Tragically, as the number of fallen soldiers increases, more and more families are faced with the trauma of death. As the wife of one marine put it, "[b]eing married to a Marine is said to be the toughest job in the Corps."[1]

Young children are especially vulnerable when a parent leaves for war. According to a Veterans Administration publication, *Iraq War Clinician Guide*, preschool children might personalize the absence of a parent, and incorrectly attribute it to disapproval. Although the armed services and Veteran Administration have established helpful support networks, some solutions are still experimental. Elaine Leeder, a sociology professor at Sonoma State University, claims that the army produced "life size cardboard cutouts" of parents who deployed; "it was so bizarre that they'd think this would be a stand-in."[2]

The activation of large numbers of National Guard and Reserve forces has added to the burden. In 2005, National Guard and Reserves comprised 46 percent of U.S. troops in Iraq. Military pay is often less than what they earned in civilian life, adding financial pressures to the equation. Families of reservists, unlike active duty families who live in a neighborhood where others experience similar issues, often "feel isolated."[3] These once part-time soldiers are on average serving tours that last a year and a half. "Eighteen months away from employers and the family is really too long," said Lieutenant General Clyde Vaughan, identified as chief of the National Guard in 2005. "Think about being away from your employer 18 months and the friction that causes back with the family," the general observed. Another General, Jack Stultz, commander of the U.S. Army Reserve Command stated bluntly that, "we've got a lot of internal turmoil."[4]

There is also political turmoil over the war across the nation. Family members opposed to the war have formed organizations such as Military Families Speak Out and Gold Star Families for Peace. They express anger, disappointment, and frustration regarding the necessity of the Iraq War. Cindy Sheehan, mother of a fallen soldier, has become a household name as one of the staunchest opponents of the Iraq War. The dissenting families point to a December 2007 *Los Angeles Times* poll that reported approximately 60 percent of military families felt that the war was "not worth it." The same poll found that 64 percent of the military families preferred that the troops withdraw by the end of 2008, compared to some 70 percent of the general population that favored withdrawal "right away."

While the oppositional family member's dissatisfaction proceeds from the mishandling of the war, the rising age of the average service member is a contributing factor. The army increased the maximum enlistment age from thirty-five to forty-five, which means that many service members leave children and spouses when they are deployed. This burden on the family unit certainly adds to the stress on soldiers and families.[5]

Families who stand behind the Iraq War have also organized, having formed groups such as Families United for A Strong America. The group follows "four basic principles." Their first principle is to emphasize that the United States was the "victim" of an attack on 9/11. The next principle is to embrace the notion that "our troops want to finish the job." Third, "democracy abroad is necessary for our security at home"; and last, "we will not be safe until the terrorists are defeated."[6]

Whatever a particular family member may think of the war, they all share the hardships and tribulations of having a loved one at war. These voices are equally important to understanding how war stretches beyond the battlefield of Iraq and directly into the homes of American citizens. The perspectives of family members are frequently overlooked in studies on the war. However, there has been a recent appearance of books on the subject, such as *Courage after Fire: Coping Strategies for Troops Returning from Iraq and Afghanistan and Their Families* (2006) and Martha Raddatz *The Long Road Home: A Story of War and Family* (2008). This chapter presents the voices of military family members to better understand the personal impact of war, which sometimes translates into radical political opposition, but more often entails a family member simple trying to cope with the anxiety of having a family member on the battlefield. These poignant reflections force us to wrestle with the meaning of war on a level that should transcend partisan politics.

Celeste Zappala

"How is it okay for my son to go and be killed in this war that no one can explain, but the people who wanted the war don't send their kids."

Celeste is the mother of Sergeant Sherwood Baker, who was the first soldier from the Pennsylvania National Guard to die in the Iraq War. Sherwood, a social worker in civilian life, leaves a wife and young son. He joined the National Guard in 1997 and deployed to Iraq in January 2004. Sherwood worked in military security for the Iraq Survey Group, which searched for the elusive weapons of mass destruction. Sherwood died as the result of a bomb explosion in April 2004. Celeste is a founding member of Gold Star Families for Peace and a member of Military Families Speak Out. She is also on the Advisory Board of the National Council of Churches and lives in Philadelphia, Pennsylvania.

My son, Sherwood Baker, served in the Pennsylvania National Guard and was deployed to Iraq in March 2004. He was killed in an explosion in Baghdad while he was protecting the Iraq Survey Group. They were the people who were looking for the weapons of mass destruction and he was assigned to look after them. Sherwood had been in Baghdad for six weeks. He was thirty years old and in civilian life he worked as a counselor for disabled adults.

The Iraq Survey Group, headed by Charles Duelfer, were still looking for the weapons of mass destruction in April 2004 after everyone had generally agreed that they were not there, but the administration was still looking for them. One day they were supposed examine a small factory. Some people said it was a perfume factory, so they were not sure if they were going to go on the mission. The morning of the mission they were supposed to take a large anti-explosive truck with them, but the truck broke down. They were told to go on the mission anyway. They arrived at the building and there was an explosion. Sherwood tried to get out of his truck to help the others. There was a second explosion that sent debris flying through the air and caught him in the back of his head. The day of his funeral in Wilkes-Barre, Pennsylvania, 1,000 people came.

Sherwood was a card-caring Democrat and did not vote for George Bush, but he took an oath to serve and he loved the guys that he served with. He was not a vengeful person; he just wanted to protect "his men." One of the things that was especially difficult for Sherwood was a training exercise. The soldiers were told that if they were in a tank they had to keep moving no matter who got in front of them. They practiced running over cardboard cut outs of kids.

While in Iraq, Sherwood called home and told me that food and water were being rationed. This was after we had to buy him equipment. We bought him a field phone and global positioning device, which was infuriating: to be expected to buy equipment for my son who was being sent off to war. When he told me that food and water was being rationed, I called newspapers and Congressional representatives, and no one cared. We sent a large package of food to Sherwood a few days before he was killed. He never got it. The package was sent back to us during Memorial Day weekend. It was waiting by our frontdoor after we visited Sherwood's grave site that weekend. I couldn't bring it into the house. I left it on the porch.

In March 2004, George Bush made a joke about looking for the weapons of mass destruction at the annual correspondents' dinner in Washington, DC, Bush was pretending to look under a desk and around the room for the weapons and it brought the house down. They found it riotously funny. Yet, people like Sherwood were still looking for the weapons for real. People were risking their lives looking for weapons that did not exist and the Bush folks made a joke out of it.

I do not think war is something to joke about. I think this war is unjustified, immoral, and illegal. People often ask me, "What is the definition of a just war?" The definition of a just war is the one that you are willing to send your own children to. The architects of the war have shown us that it's not such a just war. How is it okay for my son to go and be killed in this war that no one can explain, but the people who wanted the war don't send their kids?

I feel that the administration has betrayed the military in the way that they have casually used those people. The administration sent soldiers to a war and it still can't even agree on what the reason for going is. I do not in any way wish to denigrate the soldiers. After all, my son was a soldier.

When Sherwood was killed, I made a decision that I would not be quiet. I met other families who spoke out. I work closely with Military Families Speak Out, which now includes 3,500 families of both the fallen and soldiers currently serving. It is a powerful idea that military families themselves will speak. I also think it is important that the mothers, wives, and girlfriends of soldiers are speaking out. I recall the mothers of the "disappeared" in Argentina in the 1970s who would hold the pictures of their children and demand to know what had happened to them. This image is so informing and empowering for me.

We also have to remember the tens of thousands of Iraqis who had no say in what has happened to them. Iraqi people run over the same bombs that our soldiers are running over. We must remember the people caught in the crossfire. The U.S. presence does not help them. The vast majority of Iraqis want the United States to leave.

Teri Mackey

"It touches you in ways that you can't imagine unless you've been there."

Mrs. Mackey was born and raised in the Midwest and currently lives in Novato, California. She is a forty-seven-year-old mother of two sons who were both service members on active duty from 2003 to 2005. Her oldest son Jed deployed twice to the Middle East with the California National Guard, serving his second tour in Iraq from late 2003 to mid-2005. Jed was honorably discharged in March 2007. Mrs. Mackey's other son is in the U.S. Navy and her husband is a military officer who has served for over twenty-two years on active duty. She holds a master's degree from Sonoma State University, and completed a thesis titled, "A Study of the Intersection of War and Instantaneous Communication as It Impacts Families of Soldiers." The thesis grew out of her experience of communicating with her son by cell phone and e-mail while he was in Iraq. There were both positive and negative attributes to being able to communicate by cell phone. A phone call from Jed would reassure her that he was fine, yet the absence of a phone call often left Mrs. Mackey anxious and waiting impatiently for an update that he was alive and well in the combat zone. She movingly tells us about an incident when her son called from Iraq during an intense firefight. Wondering if it may be his last, Jed wanted to let his mother know that he loved her.

I married in 1979. I grew up in a small farm community so my husband was the first person I knew who was in the military. In the 1990s we were stationed in California and my son Jed was active in the Civil Air Patrol and volunteered with the Red Cross as a teenager. There was a large fire in western Marin and he went out there to help. The National Guard was out there as well and he was really impressed by what they did. When he graduated from high school in 1999, he joined the Guard. He had to pick an MOS [military occupational specialty], and since he scored pretty high on the ASVAB [Armed Services Vocational Aptitude Battery] test decided to go into military intelligence. I was very supportive. This was all before the Iraq War; it wasn't even on the radar.

By the time the Iraq invasion came, we knew that something was going to happen. He was activated and sent to the Middle East before the invasion and because of that deployment we were more aware of the international scene, reading several popular Middle Eastern news Web sites on a daily basis. I remember the first night when the United States went into Baghdad my husband and I just sat on the couch and cried. My reaction was, "Oh my God, what have we done." We had another son who was just in high school and knew if things got bad over there he could go over as well. I couldn't believe the collective jubilation at the time. I was very apprehensive. I had been paying attention, looking closely at the talking points as to why the United States was doing what it was doing. I was very concerned, but it seemed that most people weren't paying attention.

Jed is a solid man, a good man, and he likes the military, so when duty called he went without hesitation. When our son was over there the second time, he was stationed in Baghdad and his general patrol area was Haifa Street and Airport Road from the end of 2003 to early 2005. There were lots of causalities at the time. On the news, it seemed like everyday there was a report of a Humvee blowing up. I had a list of news Web sites that I checked and I discovered that the network and cable news are updated at six in the morning Eastern Time. Since I live on the West Coast I automatically to woke up at three in the morning to get the latest news. Richard Quest used to be on CNN at midnight just before I went to sleep; he was from the British office and reported things that you didn't always hear on the American news.

Since we are a military family we shop at the commissary, which is our grocery store. Sometimes when I was shopping I would see a man with a Vietnam Vet hat, with an arm missing or something that I knew was a battlefield wound and I would think to myself "[t]hat could be my son." I would have to leave my cart, walk out, and try to make it to my car before I would breakdown in tears. I just couldn't do it sometimes.

There was really no support network for me. My feeling was that no one really believed what you had to say. There were news organizations and certain power structures who were painting a rosy picture of what was going on. I knew it wasn't rosy. People would ask me, "How's your son doing?" Well, from my reference point, I'd say, "I know he was alive at eight last night because I got a phone call. But right this minute I can't tell you if he's dead or alive because he's out on patrol." People would just look at you; they didn't know how to respond. Some of them would say, "That's not what I heard" as if it was safe over there and I was a liar. They didn't even know the soldiers were getting mortared and attacked. One person said to me "They are really getting shot at?" I guess I can understand that point of view if you watch only certain news programs that reported things are going well, and we are making steady progress.

My son called frequently from Iraq. This is the first war that the Internet has played such an important role in collecting and distributing information and it is referred to as "network centric warfare." It is so common for soldiers to have cell phones and internet access. There was eleven hours difference between Iraq and California, so we were accustomed to answer the phone at two in the morning. One early morning the phone rang. My son was calling from a rooftop in Iraq. The phone call was to tell me goodbye because he didn't think he was going to make it. I heard helicopters, jets, bombs, and bullets. I heard it all. He told me that he loved me and I was crying. We're a military family and we move around a lot and we had just moved to a new neighborhood so I was alone when the call came. My husband was at work and there was no one to talk to. I was a basket case. I just sat there, and then called family, saying that Jed's not going to make it. Finally, he called back and said he is okay. He was sorry for scaring me. He just didn't want to die and not say goodbye. I spoke to other families for my master's degree research and they told me they would get calls like this. Sometimes they would have to wait two days to get a return call. They spoke about constantly checking emails, and waiting for the cell phone or telephone to ring.

There are certain events that you just can't shake. When I was in grad school, I would go on the internet during class breaks to get an update from the battlefield. I logged onto yahoo. There was a picture of medics dragging soldiers out of Humvees that had been blown up. One soldier was the size of my son, had a baldhead, big feet, and a big tattoo on his arm. Jed has big feet, a baldhead, and a big tattoo on his arm. I thought, "Oh my God, that's my son!" I called my husband and he didn't even say hello he knew it was me and said, "I saw it too. He has a wedding ring on. It's not him. Look closely." So we had both seen the same picture within a half hour. He had more time to process it, as I was on a ten-minute break. Okay, I just had that experience and I have to get my shit together and go back to an academic situation. I will never forget that day. But the thing is—although it wasn't my son that was somebody's son. You feel this overwhelming sense of relief that it was not yours, but that soldier is somebody's daddy, somebody's husband, or somebody's son and they are dead. They're doing the same thing I am, searching for information on the Internet but they don't get the relief of realizing that it is not their son, husband, or daddy. That's hard. It made me more aware. It's made me a better person—just to know what it's like to go through this. It is a kind of grief, a kind of guilt, all these emotions wrapped up. It touches you in ways that you can't imagine unless you've been there.

Unfortunately however, I sensed a real disconnect in the military community. I tried mother's groups. Some of the moms have sons who are stationed stateside and let me tell you—"It ain't the same." I went to a meeting expecting to meet other women like me, holding on by a thread, but everybody was mixed in. This is not to disregard anybody's service, but they mixed in mothers who had sons on the battlefield with moms with soldiers at home. It made it hard to talk about your experiences, so you keep it to yourself.

It's been a real fine line for me because I know what's going on and I don't feel like I can speak freely sometimes. I don't want to politicize my son's experience. However, I feel like I can critique the administration's handling the war. They need to be criticized because this administration was caught flat-footed and that left our soldiers ill equipped and unprepared. The experts and the academics were warning them what might happen and they did not listen and we lost kids because of it. I am furious about that! I am furious that due to incompetence, short sightedness, and groupthink our bright young men and women were lost. But, we are never going to get them back. We have to look ahead and think how we can keep this from ever happening again. They said that about Vietnam and it has happened again.

This war is not going to be told by the historians. It is going to be told by the kids who went over there and were in the shit. They sent video, pictures, and e-mails back home and they know what's going on. This war is on their computers all across the country. Once this political climate changes and some time passes I hope these images and facts are brought to light and America wakes up. Right now we're dead and it is frustrating. Americans really haven't paid a price personally, not even a tax. They haven't had to do anything. They haven't even had to pay attention.

I wish there was a draft: an all-volunteer force has made America complacent. A collective attitude of complacency and apathy has developed in the population because there is no draft. As the result of these attitudes those in power have basically been given carte blanche to do what they want. Many parents are not engaged because they have the perception that the war is not going to affect their family because their kids are not going to enlist. I have had people say to me, "Why is your son doing that, don't you have college funds?" That attitude left me with the feeling that military service was something that lower-class people do and that those families with any position or financial means do not serve or feel the need to serve. Joining the military just isn't something that people with status do. So, it is hard to avoid being political. The whole war is political. That's my own opinion. The lack of the draft, the lack of community, has allowed people in power to do whatever they want.

I went to one candlelight vigil on the anniversary of the war. I felt out of place. There were people there from the old hippie movement. For me it just seemed as if the war was their latest cause for some kind of political rally. I think I was the only one there who had a personal stake in the war. The vigil might as well have been to save the whales or save the seals. It left me with the feeling that people would show up to rally to turn the sky purple. I think a lot of people were insincere and just wanted to be part of the "in" crowd. There were people there who were pushing their agendas, one way or the other. I felt for some reason I shouldn't be there and when I left I had an overwhelming sense of sadness because I quietly realized just how alone in my community I was.

Monica Benderman

"The issues are more important than we are."

Monica lives in Hinesville, Georgia, near Fort Stewart with her husband Kevin. She works as a senior care advocate. She met Kevin on a beach in Texas in 2001 and they married before he was deployed to Iraq in 2003. Kevin was a sergeant in the U.S. Army, who served a tour in Iraq, and filed for conscientious objector status following his battlefield experiences. His application was denied. Kevin served approximately one year in prison for his beliefs, having been convicted on the charge of "missing movement." The Benderman Defense Committee has produced a video on Kevin's service titled, A Matter of Conscience.*

Mrs. Benderman discusses the impact of Kevin's military service, difficulties in filing a conscientious objector application, time in prison, and tensions with segments of the U.S. antiwar movement.

Kevin and I met in late 2001, after the Trade Center attacks. He had reenlisted in the military back in June of 2000. He had come down from leave to where I was living in Texas. We exchanged e-mails and phone calls, and we had the chance to spend some time together over the summer. He was going to the National Training Center, and he knew his unit would be deploying to Iraq. They were given a date of January 19, 2003. I went to Fort Hood, Texas, to visit Kevin. They announced that the deployment was cancelled. Kevin was with the 4th ID [Infantry Division], which was supposed go into Iraq through Turkey, but Turkey changed its mind and wouldn't allow the United States to stage operations there. This is the time when we got married.

I was working as a care director, developing care plans for residents in assisted living facilities. I had ninety-three residents in my care, and many of them were veterans or wives of veterans. I learned a lot about the military talking to them. They were very honest about their likes and dislikes. When Kevin deployed, the women there were amazing, giving me advice on what to expect. They told me to keep busy, and I took up knitting and crocheting. The men also gave me their perspective of war, telling me things that maybe Kevin couldn't tell me because he was immersed in the experience of war while they had already lived through it.

We respect the people who served, not everyone agrees with the military and why we still must have it. But the people in the military did step up. Right or wrong, they were willing to put their lives on the line for what they believed. It is not just their voices, but their lives that are being put at risk. For me, whether I agree or disagree with war, I respect the soldiers for their commitment.

The war made no sense to me. Listening to the veterans at my work and through my reading, it didn't seem necessary or justified. Think how many lives could have been saved if we tried mediation instead of a gun. I will tell you a lot of the soldiers I had the opportunity to speak with at Fort Hood had questions about the war. But there was nothing definitive—what's available in 2008 wasn't available in 2003. While the soldiers had questions, they accepted that it was their duty to fulfill their commitment. They just wanted to get it over with and come home. Many people thought it would be quick—not this terrible thing—but regardless of what I thought of the war, I supported Kevin the man when he deployed. I was more nervous about not being available for Kevin than him getting hurt. He is a survivalist. I wrote him a letter everyday and wore yellow ribbons in my hair to help remind myself and others of what the soldiers were facing and what they were missing because of their commitment.

Kevin began questioning things even before he left Iraq. But definitely after he returned and we had moved to Fort Stewart, Georgia. It was a tough, private struggle before he decided to apply for conscientious objector (CO) status. The military's very tight definition of a CO is not my (or Kevin's) definition of conscientious objection. They don't want people to be COs, so their definition means that you must oppose all wars. From our standpoint, conscientious objection is that your conscience will not allow an action that is detrimental to humanity. Your conscience objects to the action, and speaks up to stop it. It includes not only war; it could be someone who is aware of an abusive relationship, someone who knows of an action that violates the personal freedom of another and steps up to try to stop the action. There are lots of different reasons to be a conscientious objector. In this sense, Kevin has always been a conscientious objector.

When did he begin to feel this way about war? It was when he was in Iraq. One day I got a letter that he wanted me to forward to his senator.

It outlined some of the abuses he saw within the military while serving in a combat zone. He felt the orders the soldiers were given were outside their training. He worked on Bradley's on the front line. But they were handling missiles and IEDs [Improvised Explosive Device], which they weren't trained to do. Kevin saw younger soldiers get hurt as a result of orders they were given. If they had been appropriately trained, or if the orders given were appropriate for the training they had received, he felt they wouldn't have gotten hurt.

Kevin started speaking out against his command, questioning some of their decisions. He wanted to help the younger soldiers. There was some concern about what would happen if he went back. He believed the soldiers were being used. I would have supported his return to Iraq, if he felt that was what he wanted to do. Our relationship is more important than the war, than anything. A few years before Iraq happened, Kevin had spoken with this father about his own experiences with war. His father was a World War II veteran, and he did not have a good experience with war. A lot of the combat stress issues that his father experienced also factored into Kevin's decision.

When Kevin first tried to ETS [Estimated Time of Separation from Army], he was just going to retire and get out. When he submitted the ETS paperwork, they immediately stop-lossed him. He tried to talk to the chaplain and commander about filing CO status, but they didn't want to have that conversation. Before he filed his CO application, he wrote to the President on one of those veterans' Web sites that was supposed to be confidential, but it somehow made its way all over the Internet. Kevin said that he wanted to fulfill his commitment to the military but he did not want to do it as a mercenary. He went on to say that George Bush was not worth the dust off the boots of the soldiers in Iraq.

I also wrote a letter that detailed the problems we saw in the military. It mentioned that civilians were not doing a good job holding the military accountable concerning the rights of soldiers. We didn't include any names or specific companies, but I did discuss specific situations we had witnessed which were detrimental to the welfare of the soldiers. I posted it on the internet and it went all over the world.

Kevin's unit was due to deploy during the time between January 7, 2005 and January 12, 2005. On December 30, 2004, he attempted to file his CO application. On January 6, his company commander called him into a counseling meeting. When he arrived, there were fifteen NCOs and officers in the room. Kevin was told that he was being investigated for making disloyal statements and for disrespecting a superior officer. They pointed to the letter I posted online even though it hadn't named anyone specifically. Kevin was also told that he was going to be investigated by CID [Criminal Investigation Command]. The company commander read Kevin his rights. The next day, January 7, his company commander called him out of deployment and sent him to a meeting with the sergeant major of the battalion. He started asking Kevin questions. The sergeant major said something to the effect of "Let's do this hypothetical thing. If some-one asked you to deploy, what would you do?" Kevin answered, "I don't know but I probably wouldn't deploy." The sergeant major replied with something like "Oh, you just refused to deploy." When someone refuses to deploy, think about it, they send in the military police, detain the sol-dier and begin an investigation. But they simply released Kevin that day. He reported to duty on January 10 and was reassigned to the rear detach-ment unit at Fort Stewart, Georgia. The company commander had writ-ten an order that he should be put on a plane to Iraq leaving later in the week. Kevin said that no one told him of that order. On January 16, they brought him up on charges of desertion and missing movement.

People in the community were mostly supportive. We have full respect for the military. We have been working on veterans' programs and trying to establish communication between the military and community. The only negative comment that I remember was from two military wives, whose husbands were getting ready to deploy at the time of Kevin's court martial. They had signs in the back of their cars that said, "My husband is in Iraq, where's Sergeant Benderman?" It wasn't hurtful to me. They had the right to ask that question. By the same token, their husbands had the right to file for conscientious objection. They could have said no too.

I am not going to express my political views in terms of naming the President or pointing fingers. I don't want anyone influencing me about politics, so I am not going to make an effort to influence anybody else. What I do want is for people to open up their conscience. If they don't feel guilt about their decisions, I respect that. But if they feel guilt and they don't do something about it, then I have no respect. I'd rather bring issues to the conversation not politics.

The most frustrating thing for us has been the promises being made and not kept, and it comes from both sides. We did what we said we were going to do. We are standing for ourselves. I speak from my perspective and why it works for me. We have always been honest about it. People have said, "Well you're part of the antiwar movement and you're doing this for peace." We are doing it for us. Everybody has to do it for themselves. The combined effort is what's going to bring peace.

Don't get me wrong. We appreciate the people who have done what they can to support us. We are very grateful to the people who have written to us and share their words of support with us. What we really want, and hope our efforts encourage others to do, is for people step up and do the same thing for themselves; don't rely on us to do it. Take a stand to say No to abuse of their freedoms. Too many people, and it is not everybody, pay lip service to activists like Martin Luther King. They can quote him, but not live the words. Some people have said we'll be there for you, but when you call for the help, there's no answer. It is not just us. Lots of soldiers write and call us. I used to direct them to a military families peace group but the soldiers and families would say "We tried, but they don't answer." The support we are hoping for is not that they give to us in material terms—but that they give more than just words to what we have done by adding their actions to ours to strengthen the move toward a conscientious end to war, and the abuse of humanity.

What we found prevalent in the antiwar movement is that if you express a view that calls their own views into question, they don't like it, and tend to shut you out. I am antiwar, but I don't identify myself with the antiwar movement. The issues are more important than we are.

Carlos and Mélida Arredondo

"Dad on fire."

Carlos is from Costa Rica and recently obtained U.S. citizenship. While living in Hollywood, Florida, and working as a handyman, he received a visit from three U.S. Marines as he worked in his frontyard. It was Carlos's forty-forth birthday, and he thought for a moment that his son Alexander was making a surprise visit from his deployment in Iraq. Moments later he learned that his son had been killed in Najaf. Swept into a volatile mixture of denial, grief, and confusion, Carlos set the Marine's van and himself on fire. Television helicopters flew overhead as the scene unfolded, and the van engulfed in flames with Carlos's burnt body appeared on "breaking news" across the country.

With second and third degree burns on 26 percent of his body, Carlos attended his son's funeral on a stretcher. His wounds quickly healed in what one doctor described as a "miracle." Carlos signs off his e-mail with the phrase "Dad on Fire." His visceral reaction to a parent's worst nightmare has become a means by which Alex's memory can be preserved.

Alexander was twenty years old when he died as a lance corporal with the U.S. Marine Corps' Battalion Landing Team one-fourth out of Camp Pendleton, California. Mélida is Alex's stepmother. The Arredondo's share their feelings about that fateful day, the importance of keeping the memory of Alex alive, and the challenges facing military families.

Mélida: Alexander was pretty quiet about joining the military. I took him to the dentist one afternoon, where he mentioned that he wanted to join the Marines. I said to him that he didn't have to go right in. He could try ROTC in college. A few weeks later, we found out that he had enlisted at the age of seventeen.

Carlos: Alexander went to a technical high school where he was recruited. Alex told me one day he was joining and I said, "Oh, no." I didn't know what to say to him. I was concerned. I told him that I loved him and supported him, but that I didn't want him coming home in a body bag. He said, "Dad, don't worry, nothing is going to happen." I am from Costa Rica and we don't have an army. Afterward, Alex had a teacher whose husband died in the 9/11 attacks, so it brought the whole thing home. He donated blood to 9/11 victims. He had already enlisted with his mother's permission into the delayed entry program, but 9/11 really made him feel more obligated to serve.

Mélida: After Alex died, we found out he and his buddies were supposed to sign up together. They give you extra money under the "Buddy Program." Alex was the only one of the three who joined the Marines.

Carlos: A lot of kids join the military for the benefit of legal U.S. status. After two years of service, they can be granted U.S. citizenship. Then that troop can claim members of the family to gain residence. I was granted U.S. citizenship after my son's death.

Mélida: In the summer of 2002, Alex was still in boot camp and he wrote home saying that there are a lot of rumors and to send information on Afghanistan, Iraq, Iran, and the Middle East. Alex deployed with one of the very first Marine battalions that went into Baghdad.

Carlos: We didn't hear from him while he was first there. It was 2003 and they didn't have the phone, Internet, and the mail set up.

Mélida: The first time we heard from Alex in Iraq was when we were listening to the radio. Alex was on NPR. Suddenly, we heard: "We are here with Marine Lance Corporal Alexander Arredondo." We were worried all the time and it was good to hear that he was alive. Alex's brother, Brian, was freaking out. He stopped going to school, and he showed up at odd times to my job, sweating and saying things like, "The war has me nervous. I am so worried about Alex."

Carlos: Alex came home after his first tour. I didn't want to ask him to tell me what happened over there. He seemed like he wanted to tell me something. His mother told me later that Alex didn't want to go back. He wanted to take care of the family at home. His mother was worried he could get a dishonorable discharge. But he wanted to go back for his friends too; it was like a roller-coaster. He wrote home that he wanted all the children in Iraq to be free like his brother Nathanial. He wanted to accomplish that. He wanted to do something honorable for his country. Ten months after he died, we received information that he killed three insurgents, that is, he killed three human beings. Knowing the kind of kid he was, I couldn't see Alex doing that. He wanted to serve his country and was recommended for the Bronze Star, but pulling the trigger and killing people I'm sure gave him some doubts.

Losing Alex was the worst thing that happened in my life. I lost my father the same year but it was nothing like this. I stopped working. I am trying to deal with the loss of Alexander. We meet with military families to share who Alex was and share what happened to us. Some worry that it could happen to them. Since Alex died, we have had a lot of people mourning with us, families from all countries and all colors who lost children in war—Iran, Argentina, China, everywhere. So we don't feel alone anymore. It helps a lot to talk to them. I am still in denial. I looked at a picture of my son the other day and couldn't accept he was gone. Then, I feel grief.

Mélida: I am still in shock. It breaks my heart to see Alex's brother, Brian, without him. They were always together "Brian-and-Alex," one word. It is really Brian's loss in many ways. Alex was always there for him. I met Alex when he was eight and Brian was six. Carlos and I got married a few years after that. The boys have always been part of our life together. I still talk about Alex in the present tense.

Carlos: On August 25, 2004 he was in a fight against Muqtada al Sadr's militants and was shot in the head by a sniper. He was twenty years and twenty days old. It was my birthday. I had my telephone in my pocket, waiting for Alex and Brian to call.

Next thing I know this van pulls up in front of my house. I saw the Marine Corps blue uniforms, it immediately caught my attention. I thought, "Alex is here. Alex is here." I looked around. The Marines were walking toward me. I didn't see Alex. I asked them, "Why are you here? Are you recruiting?" They said "No we are here to see the family."

I said, "Wait a minute, I am the home-owner." Right there in front of my house, they asked, "Are you Carlos Arredondo?" I said "Yes." They stated, "I am sorry we are here to notify you of the death of Lance Corporal Alexander Arredondo."

I was trying to understand what was going on. I tried to translate it into Spanish and say the words to myself. My brain stopped. My heart felt like it went all the way to the ground and back up at 100 miles an hour. I just took off running. I was yelling and screaming and told my mom what these men were telling me. She broke down as well.

I tried to call Alex's mother in Maine. His brother, my son Brian answered. I said, "Brian. Brian. I am so sorry. The Marines are here telling me that Alex was killed." Brian said to me "I know dad. I know." I stopped, "How do you know?" Brian said, "They are here." I said to Brian "Where's your mom?" She wasn't there. Oh my God, I asked if they had told him what happened. He said, "No, I knew when I saw them arrive at the house." He was only sixteen and figured it out right away. I had no idea when I saw them. Once again I felt like something hit me so hard.

I couldn't figure out what was going on. I ran again, looking for my mama. I kept thinking it was a bad dream, asking God to help me. I saw the Marine uniforms and realized that it was not a dream. I asked them to please leave. They said they are waiting for my wife, who was on the way. I kept begging them to leave. I kept thinking if they left, then this would all go away. My mother took my son's picture off the wall. It was terrible. I walked away and looked at the Marines, I looked at the trees. I felt like I was in a dream again.

I dialed my son's recruiter on the phone and asked him what was going on. He said sorry you have the wrong number and hung up. I dialed again and he hung up. Later I found out the recruiter's number had changed but I couldn't understand what was going on. More than twenty minutes passed when I went into my garage and grabbed a hammer. I kept saying please leave my house to the Marines. I started to smash the Marine's van with the hammer, breaking the windows. I threw the hammer down.

I got a five-gallon can of gas from the garage and a small blowtorch. I jumped inside the van. I poured gas everywhere in the van, and I didn't realize it spilled on my shorts and my body. I saw the Marines talking on their cell phones. My mother was yelling. Suddenly she grabbed me: that's when I pressed the button and the flame came out. There was an explosion that threw me out of the van. I rolled on the ground, from one side to another. My mother pulled my burning socks off. I had flames burning me up. I heard a lady's voice: "It's going to blow, move back, move back." She was my neighbor and a firefighter. That lady and a Marine dragged me away from the truck and then it blew up. Next thing I know my wife was asking me if I was okay. I could not see anything.

It was my birthday, the day I am supposed to be celebrating life, and I was in denial, then self-destruction. Now I'm dealing with my hidden wounds.

Mélida: I was at work when Carlos called. My mother was with me at work that day. We got in the car together. As I turned the corner to my house, my mother said, "This is going to kill Carlos." We saw a fire burning and what was happening. When I parked in front of the house, the Marines told me to move since the van was going to blow. I went to the end of the block and ran back. There was a helicopter and news media all over the place. Brian called his Dad's cell phone. Luz, Carlos' mom, handed it to me. The picture of me speaking to him on the phone was on the front page. At the time, I told him to turn on the TV since I could see film crews, and he saw the live overhead shots from a news helicopter.

I told the police that my husband was having emotional problems. Carlos was put on psych watch at the hospital's burn unit.

Carlos: Next thing I know I was in the hospital, dreaming about some kind of fire. I was supposed to be in the hospital for a long time. After two weeks, I tried to walk, and I kept collapsing. But I kept trying and was able to walk out. The doctor was in shock. I healed so quickly, and he called it a miracle.

Mélida: Carlos was concerned that he would be sent to Guantanamo. He wasn't a citizen and people throughout Latin America know about Guantanamo. We realized that he didn't have the rights of a citizen.

Carlos: After I healed, I put a memorial together because I was devastated. Alex always asked me to save everything. He was very upset that the American people didn't really care.

I made my grief very public. I hit the streets with a casket memorial with crosses, pictures, his medals, boots, and uniform. I am not trying to represent or upset anybody. People for the war or against the war are all grieving. Everybody has their own way to deal with it, and we should respect that. I am honoring my son.

I have been under attack because I travel around with Alex's memorial. I will never get him back. I have been told that I dishonor my son by putting his picture on the casket and making a public memorial. Some military families think it's a dishonor but in my (Latino) culture we grieve in that way. I have walked at many marches with many people. I am not representing anyone else. I have my own beliefs and my own way of remembering Alex and the fallen troops.

It is a small group that gets extremely angry to the point of harassment and violence. We all have the right to participate and have difference of opinions. People around the country have been very supportive. We have worked with many families. This is my pain, this is my loss. Thank God we have the freedom to participate.

Mélida: The war overseas is exacerbating the war at home. There are differences of opinion and a lot of fear of people who are different. Alex explained to me that the differences (black, white, Latino, tall, short) aren't as big because all are Marines. As the peoples of this nation, we need to learn from this. We have to put our differences aside to unite. Fear is not healthy. We can't allow fear to run the nation.

FIVE

War Managers: Pundits and Policy Officials

No book on the Iraq War would be complete without some attention to the policy debates among war planners and public intellectuals. This chapter opens with two well-known pundits, Andrew Bacevich and David Horowitz, both identified as conservative, albeit with far different understandings of the term. Since this book seeks to open dialogue, a brief explanation on the inclusion of Horowitz is in order given that he is a "polarizing figure."

During the march to war in the spring of 2003, the political atmosphere in the United States made it difficult to question the legitimacy of the administration's claims over weapons of mass destruction (WMD) and Iraq's connection to 9/11. At the time, critics of the administration line needed to directly and clearly challenge the prevailing orthodoxy. Calls for "balance" were often misused to dilute and distract us from facts that contradicted the administration's now fully discredited assertions. The political climate has changed substantially since the outbreak of hostilities. The antiwar and peace movement was largely correct in its suspicions regarding the WMD issue and Iraq's alleged involvement in 9/11. Positions once seen as "leftist" or antiwar are generally accepted as common knowledge. Under these circumstances, critics of the war (like the present author) can afford to display restraint and open dialogue with the war's supporters. A fundamental theme throughout this book is that we need not ostracize those with whom they disagree.

As such, Horowitz is invited to the discussion, and he argues here that the Left has undermined the nation's efforts to defeat terrorism. This focus on a polarizing dichotomy, given this book's search for dialogue, needs to be addressed. The "Left has done the work of the enemy by sabotaging this war," Horowitz bemoans. In the course of our interview, he paused to say, "I know listening to me is painful for you, but remember you're the one who contacted me." True, it was a somewhat agonizing experience, but not because of Horowitz the individual, who was actually quite congenial and easy to talk to. The problem is that his argument conjures up the "betrayal narrative," namely, peace activists and/or the liberal media caused America to lose the Vietnam War. It is a narrative that projects all of the errors of the policy-makers on to a nebulous mass: leftists, liberals, radicals, or other vague classifications. What this chapter helps to demonstrate is that it is not the Left alone (or an imagined liberal media) who oppose this war. As we have seen, soldiers are questioning it. Equally significant is that government insiders, from libertarian conservatives to middle-of-the road thinkers to generals are aggressively criticizing the war. We hear from some of them in the following pages.

These dissenting officials are not aberrations. They are among a rather broad spectrum of voices that are "sabotaging" the U.S. invasion. Perhaps the most interesting saboteur has been Richard Perle, a former Defense Policy Board member and one of the neoconservative hawks who pounded the table for war, and has since registered second thoughts. In May 2003, he echoed Bush's "Mission Accomplished" remark, having written that the toppling of Hussein was the greatest military victory since World War II. "Relax," Perle implored us, "and enjoy it." Four years later he admitted a "successful invasion was turned into an unsuccessful occupation...I think the occupation was a mistake." Perle was also asked by *Vanity Fair* magazine that if he could go back to the start of the war would he have advocated an invasion. He answered, "I think now I probably would have said 'No, let's consider other strategies.'"[1] Notable conservatives such as George Will, Patrick Buchanan, and William Buckley, Jr., have all leveled sharp criticisms at the handling of the Iraq War. The U.S. "objective" in Iraq has "failed," Buckley wrote, and "the kernel is the acknowledgment of defeat."[2] Placing responsibility for the war's mistakes on something as vague as the Left is historically inaccurate; it is a distorted narrative that mutes the wide dissatisfaction from conservative and mainstream voices. The people who orchestrated the war ought to take responsibility for it, which incidentally, is a theme in the writings of many conservatives.

Perhaps our first interlocutor in this chapter, Bacevich, puts its best. "I don't care if you tell me if you are on the Left or the Right, what I care about is what you have to say. I am eager to hear all points of view." Categorically dismissing someone because they are on the Left or Right is a dangerous phenomenon.

Horowitz's testimony is followed by Hans Blix. He informs us about an unusual meeting with Vice President Cheney, the comprehensive scope of weapons inspections in Iraq before the invasion, and the legality of the war. Colonel Lawrence Wilkerson explains the background to Colin Powell's February 2003 speech before the UN on Iraq's weapons program. "We went up there and told the United Nation's Security Council a bunch of lies," Wilkerson exclaims. He attributes this misinformation in part to the Vice President and policy-makers such as Douglas Feith, Undersecretary of Defense for Policy, who "cherry picked" evidence to make a case against Saddam Hussein. Feith suggests in the following pages that his office simply produced policy critiques that could not have been interpreted as "intelligence products." When I asked him about the possibility that someone might have misinterpreted his reports as intelligence, he quickly jettisoned the idea as absurd.

Our next interviewee, Karen Kwiatkowski's worked in a Pentagon office associated with the undersecretary of defense, and she reports that it produced "mandated" talking points on Iraq. Kwiatkowski noticed that the President and Vice President's public speeches contained information that was "nearly identical" to what she read in these talking point memos.

Intense debates over strategy and policy among government officials stretches beyond Washington to embassies across the world. John Brady Kiesling, a former State Department political officer in Athens, Greece, resigned in protest on the eve of the invasion. Likewise, Ambassador Ann Wright submitted her resignation, and received tremendous support within the State Department, making her ponder why more resignations were not forthcoming.

It was not until the spring 2006 "revolt of the generals" did the nation witness dramatic denunciations of the war from high-ranking officials. About a half-a-dozen of recently retired military generals publicly aired their grievances against the war's central planners. Among them is Major

General Paul Eaton, one of the narrators in this chapter who deployed to Iraq. He called for the resignation of Donald Rumsfeld, and speaks about the "groupthink" atmosphere and "Rumsfeld screening" of generals assigned to Iraq.

We also hear from Terrence K. Kelly, former director of Militia Transition and Reintegration for the Coalition Provisional Authority [CPA], who also returns us to the ground in Baghdad. He wishes to avoid political debates and is generally supportive of the U.S. role and mission in world affairs. Kelly in passing, however, provides what might answer Wright's query as to why more officials did not resign. He says that he worked with many people in government who disagreed with the U.S. invasion of Iraq, but they felt that it was too important to ignore. These people attempted to do sound and productive work to help improve conditions in Iraq, regardless of their personal position on the overall mission. His expertise on militia groups is indispensable in grasping the conflicts within the country.

Finally, the best way to comprehend Iraq's internal strife is to hear from the Iraqis themselves. While including only two Iraqi voices is admittedly limited, we gain a glimpse of a perspective that has been almost entirely overlooked in the Western media. Samir Adil, president of the Iraqi Freedom Congress, discusses how his organization has established safety zones in Iraq to reduce violence. They oppose both Islamic extremists and the U.S. occupation and reach for national unity, captured in their slogan, "No Sunni, No Shia. We believe in human identity." Finally, our chapter concludes with Donny George Youkhanna, the former director of Iraq's National Museum that was looted in the early phase of Operation Iraqi Freedom. He articulates the agony of watching precious artifacts disappear before his eyes as well as what life was like under Saddam Hussein and the complexity of life after his removal.

In short, this chapter offers a range of views among high-ranking officials and public intellectuals in both the United States and Iraq. Some interviewees chastise the Bush administration, while others defend the Iraq intervention on political, moral, or tactical grounds. Critics of the invasion in this chapter do not conform to the stereotypical antiwar advocate. In fact, there are few conventional antiwar perspectives in this chapter, but there is no shortage of critical assessments of Operation Iraqi Freedom. The policy-makers cover some of the technical debates mentioned throughout the text, and readers might refer to the earlier chapters on the soldier's experiences to weigh and analyze some of the arguments made in this chapter.

Andrew J. Bacevich

"The military effort is a futile one."

Bacevich is Professor of International Relations and History at Boston University. He is a graduate of the U.S. Military Academy at West Point, and earned a Ph.D. from Princeton University in American Diplomatic History. A veteran of both the Vietnam War and the First Gulf War, Bacevich has also served as a fellow at the Paul H. Nitze School of International Affairs at Johns Hopkins University, the Kennedy School of Government of Harvard University and the Council of Foreign Relations. He is the author of numerous books on foreign policy, including the acclaimed The New American Militarism: How Americans Are Seduced by War *(Oxford University Press) and* American Empire: The Realities and Consequences of U.S. Diplomacy *(Harvard University Press). Professor Bacevich is widely published in scholarly journals and the popular press such as the* Wall Street Journal, New York Times, Los Angeles Times, *and* Boston Globe. *He is also a contributing editor for the* American Conservative.

Not only is Bacevich one of the nation's leading scholars of international affairs, he is also the father of a fallen soldier in Operation Iraqi Freedom. While Professor Bacevich views his personal loss as a private matter, he wrote a passionate reflection immediately after the tragedy in the Washington Post. *"I know that my son did his best to serve our country," Bacevich wrote in the emotional and moving essay. "Through my own opposition to a profoundly misguided war, I thought I was doing the same. In fact, while he was doing his all, I was doing nothing. In this way, I failed him," he concluded.[3] Many readers of his books and articles may disagree as Professor Bacevich's work has reached a wide and appreciative audience.*

President Bush is a limited person in many respects. On 9/11 he was confronted with a horrific attack on the United States and he had no ready response. I would not have wanted to be the guy who had the responsibility to explain to the American people what this attack meant and what needed to be done to prevent any recurrence. I think it was Bob Kagan who said that the neoconservative perspective was fully developed and available for the President to pick up. Bush needed a recipe for action, so the guy who ran for the presidency in 2000 calling for a humble foreign policy, underwent something of a conversion to explain the attacks and prepare a response.

John Mearsheimer and Stephen Walt in *The Israel Lobby and U.S. Foreign Policy* seem to argue very strongly that the neoconservatives really engineered this war; both people inside the government such as Douglas Feith, and influential outsiders such as Bill Kristol and Bob Kagan. My argument is somewhat different. If you look at the entire post-Vietnam period and the arguments that were made relating to the utility of force and the convergence between U.S. national security interests and the spread of democracy, the neoconservatives helped to create an intellectual environment in which preemptive war and the invasion of Iraq came to be seen as reasonable. Had it not been for this long-standing effort, it would not have been possible for the President to make the case for invading Iraq. The neocons offered a set of ideas that seemed reasonable, yet in my judgment ought to have been rejected out of hand. The neoconservatives didn't whisper in the President's ear and tell him what to do, but made available a reckless set of ideas that he had the bad judgment to adopt.

It is ironic is that you can trace the militarization of U.S. policy in the Middle East to the Carter Doctrine of January 1980.[4] Following the Soviet invasion of Afghanistan, Carter declared the Persian Gulf a strategic priority. His doing so set in motion a wide variety of initiatives within the national security bureaucracy that ultimately caused the Middle East to become the focal point of American strategy. I do not mean to suggest that Carter anticipated all of this. But, here is where a strategist such as Wolfowitz plays a key role. If there is one document that I'd like to see declassified, it is the Limited Contingency Study that he presided over in the late 1970s. It is the internal document that began the process of transforming the Carter Doctrine into war plans in the Persian Gulf. Carter pointed to the Middle East as a vital area of interest. The neoconservatives viewed Iraq as a staging point for their broader vision of transforming the region through military means.

My arguments have led some readers to say "Gosh, you sound just like Chomsky." I always react negatively. My historical writings have emphasized that there are continuities between Democrats and Republicans insofar as they attend to powerful interests. If you want to place a one-word descriptor on these interests, it is the money classes. To have your voice heard in Washington, you've got to have money. But I just loathe the argument that depicts the United States as a tremendous force for evil in the world. Chomsky's position strikes me as oversimplified. I do, however, argue that there is unquestionably an American Empire, and I agree with William Appleman Williams that expansionism is central to the American story. Williams certainly identified himself with the radical Left and his critics read him as warning about the great capitalist juggernaut taking over the world. He certainly emphasized the importance of economic interests to explain U.S. behavior. But I also read Williams as saying that you cannot understand American foreign policy behavior without examining its ideological component. Williams credited the builders of the empire and advocates of the Open Door for having this ideological agenda related to spreading freedom. This ideological component makes the imperial project more seductive and more difficult to unpack.

When Williams was writing in the 1960s and 1970s, there was a great backlash from orthodox historians against his work. Yet, it is remarkable that there are variations of Williams' argument arising from conservative circles today. Kagan's *Dangerous Nation*, for instance, suggests that U.S. isolationism has always been a myth. Well, that is exactly what Williams argued in his famous *The Tragedy of American Diplomacy*; he devoted a chapter to this theme, in fact. Kagan also goes on to argue that the United States has always been engaged in a great expansionist project, which is what Williams' repeatedly argued. Kagan, of course, sees it a something to be endorsed. Williams, on the other hand, views it as the tragedy of American diplomacy. Williams warned that seeing ourselves as a providential nation produces all sorts of havoc. Yet, there is a kind of convergence between many conservative writers and Williams. A new consensus sees expansionism as the core theme of U.S. policy. This represents a sharp shift from foreign policy orthodoxy thirty years ago. Both the advocates and critics of American Empire are now employing a narrative that views the expansionist project as ongoing.

As for the expansionist project in Iraq, instead of persisting with the grand strategy of transforming the region through military power, I would instead propose two things. First, revitalize the international police effort to destroy Al Qaeda and its affiliates. Let me emphasize that this is not a military operation: it is the work of intelligence agencies to ferret out these people and bring them to justice. The United States has not devoted sufficient attention to that international police effort because we have been distracted by the Iraq War. Second, recognizing that Islamic radicalism does pose a threat to the United States, we need to devise some sort of equivalent to the containment strategy of the cold war. The genius of the containment strategy was that it was based on the conviction that the internal contradictions of Communism would cause the Soviet Union to collapse. We need to take a similar approach to political Islam. Sharia law, which is an archaic form of Islam, will not respond to the needs of people living in the twenty-first century. We have already seen evidence of this in Iran. We need to contain radical Islam to encourage Muslims to recognize that it does not represent a viable alternative. Now, I can not give you the ten key points to make this operational, but if I were the President, I'd put my smartest people to work developing a strategy of containment. Part of this relates to an energy policy. We need to stop pouring billions of dollars into the Saudi monarchy. The Saudis supposedly spend $3 billion a year on madrassas [Islamic religious schools], thereby making the problem much larger.

In Iraq, the military effort is a futile one. I could support a continued military presence that advises and trains Iraqi forces to build up a legitimate government. However, once we conclude that there is no longer a legitimate government and there won't be one in the near future, then even an advisory effort makes no sense. We may already be at that point. There is no way that U.S. military power is going to bring about a happy ending in Iraq, and we need to accept that.

The United States must work to prevent instability in the region, but that is not primarily a military effort, it is a diplomatic one. My hope is that various nations in the region that may be at odds with one another on a host of issues might have a common interest in avoiding chaos. Scaremongers predict that if the United States withdraws from Iraq, political Islam will take over, giving rise to the Caliphate [Islamic government based on Muslim unification]. This is hogwash. The politics of the Persian Gulf features so many protagonists whose interests are so much at odds with one anther (Arabs versus Persian, Sunni versus Shiite, etc.) that it is highly unlikely that any one force can have its way. I just find that kind of thinking so superficial and it surprises me that otherwise thoughtful people take it seriously.

I also think the debate about "cut and run" versus phased withdrawal is a false one. For practical reasons, any withdrawal would have to be over six to nine months. Part of the vision going into Iraq was to use it as vehicle for regional transformation, which included at least semi-permanent bases in the region. At this juncture, the administration and military are probably less confident about that goal and more likely looking for access to bases elsewhere in the region. There has been a lot of talk about "over the horizon" and "off shore." U.S. strategists want an American presence, but the likelihood that it will be in Iraq is diminishing. Iraq is not going to be a congenial environment for maintaining U.S. troops. From a military point of view, stationing the navy in the Gulf, for instance, makes sense. But the navy is smaller than it once was. Under present circumstances, you probably could not maintain more than two battle carrier groups in the region. In crude military terms, it is a limited capability with respect to projecting power on a substantial basis. The United States certainly wishes to maintain a maritime presence, but American planners will want a land presence as well. I am not advocating this, simply explaining what the military strategists might have in mind concerning the Middle East, which they define as essential to national security.

In my opinion, the real strategic imperative is to reduce the importance of the region. We backed ourselves into a corner by becoming ever more dependent on foreign oil. America needs a genuine energy policy, which will require some serious changes in our domestic political and economic priorities. In the long run, it would be less costly to develop a new energy policy than trying to impose regional hegemony in the Persian Gulf.

Most of the American people have come to reject the war, and it is frustrating that public opinion has had such a limited impact. I think we see this frustration in the antiwar movement which has been so ineffective. Because of the antiwar movement's failure to stop the war, some of the war's opponent's support a soldier's lobby such as the Appeal for Redress. The argument is that if civilian attempts to stop the war are not working, then it makes sense to bring the soldier's into the debate. While I share this frustration, turning to the military is a version of praetorianism. Once you invite the military out of the barracks and into politics for a cause that you believe in, you better be ready to see them enter other causes, ones that you might not like.

There is a counterpart to the GI antiwar movement, the Appeal for Courage. It calls for Congress, and I am paraphrasing here, to prevent the media from demoralizing the soldiers by reporting negatively on the war. This implies suppressing free speech. I feel strongly that it is very dangerous for us to politicize the military; soldiers should remain apolitical.

The military needs to clearly support the chain of command; otherwise we have an army that may pose a danger to the political order. Part of the problem is the American people spoke and brought the Democrats to power, and the Democrats have failed egregiously to stop the war. Again, I share the disappointment in how little the Democrats in Congress have accomplished, but I am still very wary about politicizing our military. You can't invite the military into the debate simply because they happen to conform with your own values today. If a new president says we must put an end to the genocide in Darfur, what happens if a politicized military says: "We don't want to go to Darfur?" As for individual soldiers who conclude that they can not participate for moral reasons, they have my respect and admiration. But it would be a mistake to offer blanket amnesty to anyone who refused to take part in the war. For the good of the country, we need a military in which good order and discipline prevail.

I continue to call myself a conservative, although I am not sure it is an accurate description. I see myself engaged in a journey as I try to make sense of events. I don't care if you tell me if you are on the Left or the Right, what I care about is what you have to say. I am eager to hear all points of view.

David Horowitz

"There is no question that the war was justified."

The liberal-leaning The Nation *magazine has described David Horowitz as "outrageous," a "pugilist in the culture wars" who "plays with fire." His advocacy of conservative causes led* The Chronicle of Higher Education *to classify him as a "deeply polarizing figure."*[5] *Horowitz is indeed a controversial conservative voice in the national debate over the war, affirmative action, and the political climate on college campuses. Before he turned to conservative activism, Horowitz aligned himself with the radical Left during the 1960s. An early New Left activist in this period, he earned a bachelor's degree from Columbia University and went on to graduate study at the University of California, Berkeley. He served as an editor of a leading anti–Vietnam War magazine* Ramparts.

More recently, Horowitz founded the Center for the Study of Popular Culture (CSPC), which is now known as the David Horowitz Freedom Center. The Center directs its work against leftists, and states that it seeks to preserve individual freedom, private property, and limited government. The Center also publishes the online news magazine frontpage.com *and a directory of Left networks,* Discoverthenetworks.org. *Ironically, the original sponsor of the oral history project that led to the present book, Historians against the War, is listed on Horowitz's site. The present author's name also appears as a member of the "network."*

In 2003, Horowitz made headlines after starting an academic freedom campaign, which promoted an academic Bill of Rights. He maintains that U.S. universities indoctrinate students and fail to tell the whole story to youngsters; namely, American colleges hold a leftist bias. Horowitz is the author of numerous books, including Radical Son *(1996);* Uncivil Wars *(2002);* Unholy Alliance *(2004); and* The Professors: The 101 Most Dangerous Academics in America *(2006).*

I was a radical leftist for twenty-five years and participated in the anti–Vietnam War movement. In my book *Radical Son,* I have written about the change in my views. What I wrote was that everything the Left believed about the Vietnam War turned out to be false. What the Left accomplished was to help the Communists of Cambodia and Vietnam to kill 2.5 million peasants in Indochina. It is the main reason why I left the Left.

The interesting thing about Iraq is that the Left has spent the past thirty years complaining that the United States has supported dictators and tyranny. The Left has maintained that for all these years the United States sacrificed morality and principle by supporting dictators such as the Shah of Iran because they were allies in the cold war. So, it comes as quite a surprise, doesn't it, that when the United States overthrows a dictator in Iraq, the Left opposes American policy anyway. Instead of cheering the United States on for overthrowing a monster such as Saddam Hussein, the Left is in the streets trying to stop American efforts. The Left has no moral principles. The only principal that actually motivates it is its pathological hatred of America. "Leftism," Socialism and Progressivism are descriptions of a political religion. What Leftists yearn for is redemption in history. What they believe in is the fantasy of a better world, a world in which there can actually be social justice. This delusion blinds the Left to the reality right in front of its nose, leading to its Hitler-Stalin pact with the "Islamo-fascists."

Leftists who are principled compromise an insignificant minority among leftists. Some on the Left have criticized the U.S. alliance with

Saudi Arabia. Indeed, it is a huge problem. It is Bush's Achilles heel, or at least one of them. Politics, as the Left well knows, is not about choosing between morally pure options. In the real world, you have to make difficult choices. The United States made a decision to tilt toward Saddam Hussein in the war against Iran in the 1980s. Iran is four times the size of Iraq and declared America the Great Satan and called for our destruction. Naturally we didn't want them to win the Iran-Iraq War. Every nation in the world makes unpleasant calculations like this. Conservatives are realists. But leftists are religious fanatics. Leftsists actually believe that Hamas and the PLO [Palestine Liberation Organization] are liberators. In fact, they are Nazis. The Left was worried about the late Jerry Falwell,[6] who was a kind of teddy bear, but they are somehow not worried about Islamic fundamentalists who will saw their heads off.

The Democratic Party's behavior toward a war it first supported is one of the most disgraceful events in American history. It is criminal to send troops off to war when you have national leaders such as John Kerry and Ted Kennedy telling them that they're dying for no reason; that it's an unnecessary war and a fraud. John Kerry and the Democratic leadership argued for the war and voted for the war. When Howard Dean's campaign in 2004 took an antiwar stance and gained in the polls, Kerry, Edwards, and the Democrats generally changed their position. When these Democratic leaders put up a white flag, why should young people give their lives for what appears to be an unworthy cause? The Left has done the work of the enemy by sabotaging this war.

Don't misunderstand me—dissent is important for correcting wrongheaded war policies. I am not against dissent. But, the Left's entire political agenda is built on the belief that America is the obstacle to global progress. How can you defend your country if you think your country is the enemy? If Gore, Kerry, and the Democrats had not attacked Bush in such a vicious and uncompromising way, then perhaps the President might have modified the policy.

Liberals have a very limited picture of how the world works. Their notion that you can run foreign policy by town hall meetings is ludicrous. Most people haven't got a clue about geo-politics; they could not find Iraq on a map. Most people could not tell you which countries border Iraq. Because the Bush administration has done such a terrible job in selling and explaining the war, a vacuum has been created which has been filled by leftist ignorance and bile.

The attacks on Halliburton and Bechtel are part of the Left's fantasy life. The Left "religion" requires a devil. There is a world of suffering and it is going to be redeemed. The suffering is the work of the devil. And, the devil for the Left is corporations like Halliburton and the U.S. government, which these corporations allegedly control. In reality, corporations are responsible for bringing more people out of poverty than all the leftists put together since the beginning of time. The idea that companies such as Halliburton are the devil is ridiculous. There are only one or two big companies capable of doing the job of rebuilding Iraq. That's why Halliburton got the job. Corporations are not even right wing; they will do business with anybody. Corporations are doing business with China, which is an adversary of the United States. I don't think anything of the Left's arguments about Halliburton.

Nor do I think anything about its WMD arguments against the war in Iraq. In 1940, Germany had conquered almost all of Europe. Japan had conquered China and Southeast Asia and committed horrendous atrocities. The United States stayed out of the war until the Japanese attacked Pearl Harbor. Suppose it was discovered that Roosevelt knew about the Pearl Harbor attack in advance or even provoked it, and perhaps allowed the Japanese to destroy the Pacific fleet in order to get an isolationist public to support the war. Would anybody think it was wrong to fight World War II because Roosevelt manipulated us into it?

In fact, Roosevelt was accused of exactly this and there was a huge Congressional investigation. All of the arguments about the faulty intelligence in the invasion of Iraq are irrelevant to the question of whether Saddam should have been allowed to continue defying the UN Resolutions and expanding his weapons programs. The United States should have gone to war with Saddam Hussein earlier: in 1998, for example, when Clinton authorized the Iraq Liberation Act and called for regime change but failed to do anything because he was tied up with Monica Lewinsky.

The 9/11 attacks showed the true nature of the enemy we now face. It practically took down the American economy. If the terrorists who were based in Afghanistan had been able to take out U.S. shopping malls during the Christmas buying season, there could have been a worldwide economic collapse. What 9/11 revealed was the vulnerability of a complex, open society like ours. When you understand this, then you understand why the United States is at war. Saddam Hussein was a deranged dictator who dropped poison gas on his own people, showed his determination to violate arms controls agreements, and actively supported terrorism in Palestine. That is why we went to war. His defiance of the international order was an obvious reason to take him down.

The war was not simply about WMD. It was a war to enforce UN Resolution 1441 and to prevent Saddam from building weapons of mass destruction and put them in the hands of terrorists to be used against the West. There is no question that the war was justified. But, the administration still had to sell the war to the American public. You only get thirty-second bites in the media to sell your program to a nation as large as ours. So how do you sell a war? Well, you emphasize nuclear weapons to make Americans see the dimensions of a possible threat. The actual threat is more complex, and the evidence may always be uncertain. Even the necessity of containing Saddam proved to be an impossible sell to the French and Russians and Chinese who were arming Saddam and taking his bribes. And, they held veto power in the UN Security Council.

The corruption of the French, Russians, and UN's made it difficult for Bush to sell the war. The Bush administration did a horrible job in selling it, but the war was justified. The Bush administration should have sent 500,000 troops and locked down the country from the start rather than rushing into the creation of an independent democratic state.

Hans Blix

"How can you prove that there is no mouse in the New York Metropolitan Opera?"

Dr. Blix served as the Executive Chairman of UNMOVIC, the UN Monitoring, Verification and Inspection Commission from March 1, 2000 to June 30, 2003. Under UN Security Council Resolution 1284, Blix's team was charged with monitoring Iraq's weapons program. Media outlets across the globe covered the Commission's activities and Blix was a daily fixture in the news during the build up to war.

Dr. Blix was born in Uppsala, Sweden, in 1928 and holds a Ph.D. from Cambridge University and a Doctor of Laws from Stockholm University. From 1963 to 1976, he was an advisor on international law in the Swedish Ministry for Foreign Affairs. In 1978 and 1979, Dr. Blix served a Sweden's Minister of Foreign Affairs. He was also director general of the International Atomic Energy Agency (IAEA) from 1981 to 1997, where his tasks included monitoring Iraq's weapons program. Indeed, Blix's long and distinguished career in arms control led to his appointment to lead UNMOVIC in 2000.

Blix was selected as chairman to the Weapons of Mass Destruction Commission (WMDC) that was spearheaded by the Swedish Foreign Ministry in December 2003. The Commission's aim is to promote international cooperation to reduce the spread of weapons of mass destruction. Its work is captured in the text, Weapons of Terror: Freeing the World of Nuclear, Biological and Chemical Weapons. *Readers are encouraged to consult the commission's work and Blix's speeches at http://www.wmdcommission.org. Dr. Blix lives in Sweden and is married with two children. He is the author of* Disarming Iraq: The Search for Weapons of Mass Destruction.

I assumed the leadership of UNMOVIC in March 2000. When you get a request from the UN Secretary-General, you consider it seriously. My first response was to decline, saying that he would be able to find someone else, but I was ready if he didn't find anyone and he could come back to me.

I thought that it was important to create an inspection team that avoided all humiliation of the Iraqis. This might produce better results than UNSCOM [United Nations Special Commission] had in the 1990s. I intended to make use of all the power given to UNMOVIC under the Security Council resolutions. However, our job was not to harass, provoke, or humiliate Iraq, which happened in some of the UNSCOM inspections. They had sometimes been provocative and humiliating. Some of it was intended deliberately to provoke. The frequent Iraqi resistance led to the conclusion that Iraq was hiding something. However, now we know that there were no weapons, they were destroyed in the summer of 1991.

There were several reasons why Iraq was rebuffing the inspections, one of them being that perhaps they didn't mind the suspicions that they had weapons. It was a deterrent vis-à-vis neighbors. Other reasons probably were that Iraq simply felt humiliated by the inspections. We know that the UNSCOM inspections back in the 1990s were closely linked to U.S. and British intelligence. At the end of 1998, this was very public; the *New York Times* covered it.[7] You will find that the liaison between UNSCOM and the CIA was publicized in January 1999. One result was that in the UN Resolution 1284 [1999] it was explicitly stated that the staff of UNMOVIC should be international civil servants and recruited in the same way as other United Nations' staff. This made it clear that they must not be in alliance with any national intelligence, such as the CIA.

With UNMOVIC from 2000 to 2003, we certainly did not have any consultation with intelligence about the hiring of staff. We were entirely independent; candidates could come to us individually—not through governments. In fairness to UNSCOM we must say that they were economically dependent on the big states because for much of the time they didn't have the money from oil-for-food as UNMOVIC did. They had to turn to member states both for money and people, thereby becoming dependent on the large powers. UNMOVIC was economically independent because a small portion of the oil-for-food money came to us. Nevertheless, we had excellent cooperation from the CIA, from the French, from the Germans, and so on. We did not, however, feel in anyway on a leash. One of my motives for joining UNMOVIC was to try this method, that is, to create an independent inspectorate that was the trustee of the whole security council and not dependent on some of the members.

We conducted 700 inspections in 500 different sites in Iraq. The Iraqi's reaction to us varied, but by and large we did not have any major troubles. One reason was that we negotiated in great detail about our rights, so that we would not have to quibble with the Iraqis. Mohamed ElBaradei [director of the International Atomic Energy Agency (IAEA)] and I did that against the background of the 1990s inspections. Another reason was that the Iraqis were less inclined to resist because of the American military pressure. Nevertheless, the U-2 planes were a difficult thing, the Iraqis felt uneasy about U.S. planes under UN use. I found it was less difficult for them when we set up a whole system with the U-2 planes on the top, and then the French Mirage, and then the Russian planes that were capable of doing night surveillance. When the U-2 came on the top as part of this pyramid structure, it became less difficult for the Iraqis to accept. The other major resistance on the Iraqis part was related to inspections in the facilities owned by Saddam himself, they were called palaces but they were not all palaces. I think we carried out inspections in such places twice. The Iraqis were clearly very nervous and felt uneasy about it. But, I can't say that there was any case of denial of access or significant delay of access.

We never came out and said there are no WMD. It is difficult to prove the negative. How can you prove that there is no mouse in the New York Metropolitan opera? We felt that our job was to carry out competent, intense inspections and report on them. We did and on all occasions we reported that we had found no WMD. What was particularly significant was that we had been to perhaps three dozen sites suggested to us by U.S., UK, and other intelligence. And in none of these cases did we find any weapons of mass destruction—because there weren't any. We reported that to those who had given us the tips and to the Security Council. It should have indicated to the intelligence services that their sources were poor. In many cases, these sources were the Iraqi defectors.

In Colin Powell's speech, the United States evidently relied on other poor sources. We have learnt that he sat for hours with the CIA and that Powell threw out a lot of what they wanted him to say. Powell's speech was very well delivered; there were things that we in UNMOVIC could not check, such as the secret phone calls. For the rest, my analysts were rather skeptical. There was a site where the United States concluded that there were chemical weapons, but our conclusions were very different. I said so in the Security Council in a very courteous way. I also noted that there are things that are unaccounted for, you can not conclude that it does not exist, it may or may not. My relations with Colin Powell were always cordial and entirely civil.

Toward the end, the pressure from the administration increased. They wished that we report on some things that UNMOVIC did not find relevant. They were also anxious that we should take in someone from the U.S. intelligence side. Had we done so, everyone would have concluded that the United States took over. I hired a professional intelligence person from New Zealand and all intelligence that came into UNMOVIC came through him—or his successor—or me only.

ElBaradei and I were invited to see President Bush at the White House in the autumn of 2002. Somewhat to our surprise we first met with Cheney for what we thought was to be a courteousy conversation. In the course of the meeting, he said you realize that we will not hesitate to discredit you in favor of disarmament, which I took as a diplomatic way of saying that if we did not find weapons the United States would go ahead with other means. He was, of course, against inspection in the first place. He, like many others in Washington at the time, hoped that the Iraqis would not accept inspection. I wondered if the Vice President wanted to put us on notice in some sense.

If you ask "Was the war illegal?," I would say yes. Kofi Annan expressed himself in more diplomatic terms when he was first asked about it in the spring of 2003. He said it was not consistent with the UN Charter. It was only in the autumn of 2004 that a journalist followed up on this and asked: "So you mean it is illegal?" And Annan said yes. My view is the same as that of Kofi Annan.

The position by the United States and United Kingdom was that there was a long series of Security Council resolutions, including 1441, that Iraq had not lived up to, and this allowed them to go to war. Condoleezza Rice even said that the armed action was a way of upholding the authority of the Security Council. But it is strange to argue that one is upholding the authority of a council when we know the majority was against it. The French, and several other members, took the view that UN 1441 did not include an automatic right to go to war. The United States and others would have to return to the Security Council to use force. The United Kingdom and Spain put together a second resolution that would authorize war, but it was clear that a majority of the Security Council did not authorize it. I think that the crucial moment from the point of view of responsibility was the time when they went to war: What did they know at that time? Did they have evidence at that time? In March 2003, when they went to war, we had consistently said for a long time that we had not found any weapons of mass destruction. This is the moment one has to watch if one is interested in the question of responsibility.

In respect to the argument that Iraq transferred weapons to Syria, I don't believe it for a moment. The U.S. military has never made that contention. If they had any evidence, they would have jumped on it.

The United States did not officially argue the line that you find in the 2002 National Security Strategy: That in times of terrorism and missiles you can not wait for an armed attack to occur to exercise a right of self-defense. Bush argued in the U.S. presidential campaign in 2004 that where "there is a growing a threat" the United States should feel free to take action. His opponent, John Kerry, tried to argue that there should be some international measure by which you can compare such threats to answer that scale. The Bush administration maintained that they will not go to the Security Council for a "permission slip." The United States was even ridiculing the criteria established in the UN Charter.

There seems to be a somewhat more flexible U.S. attitude to the UN now. Whether it is just cosmetic, I don't know. Take, for example, in 1995 the Nuclear Non-Proliferation Treaty (NPT) was extended without any time limit on it. Part of the acceptance of the extension by the non-nuclear states was because of the promises given by the nuclear states, particularly on nuclear disarmament. In 2005, the Bush administration said that these were political commitments and they were made at a different time. And clearly backed out of them, and so did the French. This has caused a cynicism among many of the non-nuclear states. The original bargain in 1968 was that non-nuclear states committed themselves to remain without nuclear weapons; and the nuclear states committed themselves to negotiate toward disarmament. After the end of the cold war, it was not understood why they couldn't negotiate toward disarmament. Now there seems to be a shift: Kissinger and others published an article in the *Wall Street Journal* in support of disarmament and the NPT.[8]

For the Middle East, we [Weapons of Mass Destruction Commission] have proposed one idea that, I think, is original. It says that a Middle East zone free from nuclear weapons, while not practical now is something to reach for. It suggests, however, that we look at the example of Korea. The Denuclearization Declaration of 1992 included a commitment that neither North nor South Korea would have enrichment or reprocessing facilities and this is expected to become part of a new deal. South Korea, which has about twenty nuclear power reactors, will have to renounce having any enrichment capability in its territory. North Korea would certainly have to do away with its reprocessing capabilities. Now, looking at that experience could one not imagine a similar reasoning for the Middle East? Here is another area where the parties don't trust each other. They could all commit themselves individually against enrichment and reprocessing. That would mean that Iran and all other states in the region would stay away from enrichment. But then it would also mean that Israel would have to commit itself not to reprocess more plutonium. It would leave untouched the Israeli bombs. This is a new idea.

Another thought: looked at over the centuries I think that one must agree that there are larger and larger areas of the world in which peace extends. The United States had many wars with Mexico in the past. That is unthinkable today. European powers had innumerable wars in the past. With the creation of the European Union, it is nearly unthinkable today that you'd have an interstate war in the European Union. There are flash points of tension, of course. I do not suggest that human beings have become kinder than in the past, but there is greater interdependence than ever before.

Colonel Lawrence B. Wilkerson (Ret.)

"I do think that there will be some war crimes action against the Bush administration."

Called Colin Powell's "right-hand man" by the Washington Post, *Wilkerson is a retired U.S. Army Colonel and a combat veteran of the Vietnam War. He served as Chief of Staff to Secretary of State Colin Powell from August 25, 2002 to January 19, 2005. Wilkerson was part of Secretary Powell's innermost circle of advisors and he helped to prepare Powell's historic speech before the UN Security Council in February 2003 that incorrectly argued that Iraq possessed nuclear weapons. He led an Interagency Task Force that assembled Powell's presentation. Reflecting on this experience, Wilkerson called it the "low point" of his over thirty-year military career. He made headlines following an October 19, 2005 speech at the New America Foundation where he chastised the "Cheney-Rumsfeld cabal" that undermined the foreign policy decision making process. Shortly thereafter, the* New York Times *ran the headline: "Former Powell Aide Says Bush Policy is Run by Cabal."*

Wilkerson has a long and distinguished military career. From 1984 to 1987 he served as executive assistant to U.S. Navy admiral Stewart Ring, who described him as "the most principled individual I ever met." He was also a member of the faculty at the U.S. Naval War College in Rhode Island. He was deputy executive officer to General Powell at the U.S. Army Forces Command in Atlanta, Georgia, in 1989. Wilkerson then served as a special assistant to General Colin Powell when he was chairman of the Joint Chiefs of Staff. In the mid-1990s, Wilkerson served as both deputy director and director of the U.S. Marine Corps War College at Quantico, Virginia, where he taught the national security decision-making processes for four years. He holds two advanced degrees and teaches national security policy at the College of William and Mary and the George Washington University.[9]

One of the greatest failures of the institutions in our great democracy that are supposed to protect that democracy is the failure of the Fourth Estate [media/press]. In particular, the major beacons of the print media, the *Washington Post* and *New York Times*, in my opinion, failed miserably under this administration in speaking the truth to power. Indeed, they are still in some respects failing miserably; they are still trading access [to administration officials] for truth. I cannot tell you how many times I have talked to reporters in both visual and print media who, in my view, have traded in the truth to get into the White House to talk to the President, Vice President, or principal members of his cabinet. They have shaved their reporting for that access, and it is inexcusable. Back in 2002 and 2003, you can start with Judith Miller at the *New York Times*, carrying the administration's lies. You can point to the editorial staff of the *Washington Post* in the run up to the war and the first month of the war. It's astonishing to see what are supposed to be the best newspapers in the country supporting the administration in ways that they should never have been. The media should have been going after the administration and exercising oversight.

Anyway, I first joined Colin Powell in January 1989 when he left the White House as Reagan's final national security adviser. When we went to the State Department together in 2000, I considered him one of my best friends. I was the Task Force leader for the interagency team that put together Powell's UN speech at the CIA in late January and early February 2003. When we conducted actual run through rehearsals for the speech many key players were frequently present: Dr. Rice; then deputy secretary of state Richard Armitage; Steven Hadley [then deputy national security advisor]; Scooter Libby [the vice president's former chief of staff]; CIA director George Tenet, and his deputy John McLaughlin. And, of course, Colin Powell was always there.

There were some discrepancies in Powell's speech that are clearer to me now. In the seven days and nights that we spent at Langley [CIA headquarters] and in New York City at the U.S.–United Nation's Mission to put Powell's UN presentation together, we never heard the word Curveball [code name for an alleged Iraqi informant who testified that Iraq had mobile biological weapon's labs, but who has since been revealed as a fraud]. When we rehearsed in the UN Building in New York on the top floor, we never heard the word Curveball there or any dissent the entire time we were putting the presentation together. I subsequently have learned that then CIA director George Tenet and deputy director John McLaughlin were both talked to by the CIA European division chief, Tyler Drumheller, and informed that the Curveball evidence about mobile weapons labs was unreliable. In McLaughlin's case it was laid out in detail why it was unreliable. So, why neither of those individuals made that information available to the secretary of state or me is beyond me now. I have a big question in my mind about this. I can't attribute this withholding of information to incompetence. It looks like the director of

Central Intelligence and his deputy McLaughin were both made aware of the suspicions concerning the reliability of this Curveball source and they did not relay that information to those preparing the secretary of state's presentation, which is inexplicable to me.

Another problem concerns Ibn al-Shaykh al-Libi's testimony, a captured Al Qaeda operative. It was the straw that broke the camel's back in convincing the secretary of state that there were significant ties between the Mukhabarat, or Iraq's intelligence apparatus, and Al Qaeda. The information that was in Powell's presentation about Iraq and Al Qaeda comes from al-Libi's testimony. Again, no one told the secretary that the DIA [Defense Intelligence Agency] issued a dissent about that testimony, that they didn't believe it. As we were going into February 2003 and getting ready to make the presentation, I'm now informed that al-Libi himself recanted that testimony! I subsequently learned that he was rendered to Egypt and interrogated with no U.S. personnel present. And yet, this now discredited testimony was presented to us as solid information. You can imagine how irritated I am about this.

But it was really the detainee abuse issue that pushed me to go public. Everything from homicide—that is, murder of people in detention—to torture being used by the armed forces, CIA, and private contractors in Afghanistan, Iraq, and Guantanamo Bay in Cuba, was employed.[10] I do think that there may be some warcrimes action against the Bush administration. I will say right now if I was the vice president of the United States or I was Donald Rumsfeld and out of office, I would not travel, particularly to Europe.[11]

In the course of preparing his speech, the secretary of state was given a forty-eight page text from the White House regarding Iraq and WMD. It was crafted by John Hanna and Scooter Libby for Powell to use in his UN presentation. Powell gave it to me and I went to Langley and determined with George Tenet that this text was useless. We tossed it out. We instead used the National Intelligence Estimate (NIE) of October 2002, which became the foundation of the speech. Ironically, we know now that the NIE turned out to be about three-quarters false too.

I am prepared to say that my research has shown me that it is unquestionable that administration officials cherry picked the evidence to bolster the case that Saddam Hussein had WMD. Vice President Cheney visited the CIA probably a dozen times or so in the run up to the war. In my view as an academic and as someone who has been in government for thirty-five years, that is an unprecedented number of times for a vice president of the United States to visit a single agency. One would be naïve if one thought that was not bringing pressure on the CIA; it certainly was. If there was a central character to the cherry-picking of intelligence; if there was a central character to the delusion; if there was a central character to the misuse of the truth, it was Richard Bruce Cheney.

So much power has been accumulated in the Office of the Vice President. At the time of Powell's UN presentation, that power was being used in ways that I don't think our Constitution and our Founding Fathers ever contemplated. If they did contemplate it, then maybe it was one reason why they built the Constitution: to check and balance it. People in the administration like David Addington, John Yoo, and Alberto Gonzales reinterpreted the Constitution in a way that we had never seen before. That is to say, they interpreted the Constitution to hold that in a time of crisis the commander in chief can do anything he damned well pleased. And, that is not anywhere in the Constitution. At the heart of this reinterpretation of the Constitution, again, is Richard Cheney. Some critics of the Bush administration lay all this damage at the feet of the so-called neocons. (In fact, they are neo-Jacobins, they are not conservatives, in my view—in other words they are radicals. And these radicals, such as Richard Perle, Doug Feith, and Paul Wolfowitz allied themselves with ultranationalists like Dick Cheney and Donald Rumsfeld.) But that is not all of the picture because without the President and Vice President, none of this damage would have been so serious—the failure in Iraq, the failure with Iran and North Korea, the domestic failure with respect to Hurricane Katrina, and a host of other failures not the least of which is the fiscal irresponsibility of this administration.

With regard to Iraq's alleged weapons of mass destruction, our own State Department Bureau of Intelligence and Research did report that they did not believe that Saddam had an active nuclear program. The U.S. Department of Energy let it be known that they didn't think Saddam had a nuclear program either and they based that on their evaluation of the aluminum tubes that Iraq was acquiring. They felt the tubes were for mortar or rocket casings and not for cascades for enriching uranium. Yes, there was some dissent, but you had all these other agencies and the director of Central Intelligence saying that Iraq did have a nuclear program. So, the secretary of state went with the consensus opinion of the intelligence community, led by DCI Tenet.

In the end, we went up there and essentially told the American people, the international community and the UN Security Council a bunch of lies. It permanently affected me. I've said it was the lowest point of my professional career. I lie awake at night and think in retrospect, I wish that we had had more time and I wish that I had been braver and more courageous and said something to the effect that I am not doing this, I am out of here.

I think the President went to war because of WMD and the terrorist threat and the inevitable nexus between the two. But there are lots of other reasons in there, ranging from oil to this messianic desire about freedom and about protecting Israel and so forth. Iraq was the low-hanging fruit; you couldn't take on North Korea without the expectation of huge casualties. You couldn't take on Iran without taking on Iraq. Bush and Cheney and others saw the Gulf War of 1991 and how quickly victory was achieved and they probably thought that it wasn't followed up on. They took the wrong lesson out of the 1991 Gulf War. They thought it was going to be simple, hell, they said it was going to be a cake walk. I certainly did not think it was going to be a cake walk to take over Iraq because I was there in 1991, advising my boss General Powell that it wasn't going to be easy to run Iraq if we seized Baghdad and occupied the country—and we had almost half a million troops and a meaningful, functioning coalition!

Moreover, you can't afford to discount petroleum as a reason for the war. We and our friends and allies are so dependent on petroleum fuels and Iraq sits on the second largest known oil reserves in the world. You have to put all the factors on the board: WMD, democracy, oil, and the military-industrial complex. Lockheed shares have gone from something like twenty-six dollars a share to something like ninety-six dollars. War can be very profitable for some people. By the end of fiscal year 2007, this war was estimated to cost 1.2 trillion dollars and probably about 55–60 percent has been appropriated off line as supplemental appropriations. What this means is that it is not subject to the normal oversight. A lot of this money has been wasted, squandered. One wonders where some of the billions have gone. We need some hard oversight to determine just who should go to jail. This could reach into the upper tiers of the Pentagon.

So, you put all these things on the board, but the most critical thing is how you rank them. WMD and terrorism have to go high on the President's reasons for going to war, but I don't think he was naive about the oil situation. I don't think any of the Republicans were naive about the military-industrial complex either. Some of those folks are heavy contributors to the Republican Party.

I have mixed feelings about the future course in Iraq. Somewhere back around April or May 2003, the Iranians (through the Swiss, who represent U.S. interests in Tehran) wanted to talk to the United States. The Iranians were somewhat fearful that they might be next because at that point the war looked pretty successful. The United States marched into Baghdad and brought down the statute of Saddam. Iran said that they were willing to talk and sought to put all the issues on the table, and the administration spurned such talks, which was awfully stupid in my view.

But, I am not willing to trust to serendipity that Iraq would somehow reach a state of equilibrium if the United States pulled out, so that side of me says we can't afford to withdraw. But, the other side of me says I don't see any way to succeed given all the mistakes that we have made. I am somewhere in the middle. I very much hope that General Petraeus, the U.S. commander in Iraq, has a great deal of success, yet the realist in me sees that the odds are so heavily stacked against the United States, I don't know if he can achieve success in Iraq.

The United States might be able to achieve a moderate degree of stability with a reasonably tolerant government in Iraq. The United States might keep forces offshore—aircraft carriers and battle groups—that could come back in an instant if it really gets bad. The United States might be able to leave Iraq in a condition that is not that much different from when Saddam Hussein was there, but it would be without Saddam, and at least reasonably stable. I think that is about the best that we can hope for.

I spoke to cadets at Virginia Tech in mid-January 2007, about 70 percent of whom would soon be on active duty. I said that their major responsibility was to take care of the young men and women in uniform entrusted to their care and leadership when they get to Afghanistan or Iraq. I said not to let this administration's leadership trouble you. At the same time, you are citizens and I quoted George Washington, who said that when he assumed the soldier, he did not lay aside the citizen. If your mind is in such turmoil that your citizen component overrides the soldier component, it is your decision based on your own conscience. If that person is like Muhammad Ali in my war, Vietnam, then so be it. Some of my soldiers in the Vietnam days criticized Muhammad Ali and I said that I am not going to go along with it. He is a brave man, he didn't go to Canada, he didn't hide. He went to prison and took his punishment, he's a brave man. If you make the decision to be a soldier, though, once you are in the combat zone you must take care of the men and women in uniform. But remember too, I told the cadets, your responsibility is to make sure they don't commit warcrimes. I have infinite respect for our soldiers who are bleeding and dying for the rest of us. That's a tragedy, that less than 0.5 percent of this nation is dying and bleeding for the other 99.5 percent, but that is the way George Bush and Dick Cheney are managing this war.

I wonder—where is the rage in the body of the American people? Does it take a draft to force the American people to ask the kinds of questions that they should be asking? Does it take conscription before we throw the bastards out? It is somewhat dismaying to encounter many people who don't want to know anything about the war.

Douglas J. Feith

"We worked in the open, not conspiratorially."

Considered the "Pentagon's top policy official" by the New York Times *in 2005, Feith served as undersecretary of defense for policy from July 2001 to August 2005.[12] He was indeed one of the chief architects of the war on terrorism and a contributed significantly to U.S. policy toward Iraq. Feith advised Defense Secretary Rumsfeld and President Bush on a variety of national security matters. He helped to form the Office for Strategic Influence and the Office of Post-Conflict Reconstruction in the State Department.*

Feith's association with the Pentagon's Office of Special Plans has generated tremendous controversy. When you engage in the type of work that Feith has done, he acknowledged, "you have to expect [it] will be vigorously debated and challenged." Challenges have emerged from a range of sources, from former CIA director George Tenet to investigative journalist Seymour Hersh to the Inspector General of the Department of Defense.[13]

Born in Philadelphia, Pennsylvania, in 1953, Feith has held many significant government posts, such as the deputy assistant secretary for defense for negotiations policy from March 1984 to September 1986. Feith has also worked as a Middle East specialist in the National Security Council. He holds a law degree from Georgetown University as well as a bachelor's degree from Harvard College. Feith was awarded the Distinguished Public Service Medal in 1986 and 2005. He is currently professor and distinguished practitioner of national security policy in the Edmund Walsh School of Foreign Service at Georgetown University.

[I interviewed Mr. Feith at his Georgetown University office. My notes from that interview did not reflect the full complexity of his points and so we agreed to print here only an abbreviated answer to one of my queries. Since this is an extremely condensed response, and one based on my notes of a conversation, readers should consult <www.dougfeith.com>, last accessed July 18, 2008, and his book *War and Decision* to gain a more accurate and complete understanding of Feith's position].

Question: Democratic senator Carl Levin has charged that your office exaggerated the link between Iraq and Al Qaeda. Levin asked the IG [Thomas Gimble, inspector general, Department of Defense] to examine the activities of your office. As a result, the IG issued a February 2007 report. A summary of that report states that the actions of your office "were not illegal or unauthorized, the actions were, in our opinion inappropriate given that the intelligence assessment were intelligence products." On the one hand the report vindicates your office in finding nothing illegal, yet there is the mention of inappropriate actions. You have responded to this report. Can you give us brief overview of that reply?

Mr. Feith: The IG did confirm that what my office did was legal and authorized, contrary to what Senator Levin had charged. The IG's assertion that my office's critique of the CIA's work was taken as an intelligence product and was therefore inappropriate is preposterous. On this point, the IG was misinformed and illogical.

The IG's review resulted from questions from senators Levin and Rockefeller. When the IG's team interviewed me, the team chief told me he did not know what standards should be used to decide whether an action was "inappropriate." He said the term is not a legal term and it is unclear what it means.

The IG told the Senate that it was appropriate that people in my office briefed their critique of the CIA's Iraq–Al Qaeda analysis to both Rumsfeld and Tenet. But the IG concluded it was inappropriate to brief Hadley [then deputy national security advisor, 2001–2005] and Libby [vice president's chief of staff, 2001–2005]. It was inappropriate, his report said, because Hadley and Libby might have taken the briefing as an intelligence product. But no one in that briefing could have been so confused! And, the IG never even interviewed Hadley or Libby to ask if they took it as an intelligence briefing.

This story was garbled in news media reports and the background facts are often omitted. In Tenet's book he misdescribes the woman from my office who was the principal briefer: Christina Shelton. Tenet asserted that she had no experience in intelligence, but the fact is she had over twenty years experience working as an intelligence analyst at DIA [the Defense Intelligence Agency]. Having been detailed to my office, she was looking into information on terrorism. In early 2002, she came across reports from the 1990s on Iraq–Al Qaeda connections. She was aware that the CIA was working on this very issue at the time she discovered these documents, but they had not mentioned them—or had downplayed them. She called the DIA and asked why these older reports were ignored or downplayed. She was told that circulating them would "only strengthen the hand of [deputy secretary of defense, 2001–2005] Wolfowitz." She thought this was an unprofessional answer and immediately drafted a memo about this conversation. She said that intelligence professionals should not suppress information for such a reason.

There were various reports available on Iraq and Al Qaeda, not just the Czech government report that Mohammad Atta [9/11 ringleader] met with [Iraqi official] Al-Ani in Prague. The CIA first said that the Czech report was credible, then changed its view, but they did not say that it didn't happen. It wasn't until two years later that the CIA said they thought that it wasn't true.

Because Tina [Shelton] did not think the intelligence community should suppress information for inappropriate reasons, she developed a critique of the CIA work on the Iraq–Al Qaeda link. The project eventually pooled work of Shelton and a few other Pentagon officials. The critique—an oral briefing that made use of some written slides—was a policy product, not an intelligence report. Shelton's immediate boss brought the critique to my attention, saying that I should get the briefing, which I did. I didn't study the underlying intelligence. I did not know if it was perfect, but it was certainly put together professionally. Wolfowitz and I suggested that Rumsfeld get the briefing. He had the same reaction; he wasn't sure if it was right or wrong, but he told me to arrange to present it to Tenet.

This shows that we worked in the open, not conspiratorially. We gave a critique of the CIA directly to them. When we presented the critique to

Tenet, one slide was missing. [Senator Carl] Levin said that we concealed a slide. The fact is that we didn't include it because it was a bit harsh in tone; it was a courtesy to maintain a polite tone. None of the substance changed, just the phraseology. Levin tried to make this courtesy into something devious.

Tenet devotes a chapter to this briefing in his book, and he gets a number of important facts wrong, such as the qualifications of the briefer. Tenet's book is over 500 pages and there isn't a single footnote. In my book, I use many footnotes. They help to keep one's work more accurate.

Hadley also asked my office for the briefing, which we delivered in mid-September 2002. He received essentially the same briefing. But, between the Tenet briefing and the Hadley one, which Libby sat in on, there was a slide added about the Atta meeting. It was not a brand new topic, it elaborated on existing points. I didn't attend the briefing of Hadley and Libby and didn't discuss it with them for a year or more afterward. People have turned this into a case that my office was distorting intelligence, which is not at all true. The briefing was a good, relatively minor, short-lived piece of work—a perfectly proper criticism of intelligence by policy officials.

The problem was that the CIA had a theory that secular Baathists could not cooperate with Al Qaeda. We felt that the CIA should not filter information to support its theory. No one disputes that the CIA had evidence of Iraq-Al Qaeda contacts. We realized, of course, that eyewitness evidence could be wrong—and evidence is not necessarily proof. But the CIA was filtering and shading information to fit its theory. The CIA had done what Tina Shelton charged: they used a theory to discard alternative views.

A few weeks after the briefings of Rumsfeld, himself and Hadley and Libby, Tenet sent a letter to the Senate Intelligence Committee in October 2002. He listed in bullet points ten years of contact between Al Qaeda and Iraq. As far as I was concerned, that resolved the issue. The Senate Committee issued a report and said that the policy makers "probing questions" "improved" the CIA's intelligence products.

CIA was excluding information and it was the policy-maker's task to criticize. Intelligence is frequently wrong; it is improved when policy officials challenge it as the people in my office did. They were by no means trying to bias the intelligence, they were trying to eliminate the bias that had been introduced by some intelligence officials.

Additional details can also be found in Mr. Feith's article, "Tough Questions We Were Right to Ask," Washington Post, *February 14, 2007, p. A19.*

Lieutenant Colonel Karen Kwiatkowski (Ret.)

"I call it propaganda production."

Kwiatkowski made headlines for chastising the Pentagon's "Office of Special Plans" with her insider account on how it produced reports to justify the invasion of Iraq. She retired from the U.S. Air Force in February 2003, and had over twenty years of military service when she spoke out about the Office of Special Plans. From May 2002 to February 2003, she worked in the Office of the Under Secretary of Defense (OUSD) for Policy, Near East South Asia (NESA) and Special Plans at the Pentagon. Following Kwiatkowski's public denunciation of the Office, countless news sources have studied the office's presentation of information about Iraq. "It wasn't intelligence," Kwiatkowski says, "it was propaganda." Administration supporters attacked Kwiatkowski, arguing that she exaggerated her role in the office and had little knowledge of the prewar Iraq intelligence. However, in October 2004, Senator Carl Levin similarly charged that the under secretary for defense's office circulated exaggerated claims about Iraq's weapons program. In February 2007, the inspector general of the Department of Defense concluded that OUSD, which included the Office of Special Plans, engaged in "inappropriate" actions. That is, the office "disseminated alternative intelligence assessments" that were "inconsistent with the consensus of the intelligence community."[14] [See former under secretary of defense for Policy Douglas Feith's remarks in this chapter for his reaction to Levin's charges and the ID report].

Before working in OUSD, Kwiatkowski served in the Air Force Staff, Operations Directorate at the Pentagon and worked for the director of the National Security Agency (NSA) at Fort Meade, Maryland. Kwiatkowski holds a master's degree in Government from Harvard University and a Ph.D. in World Politics from Catholic University. She writes regularly for the libertarian Web site LewRockwell.com, and has written a bi-weekly column "Without Reservation" for the Web site MilitaryWeek.com. She resides in the Shenandoah Valley of Virginia with her husband and four children. A libertarian conservative and former Pentagon insider, Kwiatkowski offers a provocative and thoughtful account of the Bush administration's faulty arguments for an invasion of Iraq.

I joined the military because they paid for my college, and because my father had always told my brothers and I such wonderful stories of his four years in the U.S. Navy in the Pacific before the Vietnam War. I applied for and received a four year AFROTC [Air Force Reserve Officer Training Corps] scholarship in 1978. My military career was satisfying in terms of meeting people, learning new things, and travel. But I saw a great deal of stupid bureaucracy and a tremendous amount of wasted resources, energy, and talent. I wanted to, and did, work in the Air Force Total Quality Management [TQM] movement in the late 1980s. After seeing how fruitless TQM ideas are in a place where basically no employee may be fired unless they commit a crime and every boss must have a new expenditure or program for which to claim credit prior to moving on, I began to really understand how government works, and I discovered my inner libertarian.

After the cold war ended, my expectation was that many cold war institutions and acquisition programs would be ended, but in fact most were only transformed to meet new, possibly imagined, threats. I began to understand the genius and the tragedy of President's Eisenhower's farewell address in 1961, and recognizing this took some of the satisfaction out of the work.

But my assignment at the Pentagon was busy, exciting in many ways, with a sense that you are on the top of the heap, in the know, clued in to both politics and the military rumor mill. For many people, there is a sense of seriousness and grave importance to what they are doing, and it makes the work satisfying. The Pentagon itself is a like a small city, and you get to know a lot of people, and see a lot of people you knew from previous assignments. It is a networked community. Because folks from all over the military do tours in the Pentagon, it is a place where you hear great stories, anecdotes, really fantastic and often strange things that have happened—not politically important, just interesting things people have done and experienced. You also get to talk to experienced people who will share their observations, their wisdom, and their perspectives with you, on history, politics strategies, and tactics.

I worked in the Near East South Asia Directorate [NESA], the parent office to the Office of Special Plans [OSP], initially known as the expanded Iraq desk and formed from NESA assets over the summer of 2002. Bill Luti was the deputy assistant secretary of defense for NESA, and on October 1 was promoted on paper to deputy under secretary of defense for NESA and special plans (meaning his day-to-day job had not changed, just his title). OSP included the Iran desk, so it was not solely focused on Iraq and the pending invasion of Iraq.

The OSP produced talking points on terrorism, WMD and Iraq. These talking points were mandated in all documents produced by OSD Policy offices that had anything to say about terrorism, WMD and Iraq. This central control (and creative license to interpret, edit, gloss over or negate known intelligence from CIA and DIA on terrorism, WMD and Iraq) was critical to the shaping of thought and language regarding the threat Iraq posed to the United States. I wouldn't have worried much, but I noticed that many of the talking points we were being mandated to use by Bill Luti, from the OSP, were also repeated almost verbatim in some of the Presidential and Vice Presidential speeches that fall. They were also in Judith Miller's articles for the *New York Times*. Because the talking points inside and outside the Pentagon were inconsistent with the real CIA and DIA assessed threat posed by Iraq—see we actually had access to intelligence reports on these subjects—I concluded then and believe today that the OSP was a part, perhaps a major part, of the domestic political propaganda effort to convince Americans that an invasion of Iraq should be pursued, and would be rational. We knew then, and everyone knows now, that what we heard from the White House and the Pentagon in 2002 and 2003 was largely fantasy. The intelligence community was frustrated when it tried to correct this false and exaggerated picture through normal channels.

Toward the end of my final tour, I wrote a short background paper on Libya and copied into it what the intelligence agencies had reported on Libya's WMD capabilities and threat. It included the directions of the leadership in Libya, which was at the time embracing the European trading partners, and public rejection of terrorism. Libya had recently, after many years, settled the Lockerbie case, and was in general good graces with everyone but the United States. What I had failed to do in my paper was make Libya out to be a huge WMD threat. Our deputy director basically told me Luti would not pass this document forward if I didn't make it more explicitly ugly regarding Libya's intentions and capabilities. Incidentally, I remember sitting in a DASD [deputy assistant secretary of defense] briefing with our valued friend representing Tunisia. As the boss tried to make the point on how dangerous Libya was to her neighbors, the ambassador gently reminded us of the vast legitimate cross-border trade and worker exchanges that go on daily between Tunisia and Libya. In any case, I tried to make that paper scarier, but I refused to exaggerate beyond what the intelligence sources had reported. This paper was taken from me electronically, and edited I presume by the deputy, before it was sent up the chain to Luti and beyond. I did not see the final version, but I believe it had been made suitably frightening. Ironically, in this case Intel may have underestimated some of Libya's WMD dealings, at least with Pakistan, as Libya was reported in late 2003 to have received some nuclear design information from Dr. A.Q. Khan of Pakistan, and a ship carrying some sort of centrifuges was intercepted on its way to Libya.

There was pressure put on staff to produce threatening reports. I explained what I saw in the *American Conservative* articles in late 2003, and in *Salon.com* in early 2004. I explained and answered questions about what I saw in this regard to the Senate staffers working the Part I investigation on Iraq intelligence in later 2004. The Republican dominated staff was unwilling to entertain the idea that pressure on intelligence producers takes the form of a lost bureaucratic customer: political appointees going to other sources if the intelligence organ fails to produce the material they want, and job pressure on intelligence leadership to provide the kind of flavor in the reporting that the civilian leadership finds most tasty.

The Senate staff report and the Part I report concluded that I had witnessed no pressure on intelligence analysts to shape or modify their reporting, briefings and language on Iraq, WMD capabilities and terrorism. It is true, I witnessed no beatings, no threats to harm persons, and no fingernails were ripped out in my presence in order to cause a shift in content or tone of intelligence reporting. But pressure in a bureaucratic system is far more subtle than that. It is the threat of illegitimacy, the threat of being sidelined, being uninvited to key meetings. Consider that the DIA-SES [Senior Executive Service] Intelligence officer assigned, with his staff, to support Bill Luti's military intelligence, was not invited or was even prohibited from some meetings. So, pressure can mean being left out of decision-making, being deprived of influence in lieu of those who will please the political customer. In this case, the customer was Cheney and Bush, Rumsfeld and Wolfowitz, and the neoconservative cheering section at the AEI [American Enterprise Institute], the Foundation for the Defense of Democracies, and the *Wall Street Journal* and *New York Times*. Pressure on intelligence was clearly there, and at several levels below the President. But don't take it from me; take it from George Tenet in his book about his experiences in giving the politicians what they wanted to hear.

As mentioned before, once the OSP was formed and operational, anything we "wrote" on Iraq was just the copy and paste version that they emailed to us in the form of talking points. We simply wrote what they told us. I maintain that these talking points from OSP were incomplete, warped, and often (as in the talking point from OSP that insisted Mohammed Atta had met with Iraqi intelligence agents in Prague prior to 9/11) simply not true and not put forth as true by the intelligence community. You might call what they did rumor-mongering, but as it had a very clear political objective. I call it propaganda production.

I just know that in late summer, fall and winter of 2002, the *New York Times* frequently published things on how dangerous and threatening Iraq was to the United States. Things I had only seen in our OSP talking points, which was classified for our use in Pentagon papers, obviously unclassified when Judith Miller and others quoted unnamed government sources. I know the President and Vice President said things in their public speeches that were nearly identical to what we had in our OSP talking points. Perhaps OSP got their material from Dick Cheney or Scooter Libby. Or, perhaps it was produced in OSP from scratch and sent out across the river. The beauty of centralized talking points is that once they are passed around, lots of people read them, and tell other people. It was a genius way to beat the war drums for an illegal, unjust, and as we know now, poorly planned invasion and occupation.

The office relied heavily on Ahmed Chalabi, who was a "known known," as Rumsfeld might have noted.[15] He was the source, unlike some in the DIA and CIA initially, who gave them whatever they wanted to hear. They cannot claim they were tricked. They can claim they were incredibly stupid, but if anyone was doing the tricking, it was the neoconservatives, desperate and in a hurry for Bush to do a regime change before sanctions were lifted, and with the expected post-sanctions influx of foreigners and trade to Iraq, a military attack and invasion would be impossible.

Well, I think the reason the United States invaded Iraq has to do with building bases. They needed to destroy Saddam Hussein's power base, which was a secular and potentially wealthy Arab beacon of anti-Israeli and anti-Saudi political power. I also think the idea was attractive to them in light of the shift in Iraqi oil pricing from the dollar to the Euro, and the inevitability of the lifting of sanctions against Iraq. The economic sanctions related to Saddam's WMD program, and Iraq had (contrary to what you would read in the American papers) complied with UN inspections to the utmost, and nearly everything had been acceptably accounted for, and nothing new in the WMD area was being pursued. Of course, David Kay found this out the hard way after we invaded. To Bush and Cheney, and the neoconservatives, it appeared as if the second largest oil capacity in the world was soon going to be pricing that oil in Euros, effectively devaluing the dollar as a global reserve currency. When sanctions were lifted, all kinds of European, Chinese, Russian, and Japanese companies would rebuild and upgrade the destroyed and defunct country, made decrepit by a decade of U.S.-enforced sanctions and periodic bombings. With Saddam in charge post-sanctions, U.S. and UK companies would be the last to benefit from this economic activity. I think the permanent basing proposals were important to bring the U.S. military along, because it supported long range strategies for securing Middle Eastern oil flows, and would quickly allow us to remove our forces from Saudi Arabia.

It is important to understand that terrorism, Al Qaeda, 9/11, WMD, or Saddam tried to kill my daddy had nothing to do with it. When a first-rate military power decides to take down a fourth rate military power one twentieth its size and population, it does so for big fundamental reasons. We would not tolerate a powerful anti-Israel and anti-Saudi power in the heart of oil country, and we could not tolerate being left out of the imminent post-sanctions economic boom under Saddam Hussein. We needed an improved regional military footprint, new bases and training areas in the Middle East. We believed we could have it, if we got rid of Saddam Hussein and Baath Party control in Baghdad. And if Bush's first Iraq related executive order post-invasion, in May 2003, means anything, we couldn't tolerate Iraq oil priced in Euros, and with this order, we effectively took control of Iraqi oil, priced in dollars.[16]

It is illegal in a just war sense, because nothing existed, or was known to exist that justified going halfway around the world to kill people, destroy a country, conduct a forced regime change, an occupation, and a program of illegal, non-treaty based military base building. It seems as if it would be illegal to knowingly lie to domestic audiences as the President and Vice President did repeatedly to get the popular support for the invasion.

I wonder still today at how easily our American democracy is led by the nose, derailed, and made cruel and heartless. Our so-called free and independent media is as compliant as TASS and *Pravda* [Soviet Union's official news] were for their Soviet masters. I would like to think that this

Iraq experience would be a turning point, where we may again return to a Republic of the United States, a country that trades freely with all, and avoids entanglements. Instead, we have become a bumbling and hated empire, with one tool developed above all others, and that is blunt force abroad, with bald-faced lies about it to the people at home. Had I not been assigned to the particular part of the Pentagon at that particular time, I might to this day be a passive supporter of war and occupation, believing that our government would never consciously pursue such a path if it weren't justified, legal and for the good of our nation. That scares me, and makes me very concerned for the future of the American republic.

John Brady Kiesling

"What would happen if I resigned?"

Having served as a U.S. State Department Foreign Service officer for nearly twenty years, Kiesling resigned dramatically in protest of the Bush administration's policies on February 25, 2003. The resignation attracted a flood of media attention, including the Wall Street Journal's *description of Kiesling an "unlikely antiwar icon."*[17] *Kiesling's letter boldly declared that "we have not seen such systematic distortion of intelligence . . . since the war in Vietnam . . . The result, and perhaps the motive, is to justify a vast misallocation of shrinking public wealth to the military."*

Kiesling was born in Houston, Texas, in 1957 and was raised in California. He was awarded a bachelor's degree from Swarthmore College in Pennsylvania in 1979 with distinction, and a master's degree in Ancient History and Mediterranean Archeology from the University of California at Berkeley. He joined the U.S. Department of State in April 1983. Kiesling's diplomatic posts include assignments as a special negotiator for Nagorno-Karabakh, 1999–2000; political/economic counselor, at the U.S. embassy in Armenia from 1997 to 1999; senior India desk officer, U.S. Department of State from 1994 to 1996; Romania desk officer, U.S. Department of State from 1992 to 1994; political officer, U.S. embassy Athens, Greece, 1988–1992; economic officer, U.S. consulate general Casablanca, Morocco, 1985–1987; and vice consul and ambassador's staff aide, U.S. embassy in Tel Aviv, Israel, 1983–1985. The American Foreign Service Association granted him and a group of colleagues the William Rivkin award in 1994 for work surrounding the Bosnia conflict.

At the time of his resignation, Kiesling was a forty-five-year-old political counselor at the U.S. embassy in Athens, Greece. Kiesling has served as a visiting lecturer at Princeton University and is the author of Diplomacy Lessons: Realism for an Unloved Superpower. *He is a freelance writer, whose monthly column appears in the* Athens News *(Greece). Kiesling's presents himself with humility, as someone who is uncomfortable with the attention that his resignation has generated. Yet, the timing of his resignation, at the eve of war, remains a historic and powerful gesture for many.*

In graduate school, I studied ancient history and archeology. I wasn't confident I had a future as an archeologist. The idea of a career in the State Department seemed perfect: I would be paid to learn languages, travel around the world, represent the United States, and perhaps do some good in the world. For most of my career, this impression was correct. It was a fine career, one that allowed me the rare privilege of seeing up close how the world really works.

As political counselor at the U.S. embassy in Athens, I was chief of the Political Section. Our job was to maintain regular contacts with politicians, journalists, officials, and other diplomats to figure out what was happening in Greece and how the United States could achieve its goals there at the least possible cost. It was a fascinating job.

There was very little discussion about the Iraq War at the embassy, which felt odd. I was also in Greece during the First Gulf War back in 1991. There we had a clear sense of purpose. The United States in response to Iraq's annexation of Kuwait mobilized a massive diplomatic coalition. Greeks were highly skeptical of U.S. motives, and all of us at the embassy were part of the effort to explain the logic and justice of military intervention under the UN to solve this problem. But in the 2003 invasion, we felt more like passive spectators of a game being played out in Washington and a tiny bit at the UN. We never received instructions to convince the Greeks of anything, only occasional generic talking points on how evil Saddam was.

Oddly enough in the embassy there wasn't a collective sense of purpose. It seemed to me that nobody was talking about the war; nobody felt comfortable. Here was the most important policy decision that the United States was facing and we were afraid to talk about the merits of it. In bureaucracies you gradually figure out that if you don't have anything nice to say, then don't say anything at all. As diplomats we understood that America's self-image as the "democratizer" of the planet carried no weight out where we were. We enjoyed no trust; our motives in the Middle East were challenged by almost everyone in Greece. And Greece was an ally. Attitudes in the Middle East would be far more hostile.

As individuals responding to me as an individual, the Greeks were fine. Following 9/11 the Greeks were horrified and sympathetic to the United States. They placed flowers outside our embassy and came to our memorial service. There is a Greek phrase, however, *kala na pathoun* or "it serves them right." I never heard a Greek say it to us directly. But what they told each other was, "Look America has been rampaging around the world for so many years. It deserves to be reminded that it is not invulnerable." Part of this attitude was a result of Greek domestic politics, but some of this sentiment has something to do with how the United States has behaved. So widespread a sentiment should have been understood as a warning of how bad the U.S. image has become in the world.

I had finally started putting things together. Cheney's speech in August 2002 made clear that war was coming.[18] The rhetoric of American Enterprise Institute [AEI] had for a long time called for an invasion of Iraq and the radical transformation of the Middle East. These people did not know what they were talking about. In October 2002, Joshua Muravchik, a public intellectual of AEI who was involved in spreading this rhetoric, arrived at the Athens embassy to speak at a conference on U.S. foreign policy. Without his doing or saying anything to provoke me, I told him bluntly that anyone who believed that the United States could democratize Iraq, Syria and Iran by force of arms was living in a fool's paradise. I was angry. A month before I had seen a highly classified cable of a conversation in which Ariel Sharon [Israel's prime minister, 2002–2006] had jeered at Bush for dragging his feet on Iraq. The AEI has worked very hard to insist that Israel had nothing to do with the invasion of Iraq, so I'd love to see that telegram again.

Meanwhile, the Greek population was strongly opposed to the war. Greeks did not believe our contention that Iraq was an imminent threat. The ambassador asked me to nag the Greek desk at the State Department in Washington to pry loose some solid evidence on Iraq we could present to the foreign minister of Greece [George Papandreou], who was about to take over the rotating European Union presidency [Greece gained EU presidency in January 2003]. What we ended up with was a print out of the sanitized version of the CIA report and a copy of the British "dodgy dossier," a report compiled in large part from a graduate student's PhD thesis. I was carrying them in an envelope. As we walked into the Greek Foreign Minister's office, my Ambassador said to me "Don't tell them that this is an unclassified report." I rolled my eyes.

But even the secret reports were full of vague, meaningless language. Analysts who write this way do so because they don't have any firm information to present. A serious blow for me was reading the CIA's National Intelligence Estimate [NIE] on Saddam's WMD, which contained sweeping conclusions that had nothing to do with the evidence they cited. I was appalled at how little ammunition they gave us to present to the Greeks. I became convinced that because we had so little information, there was a real possibility that we were completely wrong.

Papandreou and the Arab League came up with a proposal for a last-ditch diplomatic effort to persuade Saddam to step down peacefully and go into exile. The Arab League sent a private message to Papandreou saying they thought it's possible to do this. The Arab League is not a strong organization, but still—if the goal is to force out Saddam, anything is worth a try. A negotiated solution is better than a war. I didn't have a lot of optimism, but supporting the effort would at least prove our good faith to the world; it would establish that war really was the last option.

Papandreou got on the phone with Colin Powell to sell this diplomatic effort. I got to read the secret account of the conversation. I was taken aback to read that Powell told Papandreou something to the effect that, "We don't think it is going to work, you can try, but we are not going to lift a finger to help you." This doomed it—the only way a bargain like that could be made is if the United States gave its blessing. It proved to me that we had already decided that war with Iraq was the only policy outcome that we wanted. Not disarming Saddam, but disarming him military. It destroyed any basis for our moral posture.

I saw increasing evidence that our moral posture was too weak, that we had lost just about everyone in Greece. A friend of mine, a Greek professor, wrote an article, "Blood for Oil," in a mainstream Greek newspaper, not a leftist rag. He was one of the people that the U.S. embassy counted on to understand and explain (if not always defend) the U.S. position. I was irritated by the article, because oil was not the driving force of what was going on. I called him up and chewed him out. But as I did so I silently agreed completely with his basic argument, that going to war with Iraq would be a disaster. It is one of these weird segmented things, where I was criticizing what he said, but agreeing with most of it. Why did this matter? Greece is a European country and NATO ally. If this is the way they thought in Greece, then our mission in the Middle East had no hope of success. Everyone in the Middle East held far more suspicious views of the United States and its motives.

I started to dread going to the office. I caught bronchitis and was feeling down. I remember watching Colin Powell's speech to the UN. He believed what he said, I think, but the evidence he presented was so threadbare; it was not going to make the war palatable to our allies. The United States was in the process of becoming the bad guy of the world.

Throughout my career, there may have been things that I disagreed with, but on balance I always felt we were making the world more peaceful and democratic. Sometimes, perhaps, I was deluding myself, but most of the time I wasn't. Suddenly no delusion was possible. Our Iraq policy was making the world more dangerous; the Bush administration was showing itself to the world as ignorant, incompetent and violent. At a certain point, I became totally fed up. I could not visualize myself holding out another five more years until my retirement. I didn't have any hope that U.S. policy would get better.

What crystallized my decision was a memo that I got from my ambassador. I had gotten into some bureaucratic trouble with the Office of Diplomatic Security. He drafted a memo for the files to make clear that if anything happened to me later, it wasn't his fault. And I thought to myself "Oh my god, if this is what I have to look forward to, if holding on to becoming an ambassador means a life spent in petty butt covering, then this is not a job for a self-respecting person anymore." It was a rare moment of anger for me, and anger brought clarity. For the first time I asked myself, what would happen if I resigned? And suddenly the answer was obvious. If I resigned, then I would regain the right to say what I think. Everything came together. When I decided to write my resignation letter, it was an incredibly liberating feeling. I just felt happy. It is the only major decision I've ever taken in my life that I don't have second thoughts about.

One goal of my resignation was to serve as evidence people could point to afterwards that foreign policy professionals had advised against this war. But I regret that I was so slow to recognize resignation as an option. Until I did, I had no meaningful way to fight effectively within the system. I was depressed, almost paralyzed. I could have done more to oppose the war if I had understood sooner that resignation was my proper course. There was a lot of sympathy in the State Department. Once my career was no longer an issue, I should have reached out to these people to build support within the bureaucracy. That would have raised the political cost of a disastrous policy. But when I decided to resign, I did not take time to plan out a strategy. I felt under time pressure: the war was coming. For my resignation to be a clear moral statement, it should precede the start of the war as much as possible.

Major General Paul Eaton (Ret.)

"You have the number two guy in government saying that torture is okay."

Once called the "father of the Iraqi military," Eaton served as commanding general of the Coalition Military Assistance Training Team in Iraq from June 2003 to June 2004 before passing operations to Lieutenant General David Petraeus. Eaton spent thirty-three years in the U.S. Army, and held many significant posts such as commanding general of the Infantry School at Fort Benning, Georgia. He is from Weatherford, Oklahoma, graduated from the U.S. Military Academy at West Point in 1972 and holds a Master's degree from Middlebury College. General Eaton has also served as an operations officer in Somalia and taught for three years at West Point. Among his many military decorations are the Distinguished Service Medal and the Defense Superior Medal. He is married and lives in a coastal town outside of Seattle, Washington. Two of his three children are in the U.S. Army; one was deployed to Iraq and both to Afghanistan.

Eaton created a political tremor after publishing an article titled, "A Top Down Review of the Pentagon," in the New York Times *on March 19, 2006. He was one of the first generals to call for former Defense Secretary Rumsfeld's resignation, who he said was "not competent to lead our armed forces," owing in part to "a climate of groupthink" at the Pentagon. Eaton appeared in a* Vote Vets *advertisement that criticized the Bush administration's failure to take advice from Generals and military officers.*

The way that I learned I was going to Iraq was a little odd. I was stationed in Georgia and my wife and I had gone down to the Chattahoochee River, which had flooded. While there, I received a phone call. My boss was on the line and he stated, "The Chief of Staff of the Army has selected you to go to Iraq and rebuild the Iraqi Army." This was about eight days after President Bush got on board the aircraft carrier, *USS Lincoln*, and gave the "Mission Accomplished" speech. My wife said, "Well, I would have thought that guy would have been in Iraq a long time ago." So much of what this administration has done in war and elsewhere has been reactive. The fact that we did not have a team on board prepared to go into Iraq for the reconstruction phase before hostilities began is the single most important reason for our difficulties today in Iraq.

I was, in fact, commander of the Iraqi forces. Our Coalition Assistance Training Team established three recruiting centers, which were more like processing centers. We went after the rank and file soldier. We did not have to do much recruiting in this regard. What we tried to do was bring back Saddam's Army, and fix the cultural problems that it had. We had data bases of members of that Army that we did not want: agents of the Baath party, high ranking officers, etcetera. It was an attempt to avoid bringing in potential adversaries. The ministries were meanwhile reestablished.

As I was selling the idea of an Iraqi Army, I was met with resistance. Chalabi was one of the nastier guys to challenge the notion of establishing an Iraqi armed force. We all knew what had transpired back in Washington over Chalabi and INC [Iraqi National congress]. I didn't have a lot of contact with him, but he was the most aggressive guy against rebuilding the Iraqi Army. I wrote it off at the time as a fear that bringing back the Iraqi Army was like bringing back Saddam's system.

But we were instead rebuilding the Iraqi Army's whole culture and mission. We attempted to rebuild an army that was representative of the nation. Each platoon was to have the major ethnicities and religion represented: 20 percent Kurd, 80 percent Arab with 20 percent Sunni and 60 percent Shiite. In addition, we announced to the Iraqi forces in June 2003: "Welcome to the Iraqi Army, the force that will protect Iraq from enemies from without. You will not be used inside the borders in Iraq to manage the Iraqi population. You will not be used to attack Iraqis."

As the drama of the insurgency unfolded, the situation obviously changed. Fallujah was about to explode in the spring of 2004. We were going to deploy the 2nd New Iraqi Battalion, and it was a problem. I still did not want to use the Iraqi Army internally in Iraq. They refused to deploy. We had to stand the unit down, and change its leadership and realign the Iraqi forces. We had to recruit special units to operate inside

Iraq to fight alongside the United States and against insurgents. Thomas Ricks' book, *Fiasco*, covers some of this and it was painful to read.[19] It made me so angry because it was accurate, it was what we lived, and it did not have to be so. There was a significant change in the rules of engagement for the Iraqi Army from protecting against outside attack to now fighting against fellow Iraqis. This was the single greatest problem.

The British use the term "moral component" in describing how to develop a soldier or Marine. The development of the moral component is one of the easier things to do with an American soldier, but more difficult with an Iraqi. We as American citizens take so many things for granted: the stability of our society, the notions of justice and equality. The Iraqi Arab is burdened with almost thirty years of Saddam's brutality. For the Iraqi soldier, it is hard for them to believe in their civilian chain of command. Consider the Iraqi police. An embedded reporter with us wrote about the police training, and I told him it was a complete disaster—a waste of nine months of work. As one U.S. Army sergeant said to me, "Sir, I am embarrassed. Here we are with body armor, good weapons and plenty of ammunition. We have these Iraqis with thin blue shirts, old AKs and only ten rounds each with little training." They were completely unprepared. The equipment was a disaster.

The whole Iraq reconstruction phase was simply not important to Rumsfeld and Cheney. You recall the National Guard soldier who said to Rumsfeld we have "hillbilly" armor, and Rumsfeld said you go to war with the army that you have. Until April 2004, I never had access to armored vehicles. Most of my movement around Iraq was in white SUVs. We still do not have the equipment that is needed five years later. The country knows how to do it; we just need the leadership to make it happen.

This administration promotes a party line and if you depart from it, you are out. Every Three and Four Star General went through a "Rumsfeld Screen." He created a coterie of generals who would not question the party line. General Pace and Myers are examples of guys who were emasculated, their opinions were subordinated. General Odierno was on *Fox News* and fawned all over Rumsfeld, and shortly after, he was nominated to command armed forces in Iraq. General Shinseki [former chief of staff of U.S. Army who directly challenged Rumsfeld's strategy] and Hugh Shelton [general who retired in 2001 as he felt Rumsfeld dismissed advice from the military] had the guts to do what the nation asked them to do. The dramas that we have right now, the insufficient size of our military, is the result of high ranking officers failing to follow thorough on what should have been done.

The Army Rangers have an evaluation procedure where subordinates and peers rate their leadership. I had argued that Congress needed to get military personnel of all ranks to testify before Congress. I am embarrassed to admit that I did not know that it takes the political party in power to subpoena and cause an individual to be investigated. Five or six years before the Republicans controlled the Senate, I am told that there was something like 4,000 subpoenas. After they gained power in the Senate, there was zero. You had all the power concentrated in three people: Bush, Cheney, and Rumsfeld, which, in fact, constitutes a Constitutional crisis. And, Congress went to sleep at the switch. Then you had Cheney defending water boarding. My position is that it is counter to good order and discipline. In army basic training, we teach the management of prisoners and one element is to safeguard them. You had the number two guy in government saying that torture is okay. It put us in absolute gross violation of the Geneva Conventions. Witness anything that Senator McCain has said on this issue. His comment was, "Well, they did that during the Inquisition."

I made a comment on television that there is a myth that Republicans are good for the military. I said that the Republicans are the worst thing that has happened to the armed services. We are asking American soldiers to serve fifteen month tours. General Pace and Rumsfeld resisted growing the army, rather stating we had "a spike in demand for troops." I took exception to this resistance, as do many soldiers who serve multiple, fifteen month tours. It is a failure of the administration and Congress to maintain the military we need.

There was a period when everyone in Iraq knew we were in an insurgency and Rumsfeld had denied it. There is a good article by Ollivant and Chewning on counterinsurgency.[20] It is all about getting off the monster FOBs and on to the streets. Most of our fatalities occurred on patrols, getting blown up by IEDs, and this decreased with the new strategy employed in 2007.

If the Iraqis want us to remain, then we should maintain a presence. The American military presence is a beneficial one. We do need to draw down somewhat so that we are not actively involved in governing Iraq. We are the primary security for the Iraqi government, and that has got to be drawn down. If we are going to have a democracy in Iraq, the Iraqis have to believe that its leadership will provide for their interests. But the Shia majority is looking out for the Shia majority and the Sunnis feel marginalized. The Kurds already have their stronghold in the north.

I wrote a paper on how you get out of Iraq. I broke it into the three elements of national power—military, economic, and diplomatic. The Bush administration has overemphasized the military approach, we have not done much economically and diplomatically to improve the situation. The hard diplomatic work to support the American soldier in the prosecution of this war was never properly executed. The administration has, therefore, made the United States less secure. The reason for this is that we have developed a terrific amount of international antipathy; we lost a tremendous amount of support. Our diplomatic capital is at an all time low and our military is overcommitted. Bush committed the Reserve and never reconstituted it.

When a soldier begins to understand that his civilian leadership has failed, they should be permitted to become as active as they can when they get out of the military. They should be allowed to join whatever legal organization they wish to take political action. This administration is characterized by callous, incompetent civilian leadership. It has failed the American people and the American soldier. Sooner or later, the soldier too will have an opportunity to change that. The soldiers' vote counts. The performance of the military has been fantastic, and if it was not for the incompetent leadership of this administration, we would not be in the situation that we are in, both in Afghanistan and Iraq.

In terms of the threat from Al Qaeda in Iraq, it is better to think of Al Qaeda as two or many "Al Qaedas." You have the sophisticated Al Qaeda that can penetrate our borders and swim in American society without being detected and crash airplanes into buildings. Then you have Al Qaeda in Mesopotamia who blow things up (or blow themselves up) with explosives, and executes local direct small arms and rocket attacks. What is flooding into Iraq from Saudi Arabia, Lebanon, and Syria, is not the sophisticated Al Qaeda that can penetrate our borders. Are they dangerous? Yes, but they are dangerous locally, not strategically.

Terrence K. Kelly

"They put themselves in harm's way to try to help Iraq."

Dr. Kelly was the director of Militia Transition and Reintegration for the Coalition Provisional Authority (CPA) in 2004. He worked closely in Iraq with nine different militia groups. Kelly returned to Iraq in 2006 as director of the Office of Strategic Plans and Assessments at the U.S. State Department Embassy in Baghdad, where he remained until April 2007. Previously, he served as a senior National Security Officer in the White House Office of Science and Technology in both the Clinton and Bush administrations. He is a retired U.S. Army officer and graduate of West Point, who holds a master's degree in Security Studies and a Ph.D. in Mathematics. Kelly is currently a senior researcher and policy expert at the RAND Corporation, which graciously cleared him to participate in this interview with the understanding that the views expressed here are his own and not in any way representative of RAND.

My role in the CPA was to develop a policy on how to deal with the militias, negotiate agreements with them to demobilize, and coordinate programs to implement these agreements. Typically we would meet with them for a couple of hours each week. A large part of these meetings was listening to their views on what the Coalition was doing incorrectly, discussing the politics of Iraq and the future disposition of their militias.

One key element of our approach to the militia problem was the recognition that the groups we were working with had fought, in most cases for decades, against Saddam and were therefore in a real sense genuine Iraqi heroes. This meant they deserved our and Iraq's respect, and we treated them this way. Some had goals not in line with ours, or used methods of which we could not approve, but we took the perspective that it was their actions in Iraq since the invasion that counted most and we insisted they act within the law.

The thing in all of these negotiations is that you need to have clear idea of what you want to achieve. What I thought of a group's goals was really immaterial—actions are what counted. Our goal was to remove armed organizations not controlled by the government from Iraqi society, cause the members of those groups to abide by the law, and so further peace and stability.

Negotiations with these groups were at times difficult. The Kurds, for example, were wary of any agreement that would weaken the Peshmerga [Kurdistan Security Forces]. In the words of Peter Galbraith, the only enemy that they had known for eighty-five years was the Iraqi state, and they feared oppression by Arab Iraqis. After the Transitional

Administrative Law was passed (it recognized their Constitution and the Peshmerga as the legal security force of the Kurdish region), they became easier to deal with.

Our interactions with SCIRI [Supreme Council for the Islamic Revolution in Iraq]—a political party formed by Iraqi exiles under Iranian tutelage—started off rocky, with distrust on each side. However, as long they abided by the law, there was no reason why they shouldn't be part of the government-building process. Whether or not they were subverting that process, as many believe, was and is another question. They were active in Iraqi governance during the CPA. They became part of the police forces after the CPA disbanded. There have been reports that the Badr Corps [now Badr Organization, after its conversion into a polit-ical party], SCIRI's militia, committed crimes against Sunnis. A critical question is whether or not these are individual actions or the actions of Badr as an organization. If these were individual actions then those doing them would be criminals, but if they were organizational decisions then the militia would be declared illegal under the militia law (CPA Order 91, Regulation of Armed Forces and Militias within Iraq). In thinking about this question, Western analogies are not always helpful. In Western military institutions, a colonel tells a captain who tells a sergeant to do something, and it happens. This is not a good way to understand militias. They are not as disciplined or centrally controlled. The evidence seems to indicate that there have been some organizational decisions to use vio-lence. The question now is who is going to make the decision on whether or not these are organizational decisions, and if so to declare this organi-zation an outlaw group. Today the Iraqi government would have to make that determination.

We should provide a little background on SCIRI. They were one of the splinter groups of the Da'wa Party, which was the original Shia resistance party inside to Iraq. Many of Da'wa members were forced into exile under Saddam Hussein. Splinter groups formed in Iran, Syria and Europe. The original Da'wa Party espoused a political philosophy similar to Western concepts—power comes from the individual; the cleric's role is to teach or guide, not to command. Iran rejects this philosophy and promotes an Islamic state run by clerics. Since SCIRI was created in Iran, and some would say by Iran, and is certainly funded by the Iranian gov-ernment. We were cautious in our interactions with them. But, many who fought against Saddam are close with Iran, and that in and of itself should not disqualify them from a place in the future of Iraq. For example, many Kurds have close relationships with Iran. Jalal Talabani [president of Iraq and Patriotic Union of Kurdistan leader] probably has as good a relationship with Iranian leaders as does SCIRI. If we were unwilling to deal with anyone who had relationships with the Iranians, then we wouldn't deal with anyone.

We also realized that Iran has real strategic interests in Iraq, which has been their principle enemy in the Middle East. There is now a Shia leadership in Iraq that follows a relatively secular Iraqi Constitution and does not put authority in the hands of the clerics. This can be seen as a direct contradiction to the Iranian philosophy. [Ruhollah] Khamenei [supreme leader of Iran from 1970 until his death in 1989] considered himself the leader of the Islamic revolution, which he hoped would include all Muslims, and in particular all Shias. His successor, Ali Hoseini Khamenei, also views himself as the pan-Shia spiritual leader. A successful Shia government that does not follow Iran's philosophy could be seen as a threat to Iran. Everybody understands that Iran is going to try to influence the government of Iraq. The question is how they are going to influence it.

Other groups we interacted with included Iyad Allawi's INA [Iraqi National Alliance], Da'wa, and the INC [Iraqi National Congress]. These groups either claimed they had disbanded their militias, or not to have them. For example, Chalabi's INC militia was not a potential threat, but rather a large collection of guards for INC officials and offices. These groups were significant political players, so it was important to get them to sign on to the militia project. We also worked with the Iraqi Communist Party, a secular, primarily Shia, group, Iraqi Hezb'allah (no relation to Hezb'allah in Lebanon), and the Iraqi Islamic Party—the only Sunni group. None of these groups posed major security threats.

A large reason why these groups worked with the CPA on the militia issue was because we recognized that as those who fought Saddam were genuine Iraqi heroes and should get some type of recompense. I say this genuinely. For example, we felt that they were entitled to pensions or survivor benefits from the new Iraqi government similar to the Iraqi Army.

When I left Iraq in 2004, I believed that it could be a successful enterprise. In particular, Ambassador Bremer [led CPA, 2003–2004] has gotten a bad rap. He was asked to do an incredibly difficult and important job by the President. The criticisms leveled at him are not entirely fair. What he was asked to do was not nearly as difficult as what he had to do, and he had to figure that out without the aid of a competent staff or sufficient resources. This was a failure of the U.S. government, which simply does not have the capabilities to do what it set out to do in Iraq. Asking why the CPA (and Bremer) failed is like asking why your grandmother can't run a five minute mile. The answer is, given her physical realities she can't, and neither could the U.S. government do what was needed in Iraq in 2003–2004. Were there things that could have been done better? Yes, but Bremer did about as well as anyone could have. He will be judged better by history.

In the CPA I worked with a lot of great people, but most did not have the skills required for the job. While some people were there to pad their resumes, the vast majority were there for good reasons. They put themselves in harm's way to try to help Iraq and the United States. Many people who served in Iraq disagreed with the decision to go there, but they are there to do serve their country and help Iraqis. A humanitarian administrator I knew later put it well when she was asked why she was in Iraq. She said that this is so important, how can you not go and try to make a difference.

I returned in February 2006. At that point we had a lot more data and it did not look positive. The Iraqis had demonstrated that all of the tensions that Saddam kept suppressed had flared up. For now, Sunni Arabs have decided to stop shooting at us. The various tribes have determined that their principle enemy is Al Qaeda, not the United States. They still don't want us there, but they are willing to work with us to eliminate Al Qaeda. But, we need to think about them correctly. An insurgent, by definition, is a person who fights to change the government, not someone who fights the U.S. forces there to assist the government. The Sunni groups still dislike and distrust the Shia government, and will likely oppose it when we leave. That is, they are likely still insurgents. Working with them is essential at this point, but we should be clear about who we are working with. In the Shia areas, principally the south and Baghdad, there is internecine warfare between SCIRI and the Sadrists to determine who will dominate the Shia polity. In northern and central Iraq there is a large swath of land under dispute, though one usually only hears about Kirkuk. There was supposed to be a referendum in late 2007 to resolve this dispute, but it did not occur. This is a major issue that will likely lead to rising ethnic tensions, as it pits the Kurds against the Arabs. The Arab Sunni and Shia might forget their differences in the short term to oppose the Kurds.

The strategic approach adopted in 2005 and 2006 was to form a national unity government and have this unity migrate to a local level. It did not work. General Petraeus and Ambassador Crocker have shifted the focus to protecting the population and reducing violence in local areas throughout 2007, and so to work reconciliation from the bottom up. To be fair, this began near the end of General Casey and Ambassador Khalilzad's tenures. General Odierno also deserves a lot of credit for this. But I have not seen signs of reconciliation among the leaders who command the major tools of violence; they appear to be pursuing the same maximalist goals as before. This does not mean that reconciliation is out of the question, only that I have not seen any significant indicators that it is taking place at this level.

Samir Adil

"The Iraqi people believe in unity, we love each other."

Samir was born in Baghdad, Iraq, in 1964. He earned his undergraduate degree in Mathematics at the University of Mosul in 1988, and has been involved in political organizing for most of his adult life. He was a member of the League for the Liberation of the Working Class that led to the Worker Communist Party in Iraq. In the years under Saddam Hussein, Samir worked underground and was arrested in 1992 for his activities with a rival political party. Iraqi police tortured Samir, who suffers from hearing loss and an impaired left side as a result. He fled Iraq in 1995 and resettled in Canada. In December 2002, Samir returned to Iraq as president of the Iraqi Freedom Congress (IFC), which seeks a secular, democratic Iraq. The organization promotes alternatives to both radical Islam and the U.S. occupation and has worked to reduce sectional violence throughout the nation. The IFC has circulated the slogan "No Sunni, No Shia. We believe in human identity" to promote its cause. It has also organized "safety zones" in Iraq as a means to reduce violence and ethnic rivalries. The Congress maintains an office near Ferdowsi Square in Baghdad, where coalition forces toppled a statue of Saddam Hussein on April 9, 2003.

I worked with the Communist Party of Iraq from 1986 to 1990, when Saddam invaded Kuwait. After that, I resigned and helped to establish the League for the Liberation of the Working Class in 1991. All of the parties against Saddam's government were underground. I was captured by Saddam's police in 1992. When they arrested me, they asked why we were against Saddam's government and where we got our money. They tortured me for twenty-five days, I still have problem in my back, shoulders and neck. It wasn't just me, they also tortured my comrades. There were 300 people with me, and they executed many people from the Communist Party. They released me because I didn't have any relation with governments of the countries neighboring Iraq. There was a rule in Iraq that if political groups didn't have a relationship with outside governments they didn't execute them, but they did put you in prison. There was international attention and outrage and I was released. I had to check in with the Iraqi government. At one point, they asked me to cooperate and spy for Saddam's government. I fled the country through the Kurdistan region, then I escaped to Turkey and from here I went to Canada. I returned to Kurdistan in late 2002, as we suspected that the U.S. would attack Iraq.

In December 2002, the U.S. administration, British government and Iraqi opposition groups held a conference at a hotel in London. They divided Iraq into Sunni, Shia, and Kurdish. After the occupation, Paul Bremer and the Coalition Provisional Authority [CPA] divided Iraqi society into ethnic groups. We said that this will destroy Iraqi society as we know it. For example, I have six brothers and one sister. The background of my family is Shia, and the background of our wives is Sunni. I don't remember talking about Sunni or Shia. I knew my wife since I was in university; twenty years we are together and we never talked about Shia or Sunni. My mother is Shia but she did not say to me "your wife is from a Sunni family." There was a law under Saddam's government that did not allow you to talk about Sunni versus Shia as it was considered a threat to national security. They would put you in jail, maybe for twenty years, if you talked about Sunni and Shia and Christian. Iraq has a secular and civilized history.

The Iraqi government under the occupation is not working for the people, they all have political interests. The people in Iraq aren't demanding the good life, we just want security. This government cannot bring security to Iraq; it is an ethnic, sectarian government. One of the government officials admitted that "In the morning we shake hands and greet each other and in the afternoon we send out the militia to kill the other." All of the militia—Sunni and Shia gangsters—attack innocent people. The Iraqi people are not these militias. The Iraqi people believe in unity, we love each other. The Iraqi people don't want this government as it is a band of sectarian interests with militias. We now have 4 million Iraqi refugees who left Iraq and over 100,000 inside.

Baghdad itself is divided into two parts—one part is owned by Sunni sectarian government; even American tanks have no presence there. The other part is controlled by Shiites, Sadr's Mahdi Army who attack Sunnis. You can kill anyone in the daytime in front of Iraqi police or American tanks and nobody does anything. There are few jobs and no security. I went to these areas and people there were talking about how Al Qaeda offered one hundred dollars per day to work with them. And people joined; not because they believe in Al Qaeda but because they want money to feed their family. There are stories of people selling their kidneys to make money; more and more women are forced to sell their bodies to feed their children. You can walk around the city and see mountains of garbage. There is a lack of social services. In Baghdad, there are many areas where there is no electricity for five days in a row.

This argument that the U.S. forces can't leave because Iraq will slip into civil war is just an excuse to justify the invasion. Do you remember the United States said they were coming to Iraq to stop WMDs? Then they changed it to say they are bringing democracy? Then they changed it to say that if the United States leaves Al Qaeda will take over. You know all this is a justification to stay. They argue if the United States leaves there will be chaos in Iraq. Is there not chaos now? They killed fourteen men in the daytime because their name was Omer, which is a Sunni name and the same thing happens if you are Shiite. If there is no occupation, there is no justification for Al Qaeda to attack the people. The coalition said that they were going to prevent a civil war, now we are more or less living in a civil war. A lot of people in Iraq don't believe that the United States wants to stop a civil war.

The IFC has gone into many areas and cities in Iraq to try to improve the situation. The IFC has established a secular, satellite TV station that is against political Islam and the occupation. We have established a Safety Force to prevent ethnic cleansing. In Al Awadia, 5,000 people were fleeing because of the ethnic fighting. We arrived there and raised our slogan, "No Sunni, No Shia! We believe in human identity." Most of the people there joined IFC. We prevented militias from opening an office in that area. We did not allow it because we believed that they would participate in ethnic cleansing. We have many IFC branches throughout Iraq—in

Tikrit, Nassiryah, Baghdad, Basra, Dewaneiy, Samra, Hala, and many more places.

We talk to the people. We tell them "Don't use your gun against your neighbor; he is not your enemy. You both suffered together for many, many years: under Saddam, under sanctions, and under occupation." We ask anyone to come to the Safety Force and learn about the value of human life and history of people who found ways to work together. Since September 2006 to now, there has been no killing by identity in areas where we have a presence, no gangsters killing the people: in Al Awadia between Sarfi Bridge and the Hospital; in Karentina, Haaalytadab, and Hayalskry. We also work to provide oil and gas to the people and clear garbage from their neighborhood. We talked to the UN representative in Baghdad about the killings and building up the safety forces. These forces are local; we recruit people in neighborhoods who volunteer to help in their own towns. It is established and mobilized by the IFC but it is the local people who are in it.

We have helped to organize workers against the new oil law. South Oil Union called a strike against the draft oil law. Strikes against the oil law among the oil workers were effective, far more effective than killing American soldiers. We have also organized against the American occupation; we are against the administration policy not the American people. We learned that American forces killed the head of the Safety Force, Abdelhussein Saddam. His body was found in the forensic center at the Yarmouk Hospital. The Iraqi people have had a bad experience with the recent war, and the long Iraq-Iran War in the 1980s, so the people don't believe in armed resistance, it has caused so much damage. Mothers in Iraq suffer the same as Cindy Sheehan and all the mothers in the United States. Iraqis have experienced human suffering too.

We think civil resistance can work and we continue to push for a secular government in Iraq. There was a survey in Karbala that said over 70 percent of the persons there want a secular government. This is important because Karbala is a religious city, maybe the most religious area. Other surveys say that over 70 percent of all Iraqis want the occupation to end. Under Saddam, you had one enemy. If you were not involved in politics, no one in those days asked why you left your home or why you drink alcohol. But now you are an enemy because you are Shia or Sunni, or because you are a woman or because you drink. The Iraqi people have a long history of working with secular political parties before the occupation.

Donny George Youkhanna

"This was a serious accusation; it meant killing immediately."

Dr. George is an Assyrian Christian who was born in Habbaniya in 1950, a predominately Sunni Muslim town in the Al Anbar providence of Iraq. As a child, he had a passion for fishing and the outdoors. He found the prospect of living in tents and excavating sites appealing as a young man, so he turned to archeology. Dr. George went on to earn a doctorate in prehistoric archaeology from the University of Baghdad in 1995 and is arguably one of Iraq's leading archeologists. At the time of the U.S. invasion of Iraq, Dr. George and his family lived in the Dora area of Baghdad. He was chairman of the Iraq State Board of Antiquities and Heritage (SBAH), and served as director general of the National Museum in Baghdad. Dr. George is also member of UNESCO's Iraqi National Committee for Education, Science and Culture.

Immediately after coalition forces toppled Saddam Hussein's statue in Firdos Square, Baghdad, looters ransacked the Iraqi National Museum and archeological cites, stealing some 15,000 priceless artifacts over a three day period in April 2003. An international media firestorm ensued; some accusing the U.S. occupation force of failing to protect the museums. Many of the artifacts date back thousands of years, including a Sumerian cuneiform tablet or one of the earliest known forms of writing. Dr. George later helped to recover some of the lost artifacts with the assistance of the U.S. State Department and the American forces in Iraq.

After receiving death threats, Dr. George fled Iraq to Syria. With the assistance of his colleague Dr. Elizabeth Stone and the Scholar Rescue Fund, Dr. George secured a visiting professorship at Stony Brook University in New York. His efforts to preserve Iraq's ancient artifacts and cultural heritage led the New York Times *to conclude that Dr. George is "standing guard over his country's history."*[21] *The author of several books, Dr. George lectures frequently and has appeared on PBS's "Charlie Rose" program.*

I was director general of research and studies in SBAH in Baghdad. We had to leave the museum in April 2003 during the invasion. There was firing in the street. And, there were people in civilian clothes, we don't know if they were militia, but they had RPGs [rocket-propelled grenades] and Kalashnikovs [Russian assault rifle]. They were firing and shooting at the American tanks. Then after a week or so, I think it was Sunday, April 15, 2003, we were able to return to the museum. In my office, there was two feet of debris on the floor and those were my documents, my reports, and so on. My computer and cameras were gone. When we went into the galleries, it looked like a hurricane hit it. I was thinking, "Why? Why could all this happen to a museum?" It could have very easily been prevented by placing one or two tanks in front of the museum. Even when we retuned to the museum we did not have any protection. I myself have seen cars passing by the museum, flashing their Kalashnikovs.

Almost a year before the invasion and looting, I had some information from London. Two people were sitting in a private meeting; one of them said to me, you know, Iraqis are not so good to have all these precious antiquities. People might steal these things and bring them to us in London. The second one said something like "I am waiting for the day that the American Army is going to invade Iraq and I will be with them, I will go to the Iraq museum and get what I want." I was surprised. In a meeting with the Board of Directors, I told the chairman that we need to protect the museum. We should do what the Lebanese did. They put everything in storage and sealed the doors. The directors said, "You know you are exaggerating. No one will come into Baghdad." Again, I raised the issue and said "For God's sake, let's do something." One administrator said no one will dare come into Baghdad while Saddam is here.

From my own investigations—archeologists are investigators—I understood that there might be three types of groups who entered the compound of the museum and stole artifacts. Group Number One we might call the normal people. They went into the museum, smashed the doors and took everything: furniture, computers, copy machines, and telephones. You name it; they took anything they could get their hands on. Group Number Two went through a glass window that had been blocked for, say, ten years. It was a small window that one could not see from the outside. Nobody would know the window was there unless somebody studied the plan of museum or had investigated how to get into the museum. Thus Group Number Two had some knowledge of antiquities because they passed by some replicas in the galleries. I found glass cutters left around here and there that they prepared to cut the showcases. We had some showcases on the wall that showed a series of stamped bricks of all the history of Mesopotamia. They picked up nine pieces of those, which means they knew what to take. They knew what they wanted. I saw some smashed empty showcases, which contained masterpieces before the evacuation of the small items from the museum. All over the world museums are known for containing treasures and maybe this was the opportunity for people who had an eye of these things for some time. Now, Group Number Three were the ones who went into the store rooms that were located in the cellars. They entered through a small door in the Hatra gallery. I never knew there was a door there. They went through a door that goes to the basement of the museum; it was blocked by bricks. They smashed the bricks and the door. They entered the first room and they touched nothing there. They went through boxes in the second room, where they took small items: jewelry and related precious items. This group might have had information from the inside. There was no electricity; no light, but they knew where to go in the cellar.

Colonel Matthew Bogdanos of the U.S. Marines Corps conducted an investigation. Our own investigation was conducted by a former chairman of the SBAH and he never published it. The idea was to hold a conference in the auditorium of the museum, but the ministers did not accept that idea. They had a huge report. I was surprised. We just wanted to have a hearing session and I do not understand why they did not permit it.

Scholars in the United States provided coordinates of the museums to the Pentagon with instructions on how to protect them. I was told by these scholars that they said to the Pentagon if you go to the museum you will find someone called Donny George. He is cooperative and he will help you, but they never came. I am not blaming the soldiers who were in the streets of Baghdad. If they don't have orders, they won't act. They were there, but they did not protect the museum. One of the museum staff told me that he went to a U.S. tank that was very close to the museum. He pleaded with them to move the tank in front of the museum. He remembers that there were a few hundred people in front of the museum with guns, tool bars and hammers in their hands. The man in charge of the tank made a phone call, and he said "I'm sorry, we can't move the tank, we have orders." Later that same tank and the same tank commander would protect the museum. I spoke to them both together. The tank commander said, "Yes, this man came to me. I made a phone call, but I did not have orders to move my tank." I asked him who he called, and he said "I can't tell you that." But, I am not blaming him. We can't go blaming people. Now we have to work together to restore what was lost. We did restore some 4,000 objects that were stolen.

Maybe the forces did not fully understand. They did not have sufficient information on the museum and on the history of the country. There was a picture of a looter in the Western media holding a vase and few people realized it was a sacred work. It goes back 3,200 years before Christ.

Scholars say the bands on the vase represent the Sumerian philosophy of life on earth; it is one of the most important masterpieces in the world.

Whatever was happening in Saddam's time, the security situation was much better. He had half-a-million security people just for Baghdad. Of course, he had his heavy hammer and killed opponents. But now thousands of people are coming into the country and nobody is stopping them. I used to live in a place called Dora; it is just five minutes driving distance from the Green Zone [also called the International Zone, it is a heavily fortified complex in central Baghdad, where U.S. officials reside]. They say that Sunnis announced an Islamic Republic from Dora. Can you imagine this is happening only five minutes from the Green Zone? The situation is deteriorating; no one feels safe; there are no projects; and unemployment rates are huge. Most people stay at home unless it is absolutely necessary to go out. I talked to someone there who told me that twenty liters of gasoline to fill a car costs 25,000 dinars [Iraqi currency], which is well over double the normal cost. And, you can't find it; there is a huge black market in gasoline.

You see, first there were the Sunnis and Shiites. Now they are questioning the Christians. They say simply if you are a Christian, then you must be with the Americans. In my town, Dora, there was a high concentration of Christians. I am told they are walking door to door, telling people that you have twenty-four hours to leave. You either convert to Islam or you pay a tax to us or you leave. If you don't, you will be killed. People are leaving their homes and they are not allowed to take their belongings. I heard that there was talk of doing to the Christians what they did to the Jewish in the 1940s.

I had to leave the country. I was an official at the museum, of course, and they created a new ministry of antiquities that was given to the al-Sadr party. I was under pressure. First, I was chairman of the Board of Antiquities and they would not allow me to appoint any personnel. I then received an official letter, which withdrew all my official authority as chairman. I was told by someone that the order has come that Donny should not stay because he is a Christian. But, before I heard this, there was a letter dropped on the driveway of my parent's house, where my two sons had lived. They mentioned that my sons were teasing Muslim girls and making trouble. But this was a lie, they were friends, they grew up together. My son spoke Arabic and the Muslims spoke our language. The letter also said that we know that your father works with the Americans. This was a serious accusation; it meant killing immediately. We managed to get a car and get to Damascus [Syria]. I applied for retirement and it was approved immediately.

Iraq is my country. As an Assyrian Christian, my ancestors were there even before the Arabs. I am not saying this negatively. We had many wonderful Arab friends, they were brothers. I am concerned now about the Muslim gangs who are butchering the country. We never had problems among the Christians, Sunnis, and Shiites. In my second year of college, my friend asked where I was from. He never knew. He never had the idea of dividing people into Sunni, Shiite, or Christian. He never knew that I was a Christian, nobody worried too much about it.

I would say this sectarian division is the most dangerous thing that has happened in Iraq. The Iraqi Governing Council was set up, I think, under Paul Bremer [led the CPA]. The problem was that seats were given according to this division: a certain number for Shia, Sunni, Kurds, Turkmen, and so on. It ironically fueled these sectarian divisions. Despite the hardship of living under Hussein, everybody was living together. If you did not have anything do with Saddam, you would never feel anything. Little by little things improved. Politically, of course, he crushed any kind of criticism. This was not democracy or a healthy environment for the country. But as human beings, you could go to work, go out at night, and feel safe. The normal life of Iraqis was to travel, plan vacations at summer resorts or to England. I am talking about the Iraqi people. We had a bad government. But the people lived a normal life, we were positive people. Imagine a country with fine arts institutes and a wonderful symphony orchestra. Every month I went to see the orchestra. This was the normal life in Iraq. I would like to say that Iraq was not, and is not, simply a desert country. Yes, we have deserts, but we are sometimes portrayed as riding camels. We have cities and universities and I'd say the best doctors and poets in the Middle East.

That the United States got rid of Saddam Hussein is a very good thing. But all that has happened afterward, it is the responsibility of the United States. You can't just leave a country of 20 million people burning. First, things should be done politically. The main players are the neighboring countries, particularly Saudi Arabia and Iran. I would say it is not impossible to pressure these countries. I am not encouraging an invasion of Iran, but I am encouraging the political work to discourage the Saudis and Iranians from propelling the sectarian violence within Iraq. The Saudis favor the Sunnis and fear that the Iranians will dominate Iraq by helping the Shiites. The United States is a superpower and they can influence these countries.

Notes

Introduction

1. Tom Clancy, Tony Zinni, and Tony Koltz, *Battle Ready* (New York: Penguin, 2004), p. 426. David Cloud and Eric Schmitt, "More Retired Generals Call for Rumsfeld's Resignation," *New York Times*, April 14, 2006, pp. A1 and A17.
2. Thich Nhat Hanh, *Peace Is Every Step* (New York: Bantam Books, 1992), p. 103.
3. Andrew Bacevich, "Warrior Politics," *Atlantic Monthly* (May 2007). Bacevich is correct to caution us against the glorification of the military. Yet, he also argues that soldiers in uniform should not engage in politics against the war. "Although sworn to obey," "they have undertaken to obstruct." Of course, militarism is sustained precisely by way of such oaths that encourage silence in the face of misguided policies or war crimes. If Nazi soldiers in uniform petitioned against its war machine, one should not appeal to their oath of allegiance to silence them. Bacevich feels that encouraging groups of soldiers to "join the debate is shortsighted and dangerous." Perhaps it can be dangerous, but it also can facilitate democracy. Consider that the English Civil War, which in many ways was the catalyst of modern democracy, included radical elements of Levellers who worked with Agitators, who were military men in uniform. They petitioned their commanders and demanded democratic procedures. Soldiers engaging in dissent are not, ipso facto, dangerous. For a readable account of the Agitators, see Fenner Brockway, *Britain's First Socialists: The Levellers, Agitators and Diggers of the English Revolution* (London: Quartet Books, 1980), pp. 35–57.
4. For an elaboration on this point, see Michael Frisch, *A Shared Authority: Essays on the Craft and Meaning of Oral and Public History* (Albany: State University of New York Press, 1990), pp. 175–76.
5. Michael Frisch, "Sharing Authority: Oral History and the Collaborative Process," *Oral History Review* (Winter 2003), v. 30, n. 1, p. 111.
6. Linda Shopes, "Commentary: Shared Authority," *Oral History Review* (Winter 2003), v. 30, n. 1, p. 105.
7. Staughton Lynd, "Oral History from Below," *Oral History Review* (Spring 1993), v. 21, n. 1, pp. 1–8. Lynd, "History from Below." Paper presented at the annual meeting of the Organization of American Historians, New York, March 2008.
8. Jean Krasno and James Sullivan, *The United Nations and Iraq: Defanging the Viper* (Westport, CT: Praeger, 2003).
9. Alessandro Portelli, *The Death of Luigi Trastulli and Other Stories: Form and Meaning in Oral History* (Albany: State University of New York Press, 1991), pp. 1–26.

10. For details, see Carl Mirra, "Conscientious Objection in Operation Desert Storm," *Peace Review* (April–June 2006), v. 18, n. 2, pp. 199–205. Mirra, ed., *Enduring Freedom or Enduring War? Prospects and Costs of the New American 21st Century* (Washington, DC: Maisonneuve Press, 2005).

11. In 2005, a Gallup Poll discovered that almost 60 percent of Americans wished that the United States would remove its forces from Iraq; see Susan Page, "Poll: USA Is Losing Patience on Iraq," *USA TODAY*, June 12, 2005. A December 2006 CNN poll indicated that nearly 70 percent of Americans "expressed opposition" to the Iraq War, and over 50 percent favored the withdrawal of U.S. troops within one year; see "CNN Poll: U.S. Support for Iraq War Falls to 31 Percent," December 18, 2006, available at <http://www.cnn.com/POLITICS/ blogs/politicalticker/2006/12/cnn-poll-us-support-for-iraq-war-falls.html>, accessed July 18, 2008. The Program on International Policy Attitudes, affiliated with the Center for International Security Studies at the University of Maryland, surveyed nearly 4,500 people in four Muslim countries from December 2006 to February 2007. An overwhelming majority want U.S. forces to withdraw from Muslim countries; see "Muslims Believe US Seeks to Undermine Islam: Majorities Want US Forces Out of Islamic Countries And Approve of Attacks on US Troops," available at <http://www.worldpublicopinion.org/pipa/articles/home_page/346.php?nid=&id=&pnt=346&lb=hmpg2>, accessed July 18, 2008. Republican support for the war is also in decline as the conflict unfolds, see "Poll: GOP Support for Iraq War Beginning to Waver," CNN.com, June 26, 2007, <http://www.cnn.com/2007/POLITICS/06/26/poll. iraq.schneider/index.html>, accessed August 5, 2007.

12. Johan Galtung, *Transcend and Transform: An Introduction to Conflict Work* (Boulder, CO: Paradigm, 2004), p. 59.

13. Ibid., p. 46.

14. Christian Appy, *Patriots: The Vietnam War Remember from All Sides* (New York: Penguin Books, 2003), pp. 152–153. Robert McNamara, *In Retrospect: The Tragedy and Lessons of Vietnam* (New York: Times Books, 1995), p. 216.

15. The phrase is Staughton Lynd's in reference to a debate with Bayard Rustin in 1965. Lynd, "Coalition Politics or Nonviolent Revolution," *Liberation* (June–July 1965), pp. 18–21.

16. For an assessment of the toll of the invasion on Iraqis, see Juan Cole, "9 US Troops Killed; 250,000 Civilians Dead in Bush's War?" *Informed Comment*, January 10, 2008, available at <http://juancole.com>, February 15, 2008. Nir Rosen, "The Death of Iraq," *Current History* (December 2007), pp. 409–413.

I. Iraq and the United States: A Brief Sketch

1. For background information, see Douglas Little, *American Orientalism: The United States and the Middle East since 1945* (Chapel Hill: University of North Carolina Press, 2002), pp. 156–160.

2. See "Bin Laden's Sermon for the Feast of Sacrifice," *The Middle East Media Research Institute (MEMRI)*, Special Dispatch Series No. 476, March 5, 2003. Available at <http://www.memri.org/bin/articles.cgi?Area=sd&id=sp47603>, accessed July 18, 2008.

3. Dilip Hiro, *Iraq: In the Eye of the Storm* (New York: Nation Books, 2002), pp. 26–28.

4. Roger Morris, "A Tyrant 40 Years in the Making," *New York Times*, March 14, 2003.

5. Hanna Batatu, *The Old Social Classes and the Revolutionary Movements of Iraq: A Study of Iraq's Old Landed and Commercial Classes and of Its Communists, Ba'thists and Free Officers* (Princeton: Princeton University Press, 1987), pp. 985–986.

6. Marvine Howe, "Baghdad Executes 21 Officials for an Alleged Plot," *New York Times*, August 9, 1979, p. A4. See also Said K. Aburish, *Saddam Hussein: The Politics of Revenge* (London: Bloomsbury Publishing, 2001), who discusses related crimes in a chapter titled "From Planning to Plotting," pp. 160–189.

7. Mark Pythian, *Arming Iraq: How the U.S. and Britain Secretly Built Saddam's War Machine* (Boston, MA: Northeastern University Press, 1996). Products that can be used in the manufacture of biological weapons were among the items shipped to Iraq from U.S. suppliers in the 1980s. According to a 1994 U.S. Senate Committee, "We contacted a principal supplier of these materials to determine what, if any, materials were exported to Iraq which might have contributed to an offensive or defensive biological warfare program. Records available from the supplier for the period from 1985 until the present show that during this time, pathogenic (meaning 'disease producing'), toxigenic (meaning 'poisonous'), and other biological research materials were exported to Iraq pursuant to application and licensing by the U.S. Department of Commerce. Records prior to 1985 were not available, according to the supplier. These exported biological materials were not attenuated or weakened and were capable of reproduction." See Donald W. Riegle, Jr., Committee on Banking, Housing and Urban Affairs, "U.S. Chemical and Biological Warfare-Related Dual Use Exports to Iraq and Their Possible Impact on the Health Consequences of the Persian Gulf War," U.S. Senate, 103rd Congress, May 1994, available at <http://www.gulfweb.org/bigdoc/report/r_1_2.html>, accessed August 5, 2007.

8. William Blum, *Killing Hope: U.S. Military and CIA Operations since World War II* (Monroe, ME: Common Courage Press, 1995), pp. 323–25. On Kuwait's oil maneuvers, the *New York Times* reported, "Oil formations frequently run beneath political boundaries, whether they involve unfriendly leaseholders in West Texas or neighboring Arab states, and procedures have existed for years to settle disputes that arise. Typically, participants in the same field share both production costs and revenues, using a formula that sets percentages of ownership. But Iraq refused to negotiate with Kuwait on such an agreement. So Kuwait produced oil from Rumaila without any agreement, and then adopted a policy of producing far more oil than it was allowed under the quota system of the Organization of Petroleum Exporting Countries"; see Thomas C. Hayes, "Confrontation in the Gulf; The Oilfield Lying below the Iraq-Kuwait Dispute," *New York Times*, September 3, 1990. See also Brian Becker, "U.S. Conspiracy to Initiate the War against Iraq," in *War Crimes: A Report on United States War Crimes in Iraq*, ed. Ramsey Clark (Washington, DC: Maisonneuve Press, 1992), pp. 74–82.

9. U.S. Department of Defense, "The Operation Desert Shield/Desert Storm Timeline," American Forces Press Service, available at <http://www.defenselink.mil/news/newsarticle.aspx?id=45404>. Accessed on March 1, 2008.

10. George H. Bush and Brent Scowcroft, *A World Transformed* (New York: Alfred A. Knopf, 1998), p. 489. Scowcroft served as George H. Bush's national security adviser.

11. Background on UN and unfolding of the First Gulf War in Sarah Graham-Brown and Chris Toensing, *Why Another War? A Backgrounder on the Iraq Crisis*, 2nd edition, Middle East Research and Information Project (December 2002).

12. For a brief account of the PNAC, see Andrew Bacevich, *The New American Militarism: How Americans Are Seduced by War* (New York: Oxford University Press, 2005), pp. 89–91.

13. Bob Woodward, *Bush at War* (New York: Simon and Schuster, 2002), p. 49.

14. Secretary Colin L. Powell, "Press Remarks with Foreign Minister of Egypt Amre Moussa," *U.S. Department of State*, February 24, 2001, available at <http://www.state.gov/secretary/rm/2001/933.htm>, January 5, 2007.

15. David Manning, "The Secret Downing Street Memo," *Sunday Times*, May 1, 2005.

16. Charles Lewis and Mark Reading-Smith, "False Pretenses: Following 9/11, President Bush and Seven Top Officials of His Administration Waged a Carefully Orchestrated Campaign of Misinformation about the Threat Posed by Saddam Hussein's Iraq," Center for Public Integrity Report, available at <http://www.publicintegrity.org/WarCard/Default.aspx?src=home&context=overview&id=945>, accessed July 18, 2008. "President Says Saddam Hussein Must Leave Iraq within 48 Hours: Remarks by the President in Address to the Nation" (Washington, DC: Office of the Press Secretary), March 17, 2003.

17. IAEA Update Report for the Security Council Pursuant to Resolution 1441 (2002). "No Evidence of Nuclear Weapons Program: ElBaradei," *Sydney Morning Herald*, March 8, 2003.

18. "President Delivers State of the Union," January 28, 2003, available at <http://www.whitehouse.gov/news/releases/2003/01/20030128–19.html>. Dana Priest and Karen DeYoung, "CIA Questioned Documents Linking Iraq, Uranium Ore," *Washington Post*, March 22, 2003. See also "Report on the U.S. Intelligence Community's Prewar Intelligence Assessments on Iraq," Select Committee on Intelligence, U.S. Senate, July 7, 2004. The report finds numerous agencies challenging the documents regarding the Nigerian uranium sale to Iraq. Among the responses were that it was "highly suspect"; "lacks crucial details"; and "completely implausible." Jeanne Cummings, "Security Advisers Now Share Blame In Intelligence Row," *Wall Street Journal*, July 23, 2003, p. A4. Note that the CIA's initial challenge led to the removal of the uranium claim from an October speech. See Ken Fireman, "Warning Unheeded," *Newsday*, July 23, 2003.

19. Jim Rutenberg and Scott Shane, "Libby Pays Fine, Judge Poses Probation Query," *New York Times*, July 6, 2007.

20. For specific citation and details see Stephen Shalom, "Iraq White Paper," in *Enduring Freedom or Enduring War? Prospects and Costs of the New American 21st Century*, ed. Carl Mirra (Washington, DC: Maisonneuve Press, 2005), pp. 173–176.

21. *The 9/11 Truth Commission Report: Final Report of the National Commission on Terrorist Attacks Upon the United States*, *Authorized Edition* (New York: W.W. Norton, n.d.), pp. 334–335.

22. "U.S. Troops in Iraq: 72% Say End the War in 2006," *Zogby International*, February 28, 2006, available at <http://www.zogby.com/news/ReadNews. dbm?ID=1075>, accessed July 18, 2008. To be sure, withdrawal does not mean abandonment. UN consultant, Johan Galtung, suggests a Conference on Security and Cooperation in the Middle East, chaired by Jordan or a party in the region. See Johan Galtung, "Human Needs, Humanitarian Intervention, Human Security and the War in Iraq," February 2004, available at <http://www. transcend.org>, accessed July 18, 2008.

23. Sean Rayment, "Secret MoD Poll: Iraqis Support Attacks on British Troops," *Sunday Telegraph*, October 23, 2005. "Iraqis Not So Happy," *Newsday*, September 29, 2003, p. A12. Furthermore, the Brookings Institute identifies a February 2005 poll in which 71 percent of Iraqis "oppose the presence of Coalition forces in Iraq." For this poll and several others with similar data, see Abigail Fuller and Neil Wollman, "Should the U.S. Withdraw? Let the Iraqi People Decide," *Professors for Peace*, October 13, 2005.

24. Rajiv Chandrasekaran, "How Cleric Trumped U.S. Plan for Iraq," *Washington Post*, November 26, 2003, p. A20. Juan Cole, "The Iraq Election: First Impressions," *History News Network*, January 31, 2005.

25. William Booth and Rajiv Chandrasekaran, "Occupation Forces Halt Elections throughout Iraq," *Washington Post*, June 28, 2003, p. A20.

26. Hamza Hendawi, "Iraqi Shiites Demand Elections in Peaceful Protest," *Associated Press*, January 1, 2004. The key figure behind the massive, nonviolent protest was the Grand Ayatollah Ali Husseini Sistani, a leader of Iraqi Shiites.

27. Juan Cole, "The Iraq Election: First Impressions," *History News Network*, January 31, 2005. Naomi Klein, "Getting the Purple Finger," *The Nation*, February 11, 2005.

28. In June 2005, Iraq's *Al-Mada* newspaper printed a draft of this constitution. The initial draft mirrored a "Scandinavian-type welfare system," noted one informed observer. For example, Article 18 stated that "the basis of the economy is social justice." The United States dispatched a team to help in drafting the new Iraqi Constitution. One member of the team was Zalmay Khalilzad, who participated in the Project for a New American Century. The final draft of the constitution, news sources reported, had omitted the language of Article 18 above. The final version also added a new provision that encouraged investment in Iraqi petroleum. See Herbert Docena, "Iraq's Neoliberal Constitution," *Foreign Policy in Focus*, September 2, 2005, pp. 1, 2, 5, and 7.

29. For a discussion of militias in Iraq, see the testimony of Terrence K. Kelly in chapter five.

30. For information on insurgent groups Eric S. Margolis, "Know Thine Enemy," *The American Conservative*, November 21, 2005, pp. 25–27 and Marie Colvin, "U.S. in Secret Truce Talks with Insurgency Chiefs," *Sunday Times*, October 22, 2006. On rebellion, see Camilo Mejía, *Road from Ar Ramadi: The Private Rebellion of Staff Sergeant Camilo Mejía* (New York: New Press, 2007), p. 159.

31. On Hussein, see Marc Santora, James Glanz, and Sabrina Tavernise, "Dictator Who Ruled Iraq with Violence is Hanged for Crimes against Humanity," *New York Times*, December 20, 2006. For the poll, see Robert Hodierne, "Poll: More Troops Unhappy with Bush's Course in Iraq," *Army Times*, December 29, 2006.

32. James A. Baker III and Lee H. Hamilton, *The Iraq Study Group Report: The Way Forward—A New Approach* (New York: Vintage Press, 2006), pp. 9, 16, and 30. The report is also available from the U.S. Institute of Peace.

33. As Frisch observes, "oral history can contribute a substantial counter to officially received history and officially defined policy, by empowering people to generate alternative understandings." See Michael Frisch, *A Shared Authority: Essays on the Craft and Meaning of Oral and Public History* (Albany: State University of New York Press, 1980), p. 178. Again, the testimony presented here is not offered as "The" interpretation, but one that must be included in the debate on the war.

2. The New Winter Soldiers Redux: The Patriotism of Antiwar GIs

1. Camilo Mejía, *Road from Ar Ramadi: The Private Rebellion of Staff Sergeant Camilo Mejía* (New York: New Press, 2007), pp. 230–231.

2. Van Gosse, *Rethinking the New Left: An Interpretative History* (New York: Palgrave Macmillian, 2005), pp. 99–100. For a full account, see Andrew Hunt, *The Turning: A History of the Vietnam Veterans against the War* (New York: New York University Press, 1999). I am grateful to Christian Appy for reminding me of the importance of O'Brien's book.

3. Jerry Lembke, *The Spitting Image: Myth, Memory, and the Legacy of Vietnam* (New York: New York University Press, 1998). Lembke, "Erasing Resistance: Spat-on Soldiers and the Construction of 'The Good Veteran,'" Paper presented at the annual meeting of the American Historical Association. Washington, DC, January 2008.

4. U.S. Department of Defense, "What Is Posttraumatic Stress Disorder," available at <http://www.ncptsd.va.gov/facts/general/fs_what_is_ptsd.html>, accessed September 5, 2007.

5. Charles W. Hoge, Jennifer L. Auchterlonie, and Charles S. Milliken, "Mental Health Problems, Use of Mental Health Services, and Attrition from Military Service after Returning from Deployment to Iraq or Afghanistan," *Journal of the American Medical Association* (March 2006), v. 295, n. 9, pp. 1023–1032.

6. Mental Health Advisory Team (MHAT) IV, "Operation Iraqi Freedom Final Report" (Office of the Surgeon—Multinational Force Iraq and the Office of the Surgeon General, U.S. Army Medical Command), November 17, 2006, p. 25, available at <http://www.armymedicine.army.mil/news/mhat/mhat_iv_Report_17Nov06.pdf>, accessed September 5, 2007. I first learned of this report from former soldier Aidan Delgado.

7. Robert Jay Lifton, *Home from the War: Vietnam Veterans—Neither Victims nor Executioners* (New York: Simon and Schuster, 1973), pp. 41, 99–133. Quotation in Lifton, *Super Power Syndrome: America's Apocalyptic Confrontation with the World* (New York: Thunder's Mouth Press, 2003), pp. 47–48. Sociologist Jerry Lembke has warned that Lifton's work on guilt lent itself to a model of veterans as victims, and inadvertently fueled the image of the "bad" antiwar veteran as opposed to the "good" pro-war veteran. See Lembke, *The Spitting Image: Myth, Memory and the Legacy of Vietnam* (New York: New York University Press, 1998),

p. 108. Nevertheless, Lifton's concept of animating guilt can lead to healthy, positive action.

8. Author interview of David Airhart, March 2006.

9. Mejía, *Road from Ar Ramadi*, pp. 230, 240, 300.

10. Richard Moser, *The New Winter Soldiers: GI and Veteran Dissent during the Vietnam Era* (New Brunswick, NJ: Rutgers University Press, 1996), pp. 1, 7, 17–40.

11. Author interview of Perry O'Brien, December 1, 2007. O'Brien is a veteran of the Afghanistan intervention and an active organizer in IVAW.

12. William F. Buckley, Jr., "The Nuremberg Doctrine Is Raised and It Was Just a Matter of Time," *The Atlanta Journal*, September 25, 1965.

13. "Army Lieutenant Becomes First Commissioned Officer to Refuse Deployment to Iraq," *Democracy Now!* Radio program, June 8, 2006, available at <http://www. democracynow.org/2006/6/8/army_lieutenant_becomes_first_commissioned_ officer>, accessed June 16, 2007.

14. Harvey J. Tharp, "Memorandum: Reasons for Submission of Resignation Request," November 18, 2004, in author's possession and used with permission.

15. MHAT IV, "Operation Iraqi Freedom," pp. 35 and 80.

16. William H. McMichael, "Service Members Rally against the War in Iraq," *Marine Corps Times*, January 16, 2007. Again, we should not glorify these soldiers, but we should take seriously their thoughts on the war. See this volume's introduction on this matter and Andrew Bacevich, "Warrior Politics," *Atlantic Monthly* (May 2007). While I do not agree with all of Bacevich's points, his warning that we should not succumb to blindly praising veterans as morally superior makes sense.

17. Don Van Natta, "Bush Was Set on Path to War, British Memo Says," *New York Times*, March 27, 2006.

18. Lynndie England, an Army Reservist, was sentenced to three years in prison for detainee abuse at Abu Ghraib. Photographs of England holding a naked prisoner on a leash and others with her smiling alongside naked prisoners appeared in media outlets across the globe after the Abu Ghraib torture scandal was revealed. See Mark Danner, *Torture and Truth: America, Abu Ghraib, and the War on Terror* (New York: New York Review of Books, 2004). The International Committee of the Red Cross described a "consistent pattern" of "brutal behavior," and noted that "the methods of physical and psychological coercion were used by the military intelligence in a systematic way." The Red Cross report is reprinted in Danner's *Torture and Truth*, and the above quotations appear on pp. 253 and 262.

19. Rumsfeld told a soldier who questioned him about the lack of equipment that "You go to war with the Army you have." See Robert Burns, "Facing Friendly Fire: Heat from the Troops," *Newsday*, December 9, 2004, p. A5.

20. David Montgomery, "Far from Iraq, a Demonstration of a War Zone," *Washington Post*, March 20, 2007, p. C01.

21. The British medical journal published articles that estimated Iraqi deaths at over 600,000. For example, see Gilbert Burnham, Ridyah Lafta, Shannon Dooley, and Les Roberts, "Mortality after the 2003 Invasion of Iraq: A Cross-sectional Cluster Sample," *Lancet*, October 11, 2006. There has been considerable debate over the study. See "Lancet's Political Hit," *Wall Street Journal*, January 9, 2008. Two of the authors, Burnham and Roberts, wrote separate letters to the editor,

which appeared in the *Wall Street Journal*, January 14, 2008. Opinion Research Business, a British polling group, placed the number of Iraqis killed at over 1 million, see Peter Beaumont and Joanne Walters, "Greenspan Admits Iraq Was about Oil, as Deaths Put at 1.2m," *The Observer*, September 16, 2007.

22. See Paul von Zielbauer, "Army Is Cracking Down on Deserters," *New York Times*, April 9, 2007. Amnesty International, "Public Statement/ USA: Staff Sergeant Camilo Mejia Castillo Is a Prisoner of Conscience," AI Index: AMR 51/094/2004 (Public), News Service No: 143 (June 4, 2004).

23. The School of Americas at Fort Benning is a controversial facility that is accused of training a host of human rights violators. Public scrutiny was aroused in the early 1990s. A secret memo to then Defense Secretary Cheney outlined training manuals used at the school that contained information on false arrests, beatings, and even murder. Thousands of Latin American military personnel trained at the school, including those sent by Nicaragua under Somoza's dictatorship. Many "Contras," those forces opposed to the Nicaraguan Sandinistas, are also linked to the school and human rights violations. Manuel Noriega is among the school's graduates. Congress renamed the school after these revelations to the Western Hemispheric Institute for Security Cooperation. See Lesley Gill, *The School of Americas: Military Training and Political Violence in the Americas* (Durham, NC: Duke University Press, 2004).

24. After reading this transcript, Mejía noted that this discussion was too condensed. I urge readers to consult his book for context and details. The book is also indispensable for anyone concerned with understanding GI resistance. See Mejía *Road from Ar Ramadi*.

25. Edward Wong, "Iraqi Widow Saves Her Home, but Victory Is Brief," *New York Times*, March 30, 2007.

3. From Bunker Hill to Baghdad: We Will Continue the Mission

1. Quoted in Tam Cummings, "Why I Serve: General Says Teamwork Makes Military Appealing," *Armed Forces Press Service*, February 4, 2005.

2. "Appeal for Courage," available at <http://appealforcourage.org>, accessed September 10, 2007. I wish to thank Professor Andrew Bacevich for bringing the appeal to my attention.

3. W. Thomas Smith, "Baghdad Calling: U.S. Troops Make the Case for Courage," *National Review online*, April 23, 2007.

4. "President's Address to the Nation," The Library, Office of the Press Secretary, January 10, 2007, available at <http://www.whitehouse.gov/news/releases/2007/01/20070110–7.html>, accessed September 10, 2007. The plan contains six major factors: "1. Let Iraqis lead; 2. Help Iraqis protect the population; 3. Isolate extremists; 4. Create space for progress; 5. Diversify political and economic efforts; and 6. Situate the strategy in a regional approach."

5. Thom Shanker, "Army Career behind Him, General Speaks Out on Iraq," *New York Times*, May 13, 2007.

6. John Batiste and Pete Hegseth, "Getting Beyond Stalemate to Win a War," *Washington Post*, December 8, 2007, p. A17.

7. Ralph Peters, "Year of Wonders," *New York Post*, December 31, 2007. Dahr Jamail, "Challenges 2007–2008: Iraq Progresses to Some of Its Worst," *Interpress Service*, December 29, 2007. *icasualties.org* reports 817 U.S. casualties from the start of the surge in February 2007 to December 31, 2007.

8. Michael R. Gordon and General Bernard E. Trainor, *Cobra II: The Inside Story of the Invasion and Occupation of Iraq* (New York: Pantheon Books, 2006), pp. 497 and 507.

9. "President Celebrates Independence Day in West Virginia" (Morgantown, WV: West Virginia University, and Office of the Press Secretary), July 4, 2005, available at <http://www.whitehouse.gove/news/releases/2005/07/200050704.html>, accessed September 10, 2007. I am grateful to Richard E. Killbane, U.S. Army Transportation Corps Historian, Fort Eustis, Virginia, who provided the following two unpublished essays to confirm the testimony of Captain McCormick: "Battle of BIAP, 11 April 2004" and "Firefight on ASR Heart, 30 January 2005." Captain McCormick also asked him to assist in editing the transcript.

10. Andrew J. Bacevich, "Warrior Politics," *Atlantic Monthly* (May 2007); Bacevich "Vietnam Relevant, but Not How Bush Cited It," *Stars and Stripes* (August 2007).

11. Michael Gordon and Bernard Trainor, *Cobra II: The Inside Story of the Invasion and Occupation of Iraq* (New York: Vintage, 2007).

12. The Wounded Warriors project explains its mission is "to raise the awareness and enlist the public's aid for the needs of severely injured service men and women, to help severely injured service members aid and assist each other, and to provide unique, direct programs and services to meet their needs." See <https://www.woundedwarriorproject.org/>, accessed November 10, 2007.

4.   The Sacrifice of Military Families

1. Scott Jason, "Left Behind: Wife and Son Wait for Marine to Return," *Merced Sun Star*, December 19, 2007.

2. Col. Douglas Waldrep, Col. Stephen J. Cozza, and Col. Ryo Sook Chow. "Chapter XII. The Impact of Deployment on the Military Family" in National Center for Post-Traumatic Stress Disorder, *Iraq War Clinician Guide,* 2nd edition, (Washington, DC: Department of Veteran Affairs, June 2004), pp. 83–86. Jason, "Left Behind."

3. Waldrep et al. "Impact of Deployment on the Military Family," pp. 83–86.

4. Deployment statistics and quotations from generals in this paragraph from Ann Scott Tyson, "Possible Iraq Deployments Would Stretch Reserve Force," *Washington Post*, November 5, 2006.

5. Faye Fiore, "Military Kin on U.S. Handling of War," *Newsday*, December 7, 2007, p. A32.

6. "About Us," available at <http:familiesunited.com/docs/about/>, accessed September 10, 2007.

5.   War Managers: Pundits and Policy Officials

1. Richard Perle, "Relax, Celebrate Victory," *USA Today*, May 1, 2003. David Rose, "Neo Culpa," *Vanity Fair* (November 2006). The *Vanity Fair* article generated

controversy, and was accused of misrepresenting Perle's words. Perle's statement that the occupation was a mistake was on the BBC program, *Hard Talk*, and the video is available at <http://news.bbc.co.uk/2/hi/programmes/hardtalk/7108199. stm>, accessed July 18, 2008.

2. William Buckley, Jr., "It Didn't Work," *National Interest* (February 2006). Available at <http://www.nationalreview.com/buckley200602241451.asp>, accessed July 18, 2008. George Will, "A War Still Seeking a Mission," *Washington Post*, September 11, 2007, p. A16. Patrick J. Buchanan, "Stay the Course Is Not Enough," in *The Right War? The Conservative Debate on Iraq*, ed. Gary Rosen (Cambridge: Cambridge University Press, 2005), pp. 201–203.

3. Andrew Bacevich, "I Lost My Son to a War I Oppose. We Were Both Doing Our Duty," *Washington Post*, May 27, 2007, p. B01.

4. For a discussion and context on Carter see Andrew Bacevich, *The New American Militarism: How Americans Are Seduced by War* (Oxford: Oxford University Press, 2005), pp. 175–204. The Carter Doctrine states, "An attempt by any outside force to gain control of the Persian Gulf region will be regarded as an assault on the vital interests of the United States of America, and such an assault will be repelled by any means necessary, including military force."

5. Scott Sherman, "David Horowitz's Long March," *The Nation*, July 3, 2000. Jennifer Jacobson, "What Makes David Run: David Horowitz Demands Attention for the Idea That Conservatives Deserve a Place in Academe," *The Chronicle of Higher Education*, May 6, 2005: p. A9.

6. Falwell is a television evangelical preacher, whose remark that homosexuals and abortionists are in part to blame for the 9/11 attack created a storm of controversy. He later apologized for the following comment: "I really believe that the pagans, and the abortionists, and the feminists, and the gays and the lesbians who are actively trying to make that an alternative lifestyle, the ACLU, People for the American Way—all of them who have tried to secularize America—I point the finger in their face and say, 'You helped this happen.'" See John F. Harris, "God Gave U.S. 'What We Deserve,' Falwell Says," *Washington Post*, September 14, 2001, p. C03.

7. See Tim Weiner, "The Case of the Spies without a Country," *New York Times*, January 17, 1999 and Hans Blix, *Disarming Iraq* (New York: Pantheon Books, 2004), pp. 36–37.

8. George P. Shultz, William J. Perry, Henry Kissinger, and Sam Nunn, "A World Free of Nuclear Weapons," *Wall Street Journal*, January 4, 2007.

9. Right-hand man quotation in Dana Milbank, "Colonel Finally Saw Whites of Their Eyes," *Washington Post*, October 20, 2005. Brian Knowlton, "Former Powell Aide Says Bush Policy Run by Cabal," *New York Times*, October 21, 2005. Ring quoted in Richard Leiby, "Breaking Ranks," *Washington Post*, January 19, 2006.

10. See Mark Mazzetti, "US Army Says Prison Deaths Are Homicides," *Boston Globe*, March 26, 2005; "US Acknowledges Torture at Guantanamo; in Iraq, Afghanistan—UN," *Forbes.com*, June 24, 2005, available at <http://www. forbes.com/work/feeds/afx/2005/06/24/afx2110388.html>, accessed August 10, 2007. For further documentation, consult Human Rights First, "One Year after the Abu Ghraib Torture Photos: U.S. Government Response 'Grossly Inadequate,'" A Human Rights First Assessment, April 26, 2005, available at

<http://www.humanrightsfirst.org/us_law/etn/statements/abu-yr-042605.htm>, accessed August 10, 2007.

11. Lawsuits were filed in Germany and France against Rumsfeld over the mistreatment of detainees; see Adam Zagorin, "Exclusive: Charges Sought against Rumsfeld over Prison Abuse," *Time*, November 10, 2006. Rumsfeld reportedly made a hasty exit from France because of such lawsuits, see "Rumsfeld Flees France, Fearing Arrest," *Alternet*, October 29, 2007, available at <http://www.alternet.org/story/66425>, accessed March 12, 2008.

12. Quotation on Feith as top planner and the following Feith comment in Eric Schmitt, "Controversial Pentagon Official Is Stepping Down," *New York Times*, January 27, 2005.

13. George Tenet, *At the Center of the Storm: My Years at the CIA* (New York: HarperCollins, 2007), see especially Part III. Seymour Hersh, "Selective Intelligence," *New Yorker* (May 2003). Inspector General, United States Department of Defense, "Review of the Pre-war Activities of the Office of the Under Secretary of Defense for Policy," Report No. 07-INTEL-04, February 9, 2007. To be sure, the Inspector General report does not specifically address the Office of Special Plans.

14. See Hersh, "Selective Intelligence"; Robert Dreyfus and Jason West, "The Lie Factory," *Mother Jones* (January/February 2004); and Inspector General, "Review of the Pre-war Activities."

15. Former U.S. defense secretary Donald Rumsfeld was given a "foot in the mouth" award by the British Plain English Society. The award is for public officials who make outlandish or confusing remarks, and Rumsfeld impressed the society when he said: "Reports that say that something hasn't happened are always interesting to me, because as we know, there are known knowns; there are things we know we know. We also know there are known unknowns; that is to say we know there are some things we do not know. But there are also unknown unknowns— the ones we don't know we don't know." See "Rum Remark Wins Rumsfeld an Award," *BBC News*, December 2, 2003. Ahmed Chalabi is a controversial figure who was one of the leaders of the Iraqi National Congress that promoted the overthrow of Saddam Hussein in the 1990s. Chalabi is allegedly wanted for bank fraud in Jordan.

16. Executive Order 13303 appears to protect U.S. corporations that do business in Iraq with special attention to oil. It states, "any attachment, judgment, decree, lien, execution, garnishment, or other judicial process is prohibited, and shall be deemed null and void, with respect to the following…all Iraqi petroleum and petroleum products, and interests therein, and proceeds, obligations, or any financial instruments of any nature whatsoever arising from or related to the sale or marketing thereof…" See "Executive Order Protecting the Development Fund for Iraq and Certain Other Property in Which Iraq Has an Interest," May 22, 2003, available at <http://www.whitehouse.gov/news/releases/2003/05/20030522–15.html>. Accessed on June 21, 2007.

17. Peter Waldman, "Resigning in Protest, a Career Diplomat Turns Peace Envoy— Letter to Powell Makes Him an Unlikely Antiwar Icon," *Wall Street Journal*, April 1, 2003.

18. Cheney delivered a speech at the Veterans of Foreign Wars National Convention in Nashville, TN, in August 2002. The vice president argued that "[t]here is no

doubt that Saddam Hussein now has weapons of mass destruction.... What we must not do in the face of a mortal threat is give in to wishful thinking or willful blindness. We will not simply look away, hope for the best, and leave the matter for some future administration to resolve.... Regime change in Iraq would bring about a number of benefits to the region. When the gravest of threats are eliminated, the freedom-loving peoples of the region will have a chance to promote the values that can bring lasting peace." See "Full Text of Dick Cheney's Speech," *Guardian* (London), August 27, 2002.

19. Thomas E. Ricks, *Fiasco: The American Military Adventure in Iraq* (New York: Penguin Press, 2006), pp. 329–340. Ricks describes what he calls the 2nd Battalion's "near mutiny," and that this first use of Iraqi forces for internal operations indicated a "strategic failure for the entire U.S. approach."

20. Douglas A. Ollivant and Eric D. Chewning, "Producing Victory: A 2007 Postscript for Implementation," *Military Review* (March–April 2007), v. 87, pp. 109–110.

21. Roger Cohen, "The Ghost in the Baghdad Museum," *New York Times*, April 2, 2006.

Bibliography

The 9/11 Truth Commission Report: Final Report of the National Commission on Terrorist Attacks upon the United States, authorized edition (New York: W.W. Norton, n.d.).

Appy, Christian. *Patriots: The Vietnam War Remembered from All Sides* (New York: Penguin Books, 2003).

Arnove, Anthony. *Iraq: The Logic of Withdrawal* (New York: New Press, 2006).

Bacevich, Andrew. *American Empire: The Realities and Consequences of U.S. Diplomacy* (Cambridge, MA: Harvard University Press, 2002).

———. *The Imperial Tense: Prospects and Problems of American Empire* (Chicago, IL: Ivan Dee, 2003).

———. *The New American Militarism: How Americans Are Seduced by War* (New York: Oxford University Press, 2005).

Baker III, James A. and Lee H. Hamilton. *The Iraq Study Group Report: The Way Forward—A New Approach* (New York: Vintage Press, 2006).

Batatu, Hanna. *The Old Social Classes and the Revolutionary Movements of Iraq: A Study of Iraq's Old Landed and Commercial Classes and of Its Communists, Ba'thists and Free Officers* (Princeton, NJ: Princeton University Press, 1978).

Benderman, Kevin. *Letters from a Fort Lewis Brigg: A Matter of Conscience* (Guilford, CT: Lyons Press, 2007).

Blix, Hans. *Disarming Iraq* (New York: Pantheon Books, 2004).

Blum, William. *Killing Hope: U.S. Military and CIA Interventions since World War II* (Monroe, ME: Common Courage Press, 1995).

Bremer, L. Paul. *My Year in Iraq: The Struggle to Build a Future of Hope* (New York: Simon & Schuster, 2006).

Brockway, Fenner. *Britain's First Socialists: The Levellers, Agitators and Diggers of the English Revolution* (London: Quartet Books, 1980).

Bush, George H. and Brent Scowcroft. *A World Transformed* (New York: Alfred A. Knopf, 1998).

Buzzell, Colby. *My War: Killing Time in Iraq* (New York: Putnam, 2005).

Chomsky, Noam. *Hegemony or Survival: America's Quest for Global Dominance* (New York: Metropolitan Books/Henry Holt, 2003).

Clancy, Tom, Tony Zinni, and Tony Koltz. *Battle Ready* (New York: Penguin, 2004).

Cole, Juan. *Napoleon's Egypt: Invading the Middle East* (New York: Palgrave Macmillan, 2007).

Cordesman, Anthony. *The Iraq War: Strategy, Tactics, and Military Lessons* (Westport, CT: Praeger, 2003).

Delgado, Aidan. *The Sutras of Abu Ghraib: Notes from a Conscientious Objector* (Boston, MA: Beacon Press, 2007).

Feith, Douglas. *War and Decision: Inside the Pentagon at the Dawn of the War on Terrorism* (New York: Harper Collins, 2008).

Franks, Tommy. *American Soldier* (New York: Harper Collins, 2004).

Frisch, Michael. *A Shared Authority: Essays on the Craft and Meaning of Oral and Public History* (Albany: State University of New York Press, 1990).

Galtung, Johan. *Transcend and Transform: An Introduction to Conflict Work* (Boulder, CO: Paradigm, 2004).

———. *Pax Pacifica: Terrorism, the Pacific Hemisphere, Globalisation and Peace Studies* (London: Pluto Press, 2005).

Gardner, Lloyd and Marilyn Young, eds. *Iraq and the Lessons of Vietnam: Or, How Not to Learn from the Past* (New York: New Press, 2007).

Gill, Lesley. *The School of Americas: Military Training and Political Violence in the Americas* (Durham, NC: Duke University Press, 2004).

Gordon, Michael R. and Bernard E. Trainor. *Cobra II: The Inside Story of the Invasion and Occupation of Iraq* (New York: Pantheon, 2006).

Gosse, Van. *Rethinking the New Left: An Interpretative History* (New York: Palgrave Macmillian, 2005).

Hanh, Thich Nhat. *Peace Is Every Step* (New York: Bantam Books, 1992).

Hayden, Tom. *Ending the War in Iraq* (New York: Akashic Books, 2007).

Hersch, Seymour. *Chain of Command: The Road from 9/11 to Abu Ghraib* (New York: Harper Perennial, 2004).

Hiro, Dilip. *Iraq: In the Eye of the Storm* (New York: Nation Books, 2002).

Hunt, Andrew. *The Turning: A History of the Vietnam Veterans against the War* (New York: New York University Press, 1999).

Johnson, Chalmers. *The Sorrows of Empire: Militarism, Secrecy, and the End of the Republic* (New York: Metropolitan Books, 2004).

Kaplan, Lawrence and William Kristol. *The War over Iraq: Saddam's Tyranny and America's Mission* (San Francisco, CA: Encounter Books, 2003).

Kaplan, Robert. *Imperial Grunts: On the Ground with the American Military, from Mongolia to the Philippines to Iraq and Beyond* (New York: Vintage, 2006).

Keegan, John. *The Iraq War* (New York: Knopf, 2004).

Kiesling, John Brady. *Diplomacy Lessons: Realism for an Unloved Superpower* (Washington, DC: Potomac Books, 2006).

Kovic, Ron. *Born on the Fourth of July* (New York: Simon and Schuster, 1976).

Krasno, Jean and James Sullivan. *The United Nations and Iraq: Defanging the Viper* (Westport, CT: Praeger, 2003).

Lembcke, Jerry. *The Spitting Image: Myth, Memory and the Legacy of Vietnam* (New York: New York University Press, 1998).

Lifton, Robert Jay. *Home from the War: Vietnam Veterans—Neither Victims nor Executioners* (New York: Simon and Schuster, 1973).

Little, Douglas. *American Orientalism: The United States and the Middle East since 1945* (Chapel Hill: University of North Carolina Press, 2002).

Lockman, Zachary. *Contending Visions of the Middle East: The History and Politics of Orientalism* (Cambridge: Cambridge University Press, 2004).

Lynd, Staughton and Thomas Hayden. *The Other Side* (New York: New American Library, 1966).

McNamara, Robert S. *In Retrospect: The Tragedy and Lessons of Vietnam* (New York: Times Books, 1995).

Mejía, Camilo. *The Road from Ar Ramadi: The Private Rebellion of Staff Sergeant Mejía* (New York: New Press, 2007).

Mirra, Carl, ed. *Enduring Freedom or Enduring War? Prospects and Costs of the New American 21st Century* (Washington, DC: Maisonneuve Press, 2005).

———, ed. *Join Us? Testimonies of Iraq War Veterans and Their Families* (Somerville, MA: Historians against the War, pamphlet#5, 2006).

Moser, Richard. *The New Winter Soldiers: GI and Veteran Dissent during the Vietnam Era* (New Brunswick, NJ: Rutgers University Press, 1996).

O'Brien, Tim. *If I Die in a Combat Zone: Box Me Up and Ship Me Home* (New York: Broadway Books, 1976).

Phythian, Mark and Nikos Passas. *Arming Iraq: How the U.S. and Britain Secretly Built Saddam's War Machine* (Boston, MA: Northeastern University Press, 1996).

Portelli, Alessandro. *The Death of Luigi Trastulli and Other Stories: Form and Meaning in Oral History* (Albany: State University of New York Press, 1991).

Prados, John. *Hoodwinked: The Documents That Reveal How Bush Sold Us a War* (New York: New Press, 2004).

Ricks, Thomas. *Fiasco: The American Military Adventure in Iraq* (New York: Penguin Books, 2006).

Swofford, Anthony. *Jarhead: A Marine's Chronicle of the Gulf War and Other Battles* (New York: Scribner, 2003).

Tenet, George. *At the Center of the Storm: My Years at the CIA* (New York: HarperCollins, 2007).

Williams, William Appleman. *The Tragedy of American Diplomacy*, new edition (New York: HarperCollins, 1972).

Wilson, Joseph. *The Politics of Truth: A Diplomat's Memoir, Inside the Lies That Led to War and Betrayed My Wife's CIA Identity* (New York: Carroll & Graf, 2004).

Woodward, Bob. *Bush at War* (New York: Simon and Schuster, 2002).

———. *Plan of Attack* (New York: Simon and Schuster, 2004).

Wright, Ann and Susan Dixon. *Dissent: Voices of Conscience: Government Insiders Speak Out against the War in Iraq* (Kihei, HI: Koa Books, 2008).

Zinn, Howard. *The Unraveling of the Bush Presidency* (New York: Seven Stories Press, 2007).

Index